Lincoln's Sanctuary

Lincoln's Sanctuary

Abraham Lincoln
and the Soldiers' Home

MATTHEW PINSKER

OXFORD
UNIVERSITY PRESS
2003

OXFORD
UNIVERSITY PRESS

Oxford New York
Auckland Bangkok Buenos Aires Cape Town Chennai
Dar es Salaam Hong Kong Istanbul Karachi Kolkata
Kuala Lumpur Madrid Melbourne Mexico City Mumbai Nairobi
São Paulo Shanghai Taipei Tokyo Toronto

Published by Oxford University Press, Inc.
198 Madison Avenue, New York, New York, 10016
www.oup.com

Library of Congress Cataloging-in-Publication Data
Pinsker, Matthew.
Lincoln's sanctuary : Abraham Lincoln and the Soldiers' Home /
Matthew Pinsker.
p.   cm.
Includes bibliographical references.
ISBN 0-19-516206-4
1. Lincoln, Abraham, 1809–1865—Homes and haunts—Washington
(D.C.). 2. Cottages—Washington (D.C.)—History—19th century.
3. United States Soldiers' Home—History—19th century. 4. Lincoln,
Abraham, 1809–1865—Family. 5. Washington (D.C.)—History—
Civil War, 1861–1865. 6. Washington (D.C.)—Buildings, structures, etc.
7. United States—Politics and government—1861–1865. I. National
Trust for Historic Preservation in the United States. II. Title.
E457.64 .P56 2003
973.7'092—dc21   2003001215

9 8 7 6 5 4 3 2 1

Printed in the United States of America
on acid-free paper

For Rachel,
whose love is my sanctuary

CR

August 12th. [1863]—I SEE the President almost every day, as I happen to live where he passes to or from his lodgings out of town. He never sleeps at the White House during the hot season, but has quarters at a healthy location some three miles north of the city, the Soldiers' home, a United States military establishment. I saw him this morning about 8 1/2 coming in to business, riding on Vermont avenue, near L street. He always has a company of twenty-five or thirty cavalry, with sabres drawn and held upright over their shoulders. They say this guard was against his personal wish, but he let his counselors have their way. The party makes no great show in uniform or horses. Mr. Lincoln on the saddle generally rides a good-sized, easy-going gray horse, is dress'd in plain black, somewhat rusty and dusty, wears a black stiff hat, and looks about as ordinary in attire, &c., as the commonest man. A lieutenant, with yellow straps, rides at his left, and following behind, two by two, come the cavalry men, in their yellow-striped jackets. They are generally going at a slow trot, as that is the pace set them by the one they wait upon. The sabres and accoutrements clank, and the entirely unornamental *cortège* as it trots towards Lafayette square arouses no sensation, only some curious stranger stops and gazes. I see very plainly ABRAHAM LINCOLN'S dark brown face, with the deep-cut lines, the eyes, always to me with a deep latent sadness in the expression. We have got so that we exchange bows, and very cordial ones. Sometimes the President goes and comes in an open barouche. The cavalry always accompany him, with drawn sabres. Often I notice as he goes out evenings—and sometimes in the morning, when he returns early—he turns off and halts at the large and handsome residence of the Secretary of War, on K street, and holds conference there. If in his barouche, I can see from my window he does not alight, but sits in his vehicle, and Mr. Stanton comes out to attend him. Sometimes one of his sons, a boy of ten or twelve, accompanies him, riding at his right on a pony. Earlier in the summer I occasionally saw the President and his wife, toward the latter part of the afternoon, out in a barouche, on a pleasure ride through the city. Mrs. Lincoln was dress'd in complete black, with a long crape veil. The equipage is of the plainest kind, only two horses, and they nothing extra. They pass'd me once very close, and I saw the President in the face fully, as they were moving slowly, and his look, though abstracted, happen'd to be directed steadily in my eye. He bow'd and smiled, but far beneath his smile I noticed well the expression I have alluded to. None of the artists or pictures has caught the deep, though subtle and indirect expression of this man's face. There is something else there. One of the great portrait painters of two or three centuries ago is needed.

—Walt Whitman, "Abraham Lincoln,"
No. 45 (August 12, 1863), *Specimen Days*

Contents

Foreword

LINCOLN IS THE MIRACLE OF DEMOCRACY, AND INTEREST IN HIM IN THE UNITED States—and around the globe—seems insatiable. The reading public, however, also wonders how, after so many years and so many books on the Civil War president, new and important work continues to be written about him. It is a cliché that each generation needs to reinterpret Lincoln. It is also true. As new students enter the field, they bring the fresh perspective of a new generation and also substantial talents. We are rewarded not only by new voices and new emphases but also by new avenues explored and new understanding.

Matthew Pinsker proves to be a sparkling new voice and a careful historian. He constantly measures the reliability of his materials so that his readers secure fine lessons on how to read historical sources. With *Lincoln's Sanctuary: Abraham Lincoln and the Soldiers' Home*, the young historian puts himself in the vanguard of a new generation of Lincoln scholars.

The literate public knows very little about the Soldiers' Home. Scholars have known that Lincoln spent some of his summers at the cool retreat of a "cottage" in the Washington suburbs, but how important a part that place played in his story is quite new. Pinsker's book suggests that the privacy afforded the president by the Soldiers' Home, the quiet it gave him to think deeply, and the interaction with common people that the place and the daily travel to and from the White House allowed provided Lincoln with an important part of the power he needed to lead as perhaps no other president has done before or since.

The house that came to be known as the Soldiers' Home was built in 1842 for George W. Riggs of banking fame; not much later the government acquired it. Surrounded by other buildings, the place provided a tranquil "asylum" for disabled veterans of old wars, the majority of whom turn out to be immigrants—

Irish, German, and others. This is not surprising, as relatives who might have cared for them often stayed in the old country. Lincoln, who made the place his home for a quarter of his presidency, gets to know these people.

The Lincolns had hoped to have a quiet retreat in the Riggs house and indeed found some of that. One of the wonderful elements of Pinsker's work is the light it sheds on the presidential family. We find Abraham and Mary in bed together—as a soldier did and reported on it years later in an interview with famed Lincoln scholar and muckraker Ida Tarbell. We glimpse the happiness of a mother and father with their son Tad, whose slightly older brother, Willie, died early in 1862. We see the lively boy making friends of the soldiers guarding the presidential retreat. We see Aunt Mary, the escaped slave woman who cooks for them (for wages), growing intimate with the family for a short time.

We get wonderful illustrations of the gender roles of the day, with Mary successfully reaching beyond the limitations placed on women while also retaining control of the domestic sphere. The book tells the charming story of how the man who issued the Emancipation Proclamation and had to make life and death decisions day in and day out had to ask the permission of his wife, visiting Boston, to let their cook leave the cottage as winter approached.

We get to feel Lincoln's loneliness when Mary takes Tad up to the cool of Vermont, away from the summer pestilences of the Washington area. We see the president finding companions among the guards of the Soldiers' Home. One of the wonderful treasures Pinsker found are letters from a Pennsylvania soldier who had guarded the commander in chief. From soldiers we hear of Lincoln restlessly pacing the night in the ever-expanding cemetery nearby— the precursor of Arlington.

However much the beleaguered leader needs a haven away from the White House, the war and the every day chores of the job follow him. People find him at the Soldiers' Home. Uninvited, even inebriated guests show up late at night, but Lincoln sees them. At midnight a lawyer bursts upon him, requesting respite for men condemned to die on the morrow. When a servant tries to keep visitors from abroad away, he is instructed that the guests had come three thousand miles to see the president. He sees them. When his patience becomes exhausted and he roughly sends away a clemency seeker, he frets about it, then apologizes on the next day.

The private life of the Lincolns is rarely fully private, and many significant events take place during the three long summers they spend at this "hideaway." The commander in chief follows battle after battle year after year. He makes difficult decisions. He fires General George McClellan, who has the "slows"— and other generals, too. He works on his Emancipation Proclamation that transforms the character and the goals of the war and with it the American future.

He follows the Battle of Gettysburg and begins to incubate the thoughts that would create the Gettysburg Address.

Lincoln deals with friendly politicians, hostile ones, and the ones in between. He makes deals. We see his difficult struggle for reelection in 1864—probably the most momentous election of American history, when his defeat might have meant the continuation of slavery and the end of the United States. The man who not so long before found it necessary to advocate the colonization of black people away from a prejudiced United States now talks to Frederick Douglass about the need to free the slaves by helping them escape from the South—should the election be lost.

Secretary of War Edwin Stanton, the lawyer who before the war dismissed lawyer colleague Lincoln as a backwoods incompetent, also spends his summers in one of the Soldiers' Home cottages. The book convincingly argues that he thus grew into the president's closest confidant among his cabinet members. By digging deeper than others before him, by digging in different and previously untouched ground, Pinsker gives us new insights. Stories we have long known take on new significance.

We find Lincoln riding to the White House in the morning and back to the Soldiers' Home in the evening. Along the way he connects with the people. We see him trotting along a row of ambulances, talking with the wounded soldiers. We see him with escaped slaves in their contraband camps—as they came to be known. We see Walt Whitman bowing his greeting, and the president returning the bow. We see Lincoln going out for a late night ride; we hear a shot, and the president gallops back without his hat. A soldier goes out to retrieve it and finds a bullet hole in it.

Physical danger lurks all around. News comes of kidnapping plots. Lincoln dismisses them and repeatedly shows his annoyance at the precautions forced on him. Days after the president moves to his summer place in 1864, a Confederate army under Jubal Early comes within a mile of the Soldiers' Home. "Great Battle at Seventh Street," the newsboys hawk their papers. Lincoln goes to the fort protecting that most vulnerable part of the city and becomes (and remains to this day) the only commander in chief to be directly exposed to enemy fire.

We remember him the most for his address at Gettysburg and for that great American sermon, the Second Inaugural. We remember him for his high-minded official prose—best expressed in unforgettable words: "Four score and seven years ago . . ." "the government of the people, by the people, for the people . . ." "With malice towards none." Sacred words to so many Americans. Yet we also know he was a man of common touch. Surely some readers will find most interesting that thread of a summer White House story that shows Lincoln in carpet slippers rather than on dress parade.

The soldiers who guarded him remembered Lincoln visiting their tents, chatting easily with them, telling stories. One of these recalled by many of them was dubbed "The Pigtail Story":

> You boys remind me of a farmer friend of mine in Illinois, who said he could never understand why the Lord put the curl in a pig's tail. It never seemed to him to be either useful or ornamental, but he reckoned the Almighty knew what he was doing when he put it there. (see p. 153)

"The Almighty has his own purposes," is how Lincoln put it in the Second Inaugural. That's what the war had taught him.

We have here a fine new history. Perhaps half of it comes from sources not normally used in Lincoln biographies. The author modestly writes that the book provides only some fresh "snapshots." In fact, it opens a new window on the Lincoln presidency.

February 12, 2003   Gabor Boritt
Farm by the Ford

Lincoln's Sanctuary

Introduction
"I see the President"

"I SEE THE PRESIDENT ALMOST EVERY DAY," NOTED POET WALT WHITMAN IN AN entry from his wartime journal, dated Wednesday, August 12, 1863. "I saw him this morning about 8 1/2 coming in to business." Whitman, who visited the wounded at Union hospitals and lived on L Street in Washington during part of the conflict, observed that Abraham Lincoln, "somewhat rusty and dusty," along with an "unornamental *cortège*" of twenty-five or thirty cavalry troops, made absolutely "no sensation" on the city's streets. The Long Island native was less immune to the routines of the nation's capital and maintained a careful vigil over the president's daily commute while he lived in the city. He reported that in their brief encounters, Lincoln's "dark brown face" with its "deep-cut lines" was often plainly visible to him, adding wistfully that there was a "deep latent sadness" evident in his eyes. The close scrutiny apparently did not go unnoticed. "We have got so that we exchange bows," Whitman claimed, "and very cordial ones."[1]

This striking portrait of President Lincoln heading to work raises a provocative question. Where was he spending his nights if not at the White House? Most Americans, and even some scholars, have been unaware that Lincoln maintained a wartime retreat from 1862 to 1864, spending over a quarter of his presidency in residence there, usually each year from early summer to late autumn. He was actually one of a handful of nineteenth-century presidents to use this place called the Soldiers' Home as his sanctuary and private White House.[2]

Telling the story of Lincoln's three seasons at the Soldiers' Home is the first object of this book but not its only purpose. Whitman's fascinating journal entry suggests a larger meaning. As any photographer knows, a slight shift in focus or subtle change of lens can sometimes create dramatic new images from

1

otherwise familiar scenes. Few scenes in American history are more familiar than Lincoln's presidency, but no study of that period has ever attempted to see the president from the perspective of his daily journeys between the Soldiers' Home and the White House. This is a book that takes the fleeting glimpse of a poet and tries to make it the starting point for a new look at Abraham Lincoln's presidential leadership. The result is as much metaphor as narrative, offering a window into the elusive boundary that separates a president's public and private experiences.

CR

Originally known as the Military Asylum, the Soldiers' Home was an institution created in the early 1850s for disabled army veterans who could not support themselves. The federal government had purchased land for the proposed community near the District's northwestern boundary, about three miles from the White House, along the road toward Silver Spring, Maryland. By nineteenth-century standards, this venture was unprecedented, a significant expansion of government services and an untested experiment in accommodating people with disabilities. Not surprisingly, the operation struggled at first. Political support flagged and there was talk of abandoning the effort. Anxious to cultivate more allies in Washington, the military commissioners in charge of the Home soon began the practice of inviting presidents and secretaries of war to spend summers at private cottages on their grounds.

The cottages at the Soldiers' Home offered an attractive alternative to the White House, especially in hot weather, because they were well situated on cool, shaded hills. They also offered the advantage of being outside the city while not too far from the presidential office. It took an ordinary carriage driver about half an hour to navigate the three-mile journey across the District. In the Civil War era, the grounds covered nearly three hundred acres, offering a panoramic view of the capital and surrounding countryside. At the outset of the Lincoln administration, a local newspaper praised the area as "one of the most charming rural retreats in the vicinity of Washington."[3]

There were five principal buildings clustered together at one corner of the grounds; an imposing main hall for approximately 150 residents, or inmates as they were then called, and four rustic but still elegant domiciles scattered nearby. Local banker George W. Riggs, Jr., the previous owner of the property, had built the largest of these cottages in the early 1840s to serve as his family's "country" residence. With attractive gables, a stucco-covered brick exterior, and a prominent porch, the country home was designed in the English Gothic Revival style that had been popularized by prominent nineteenth-century designer Andrew Jackson Downing. The government had built two of the other cottages, called Quarters 1 and 2, in the mid-1850s, at the same time that they constructed the Scott Hall, the main edifice named after General in Chief Winfield Scott, who had been one of the founding spirits behind the Soldiers' Home. The other building, known as the Corlisle Cottage, was situated slightly apart from the others in a more secluded grove. All of these residences typically served as housing units for officers or personnel associated with the institution.

James Buchanan, the first president to reside at the Soldiers' Home, stayed at Quarters 1. The bachelor president was satisfied with his decision and reported to his niece Harriet Lane in 1858 that he "slept much better at the Asylum than at the White House." It was probably Buchanan who first recommended the Soldiers' Home to Lincoln during their brief encounters in 1861. Within a few days after the Inaugural, the *New York Times* reported that both the new first lady and her husband had separately ridden out to look over the grounds. By April, a local newspaper announced that President Lincoln and his family intended to follow Buchanan's example and occupy the same "charming spot" that the previous incumbent had enjoyed so much.[4]

The report about Lincoln's summer plans appeared on Sunday, April 14, 1861—the same day that Federal troops surrendered Fort Sumter. In the gathering storm of southern rebellion, the prospect of a presidential vacation suddenly appeared far less charming. Mary Lincoln continued to hold out some hope for a temporary escape, but it was to no avail. In mid-July, she wrote to a friend that the family expected to go out to the Soldiers' Home, "a very beautiful place,"

A wartime image of the Soldiers' Home (far right) and its adjacent cottages, published by popular printmaker Charles Magnus. LIBRARY OF CONGRESS.

within about three weeks. "We will ride into the city every day, & can be as secluded, as we please," she predicted hopefully.[5] Just ten days after this note, Union forces suffered a devastating setback at Bull Run in the war's first major engagement. With her husband now more preoccupied by work, Mary Lincoln remained at the White House, continuing with her plans to renovate the presidential mansion and dutifully visiting wounded soldiers. In August, however, she struck out on her own, heading to the fashionable resort at Long Branch, New Jersey, and then for an extended social and shopping excursion across New York.

It was not until the beginning of the next summer that the Lincolns made good on their plans to occupy a cottage at the Soldiers' Home. By then, the need for a family retreat had become both more pressing and more personal. In February 1862, twelve-year-old Willie Lincoln had died after a bout with what the newspapers had labeled pneumonia but what was probably typhoid fever. This blow was especially hard for his doting mother, who had already lost one child, Eddie, to illness years before. In the aftermath of Willie's death, Mary Lincoln found life at the White House too distracting for proper mourning. Subsequently, the president agreed, despite his ever-increasing workload, to move the family out to the Soldiers' Home in June 1862.

In retrospect, it is startling to consider how disorganized and informal the process of relocating the first family was in that era. Senator Orville Browning, a close friend from Illinois, showed up at the White House one evening only to discover that the Lincolns had already vacated the official residence for the season. There were no special security measures taken on their behalf—no guards or escorts at their disposal. The president left for the Soldiers' Home with his wife, their youngest son Tad, and probably only a handful of servants: a cook, a housekeeper, and perhaps a valet. There are no official records of their new residency—no documentation for which cottage they inhabited, no inventory of the White House belongings they carried along with them, and no register of the many guests who soon began visiting their "country retirement," as Mary Lincoln proudly called it.[6] Everything about their experience at the Soldiers' Home must be pieced together from fragments principally found in diaries, letters, recollections, and newspaper accounts.

Following their arrival, the Lincolns apparently decided that unlike President Buchanan, they would displace the acting governor of the Home, who was then occupying the former Riggs country residence.[7] Situated directly next to the asylum, the Riggs home was comfortable but offered constant reminders about the painful stakes of military conflict. Crippled veterans regularly filled the nearby paths. One side of the elegant cottage now also faced a national military cemetery, hastily dedicated after the defeat at Bull Run and, by the summer of 1862, full of fresh graves. Thus, even while attempting to escape from their private grief and the national crisis, the Lincolns still found themselves surrounded by the somber echoes of war.

Yet nothing about the sorrowful nature of their surroundings appeared to diminish the joy that the Lincolns found in their temporary seclusion. "How dearly I loved the 'Soldiers' Home,'" the first lady later recalled.[8] The president's feelings have not been similarly recorded, but he returned each summer and stayed as long as weather permitted, even when his wife and his sons were out of town. In 1862, the Lincolns remained in residence from mid-June until early November, a total of nearly five months. The next year, the president returned for another period of about four and a half months. His stay in 1864 was slightly more compressed, extending from early July until sometime after mid-October. Altogether, President Lincoln lived at the Soldiers' Home for about thirteen out of his forty-nine months in office. For most of that period, his wife and youngest son Tad were with him, though Mary Lincoln traveled outside of Washington frequently, shopping in New York or vacationing in Vermont, leaving her husband alone at the cottage for weeks at a time. Eldest son Robert was usually away at college or traveling with friends. He spent no more than a few weeks with his father each summer.

Like many modern-day commuters, Lincoln scrambled in the mornings to avoid traffic and get a head start on his daily work. "He rose early," recalled John Hay, one of his top aides. "When he lived in the country at Soldiers Home, he would be up and dressed, eat his breakfast . . . and ride into Washington, all before 8 o'clock."[9] Others involved in the daily presidential routine shared similar recollections. An Army captain responsible for accompanying the president during a period of rising military tension recalled that he used to enter the cottage each day at about 6:30 A.M., often discovering that Lincoln was already awake, "reading the Bible or some work on the art of war."[10] Not surprisingly, some contemporary observations, like Whitman's journal entry, hint at a less punctual president, but the phenomenon of rising early and heading off to work was a deeply ingrained part of Lincoln's wartime life.

During his first summer at the Soldiers' Home, Lincoln often rode without any escort, but after some nervous consultations among friends, political advisers, Union military commanders, and his anxious wife, the president was compelled to accept at least some minimal show of protection. The army ordered a Pennsylvania infantry company to guard the cottage and by the autumn of 1862, members of a New York cavalry unit that Whitman so memorably dismissed as an "unornamental *cortège*" began accompanying Lincoln on almost all of his daily trips. From December 1863 until the war's end, a unit specially recruited from Ohio replaced them and provided the president with his primary escort.

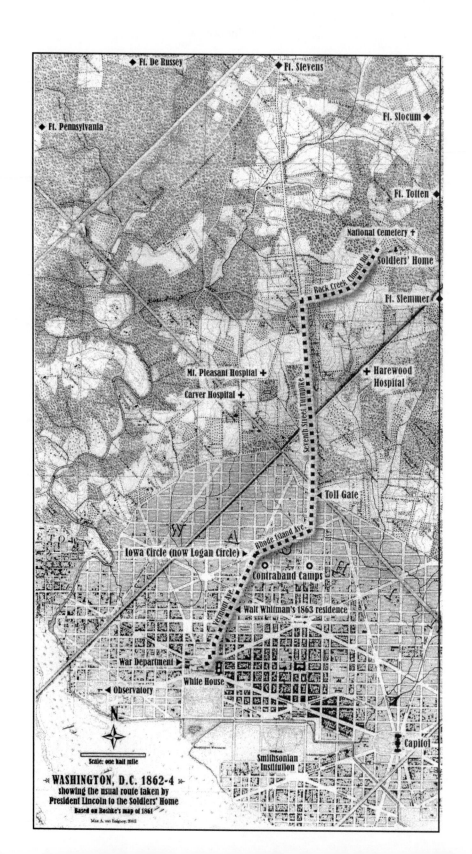

◆ Ft. De Russey   ◆ Ft. Stevens

◆ Ft. Pennsylvania   Ft. Slocum ◆

                                                         Ft. Totten ◆

                                          National Cemetery ✚
                                                    Soldiers' Home
                                   Rock Creek Church Rd.
                                                      Ft. Slemmer ◆

                      Mt. Pleasant Hospital ✚   ✚ Harewood
                                                        Hospital
                      Carver Hospital ✚

                                    Seventh Street Turnpike

                                                ▶ Toll Gate

                                   Rhode Island Ave.
            Iowa Circle (now Logan Circle) ▶
                                    Contraband Camps

                              ▶ Walt Whitman's 1863 residence
                    Vermont Ave.

            War Department ▶
            ◀ Observatory   White House

            N   ▮ Capitol

            Scale: one half mile   Smithsonian
                                           Institution

≫ WASHINGTON, D.C. 1862-4 ≪
showing the usual route taken by
President Lincoln to the Soldiers' Home
Based on Boshke's map of 1861

Max A. van Balgooy, 2002

The president and his cavalry escort had a choice of routes into the city, either via the Seventh Street Turnpike or North Capitol Street or Fourteenth Street. The turnpike was then the principal route in and out of the city, complete with a tollgate that the president was generously allowed to ignore. The road had strategic as well as political value. A key element of the city's elaborate defense network, Fort Massachusetts (later renamed Fort Stevens) sat perched just inside the District line along this pike. It was one of sixty-eight major forts that ultimately ringed the city, a martial beltway that stretched across the District lines into Maryland and through Union-occupied northern Virginia. The Soldiers' Home was not officially part of this network, but the tower at the main hall provided a communications outpost that ultimately proved vital for the defense of the city when it fell under attack in 1864.

As Lincoln and his escort crossed Boundary Street, the turnpike became Seventh Street Road, and they officially entered a city that was then expanding rapidly within the District. However, for several blocks the dusty road remained sparsely inhabited and hardly resembled a major avenue in a national capital. As many noted both at the time and since, the city was as incomplete as the nation torn apart by sectional conflict. The Washington Monument stood half-finished, looking more like a Roman ruin than a great national symbol. Until 1863, the capitol dome was also still under construction. There was a handful of spectacular buildings—the White House, Treasury Department, Post Office, Patent Office, and Smithsonian "castle"—but there was also an inescapable sense of underachievement about Washington. Depending on the season, the city's wide avenues were either dusty or muddy, with adjoining land often barren of buildings and whole sections of the town simply cut apart and isolated by open and filthy waterways. "The whole place looks run up in a night," wrote London journalist Edward Dicey, ". . . and it is impossible to remove the impression that, when Congress is over, the whole place is taken down, and packed up again till wanted."[11]

For Abraham Lincoln, though, the city must have seemed large enough with its 61,000 people at the start of the war and 230 miles of streets. Prior to becoming president, he had spent the previous twelve years living in a modest wood frame house in Springfield, Illinois, a town with only a few thousand inhabitants. He had lived in Washington once before, during the late 1840s as a homesick congressman holed up in a boardinghouse near Capitol Hill, but the town was even less developed then. Moreover, by the end of the war, the

---

(Facing page) A map showing Lincoln's principal route to and from the Soldiers' Home.
MAX VAN BALGOOY, NATIONAL TRUST FOR HISTORIC PRESERVATION.

city's population had tripled, approaching 200,000 people, and was considered, by most Americans at least, to be a bustling, engaging place.

Once in the city, Lincoln and his entourage probably turned off Seventh onto Rhode Island and there connected to Vermont Avenue. It was on this stretch of the route that the president would have passed by Walt Whitman's home near the corner of Vermont and L Street in the mornings on his way toward Lafayette Square and days full of crisis at the wartime White House.

While her husband tended to the nation's business, Mary Lincoln strained in her own way to contribute to his cause. Frustrated by her private grief and poor health, nineteenth-century gender conventions, and her husband's near constant state of exhaustion, the first lady found it difficult to connect to him and to support him in his enormous endeavors. An interview conducted years after the war by journalist and Lincoln biographer Ida M. Tarbell reveals Mary Lincoln's dilemma in poignant fashion. Charles Derickson, one of the young Pennsylvania infantrymen assigned to guard the Soldiers' Home, informed the author that the first lady often watched the daily departure from the cottage without her husband's knowledge. "Mr. D. tells of seeing Mrs. L. often standing in her night gown & night cap at the window in the morning," reported Tarbell in her unpublished interview notes, offering a vivid portrait of a wife unable to fully express her emotions, but caring too much to look away.[12]

Mary Lincoln subsequently invested herself in projects that she imagined might help her husband. Some of these experiments proved to be spectacular and costly political failures, such as her extravagant spending on White House renovations or her occasional attempts to punish the spouses and daughters of the president's more prominent rivals. Other efforts were more helpful, such as her admirable habit of visiting Union hospitals, several of which were located near the cottage. The first lady often made the rounds of hospital wards without seeking any press coverage, making them straightforward exercises in charity. Moreover, these were not encounters for the faint-hearted. A Union soldier stationed at nearby Fort Stevens described the hospitals most frequently visited by Mary Lincoln in a letter to his father:

> I went toward Washington yesterday to visit the hospitals on the edge of the city. I went to three—Mount Pleasant, Carver, and Columbia College. They all seem neat and well kept . . . [but] wounds are everywhere. Some are most shockingly mangled. I did not go about much, for I do not like such scenes.[13]

If such scenes so disturbed a combat soldier, it is difficult to imagine how they affected Mary Lincoln, who normally recoiled from bloodshed.

President Lincoln visited the wounded as well, but most of his day was invariably spent working inside the White House. His office was a magnet for visitors, both serious and laughable, though there was little effort to distinguish between them. In a wickedly biting recollection, one English visitor described the casual collection of guests who congregated at the White House prior to the president's arrival on typical summer mornings. "If you had only been with us that morning upon the steps of the White House," George Borrett wrote with tongue planted firmly in cheek, "where we waited, with one or two more loungers like ourselves, to see the President come in from his country house." He ridiculed the entire proceedings, from the "bow-legged, cow-quartered, dead-alive quadrupeds" that served as the cavalry escort's horses to the presidential carriage that "might have been centuries since it was washed or painted." "The Constitution has some queer provisions," he noted dryly, "I wonder whether it compels the President's coachman to brush his hat the wrong way."[14]

Lincoln's office was on the second floor of the White House, along the southern side of the building. Here even greater crowds spilled out into the hallways and down the stairs. The wartime president had only a handful of aides to help him manage his affairs. The result was inevitably chaotic, a situation only exacerbated by Lincoln's peculiar style of conducting business. "Sometimes there would be a crowd of senators and members of Congress waiting their turn," remembered Illinois congressman Isaac Arnold. "While thus waiting, the loud ringing laugh of Mr. Lincoln—in which he would be joined by those *inside*, but which was rather provoking to those *outside*—would be heard by the waiting and impatient crowd."[15] Nothing seemed to alleviate the delays. "The House remained full of people nearly all day," reported aide John Hay, noting that at lunchtime the president "had literally to run the gantlet through the crowds who filled the corridors."[16]

During the wartime period, Lincoln was only in his mid-fifties, but the pressures and tragedies of the conflict aged him dramatically. Old friends such as Isaac Arnold "were sometimes shocked with the change in his appearance" and could barely recognize a man they had once considered blessed with "a frame of iron and nerves of steel."[17] Many wartime observers echoed Whitman in commenting on the president's "deep latent sadness." Journalist Noah Brooks, who had met Lincoln in the 1850s, described the nation's commander in chief as having been "grievously altered" since his days as a "happy-faced lawyer."[18] Artist Francis B. Carpenter, who worked on a canvas at the White House for a period of about six months, simply called Lincoln's countenance "the saddest face I ever painted."[19]

The tension so evident in the president's appearance underscores the importance of his attempts to find sanctuary at the Soldiers' Home. In the evenings when the Lincolns were together in their cottage, they tried earnestly to relax. As with many families from that era, they found their greatest release in social activities, usually in the parlor, often in reading aloud. Although the president was known for his storytelling, recollections by guests at the cottage suggest that he was more likely to turn to his favorite poets or dramatists when he was outside the office and not trying to make a political point or neutralize an unwanted request. There were evenings full of the famous anecdotes and even some sentimental ballads, but they appeared to be less common. The Lincoln parlor generally embodied a dignified nineteenth-century ideal.

"Where only one or two [friends] were present [Lincoln] was fond of reading aloud," John Hay insisted. "He passed many of the summer evenings in this way when occupying his cottage at the Soldiers' Home." According to the loyal aide, who once drifted to sleep while listening to lines from *Richard III*, the President would read from Shakespeare "for hours with a single secretary for [an] audience." Lincoln appeared to Hay to be especially fond of the famous soliloquy in *Richard II* in which the King contemplated the meaning of death, a passage that the young assistant claimed he had heard Lincoln recite "at Springfield, at the White House, and at the Soldiers' Home."

> For God's sake, let us sit upon the ground,
> And tell sad stories of the death of kings:—
> How some have been depos'd, some slain in war,
> Some haunted by the ghosts they have deposed;
> Some poisoned by their wives, some sleeping kill'd;
> All murthered. . . .[20]

Naturally, many of the Shakespearean plays and passages that Lincoln seemed to admire most dwelled on themes of rebellion, usurpation, and ambition run amok. The historical dramas that he quoted from so freely, such as the plays about the Henrys or the Richards, depicted an England divided by civil war as two rival clans, the House of York and the House of Lancaster, vied for control of the realm. The tragedies he preferred, like *Macbeth* or *Hamlet*, concerned the nature of evil and civil disorder created by disruptions in the succession of kings. These are themes that he appreciated long before the war, but ones that developed special resonance for him as the conflict erupted in the aftermath of his own election. "Some of Shakespeare's plays I have never read," he explained, "while others I have gone over perhaps as frequently as any unprofessional reader."[21]

Not all of Lincoln's readings invoked such dark and brooding topics. He was also fond of comic verse from popular poets such as Thomas Hood or Fitz-Greene Halleck. He favored a group of nineteenth-century American prose humorists, men such as Petroleum V. Nasby (a pen name for David R. Locke) who posed as a crude southern sympathizer in a series of wonderful wartime satires. The president often read from Artemus Ward (Charles F. Browne), probably the best-known nineteenth-century American humorist before the emergence of Mark Twain. Lincoln also appreciated the character Orpheus C. Kerr (Robert H. Newell), whose biting commentary on the ways of the nation's capital struck a special chord with the politician. A number of cottage guests testified to Lincoln's talent for mimicry, which he employed with delightful effect when reading from comic pieces by one of these authors.

Recreating the physical scene where these readings and intimate social gatherings took place is a difficult task. Most of the guests recorded only fleeting observations about the interior design of the cottage, the layout of the parlor or the style of the furniture. Still, some interesting details have emerged. A receiving parlor at the former Riggs cottage appears to have been opposite the front entryway. It had windows that opened onto a porch facing one edge of the grounds. A fireplace occupied one wall, useful during late autumn evenings when the air around the cottage grew chillier. The residence was also equipped with gaslights. By the standards of the Victorian era, the parlor was only lightly furnished with a handful of sofas and chairs. Mary Lincoln tried to refurbish the interior of the cottage in the spring of 1864 by hiring a local upholsterer to add wallpaper to several of the rooms and to lay down what was then considered seasonal grass matting on the hallways and various rooms.[22]

President Lincoln invariably removed his boots when entering the cottage and walked around in his slippers. When it was particularly hot, he also carried a large palm-leaf fan to help circulate the air. The image he presented to visitors was casual—a rumpled, often tired country gentleman preparing for bed. Englishman George Borrett recalled during his 1864 visit that he and other guests were "ushered into a moderate-sized, neatly furnished drawing-room." After waiting a few minutes, they were informed by a grumpy valet that Mrs. Lincoln had already retired for the evening and did not feel well. They prepared to leave, but then suddenly, "there entered through the folding doors the long, lanky, lath-like figure" of President Lincoln. Borrett described the president "with hair ruffled, and eyes very sleepy," noting with amusement that his large feet were "enveloped in carpet slippers." Lincoln then proceeded to hold forth with his visitors on various political and legal topics before ending the audience with a recitation from Alexander Pope's famous poem, "Essay on Man."[23]

It is impossible to specify an exact number of visitors who spent such evenings at the Soldiers' Home cottage. There were probably hundreds who passed through the parlor during the first family's three seasons in residence, with a core group of about a dozen regulars and an unknown number of overnight guests. This book contains stories or insights from about seventy-five of these visitors. No easy label captures them. They were Union generals and lower-ranking officers, cabinet members and mid-level political appointees, journalists and old Illinois friends, congressmen and their wives, Washington socialites, and foreign dignitaries. Most were friends but some were strangers. It was an eclectic assortment of human diversions for a family in sore need of distraction.

The cottage visitors were certainly a fortunate group, and not just because of their proximity to greatness. Some were simply lucky to find the place. Although the Soldiers' Home was a public destination, favored by local residents for Sunday drives and afternoon strolls, it was not always easy to locate in the evenings. Several guests reported that their hacks or taxi drivers got lost on the path to the cottage. "Our driver missed the way," recalled one of the president's old acquaintances visiting from Illinois, "passing by the Home into the forest below." The man claimed that he and his other friends did not make it out of the "labyrinth" until nearly two o'clock in the morning and missed a chance to see the president.[24] Traveling on the Seventh Street Turnpike at such hours could be dangerous as well. There was a racetrack nearby and several taverns and houses of prostitution in the vicinity. "Rode home in the dark amid a party of drunken gamblers & harlots," reported John Hay in his diary, after returning from an evening with the president.[25]

But for the Lincolns, practically nothing could disturb their image of an idyllic country retreat. "We are truly delighted, with this retreat," Mary Lincoln happily concluded early in their first season, "the drives & walks around here are delightful, & each day, brings its visitors."[26] The family not only came out each season after 1862—and would have done so again in 1865—but also husband and wife made the Home a frequent destination for their regular afternoon carriage rides. They began riding out in March 1861 and continued the habit throughout the next four years. Walt Whitman reported seeing them together in the summer of 1863 "toward the latter part of the afternoon, out in a barouche, on a pleasure ride through the city." He noted that over a year after Willie Lincoln's death, Mary Lincoln was still "dressed in complete black, with a long crape veil." According to the poet, these rides were taken without military escort. "The equipage is of the plainest kind," he wrote in his journal, "only two horses, and they nothing extra."[27]

The day before President Lincoln was fatally shot in April 1865, he took an afternoon ride on horseback without his wife, though accompanied by a small cavalry escort trailing behind him. Maunsell B. Field, who was then a senior political aide in the Treasury Department, recalled that he was himself heading out toward the Soldiers' Home when the president and his entourage came up behind him. Field claimed they "conversed together upon indifferent subjects" for a brief period. He noticed that the president was in a melancholy mood and seemed tired. Then Lincoln spurred his horse and headed off, presumably for his own customary ride around the grounds before returning to work at the White House. If Field's memory was accurate, this was the last time anyone would see the president traveling between his public and private worlds.[28]

❦

The story of the Soldiers' Home frames Lincoln's entire presidential experience. He first rode out to the retreat a few days after his inauguration. He last returned on the day before he was killed. Between those moments, he lived there for a total of thirteen months. Even more critically, he lived at this retreat during some of the key periods of the conflict, such as when he developed his emancipation policy in 1862 or maneuvered successfully toward reelection in 1864. Lincoln's challenge as a national leader was unprecedented. In that era of grave crisis, he naturally sought support within his private life to help sustain his public duty. The Soldiers' Home offered a sanctuary where he could work out this vital struggle.

It was not easy. During his first season at the Soldiers' Home, Lincoln faced critical decisions over emancipation, conscription, and the controversial fate of his leading general, George B. McClellan. All these grave decisions were related to one frustrating and tragic reality—the war was not ending. In the first year of the conflict Lincoln had done his part, holding together an improbable Union coalition that included both Democrats and Republicans and ultimately four out of the fifteen slave states. But the slow pace of mobilization and the failure of Union military commanders to win decisive victories created pressure on President Lincoln to raise the stakes of the war.

The first section of this book describes how he wrestled with each of the decisions that escalated both the war's level of violence and its larger meaning. As the president veered back and forth between his difficult choices in the summer and autumn of 1862, he sometimes stumbled and lost his poise. He persevered, however, and ultimately found a workable balance by year's end. The first four chapters of the book suggest that this achievement was due at least in part to the sustenance Lincoln discovered both inside his newfound sanctuary and through the rhythm and unanticipated interactions of his daily commute.

Even well-versed students of the Civil War period might be surprised to discover some of the connections between this side of Lincoln's private life and his public decisions. On the evening before he issued a call for 300,000 more men in the war's second year, the president sat on the steps of the Soldiers' Home cottage, reciting poetry and brooding over the fate of Union armies. During the Confederate invasion of Maryland in September 1862, which led to the pivotal battle at Antietam, the president and the nervous young soldiers guarding his cottage actually heard the distant sound of cannon fire. While riding to the Soldiers' Home after issuing a controversial order suspending civil liberties, President Lincoln grumbled to an aide about high-level traitors in the Union army. Each private moment provides context for the public action.

The second section of the book describes the summer of 1863, which marked a turning point for the war and the Lincoln family. As the president waited anxiously for news from the battlefields at both Gettysburg and Vicksburg, his wife was thrown from a carriage on a road outside the Soldiers' Home. The first lady's wounds were initially considered minor, but they soon became infected and she nearly died. Robert Lincoln, rebuked by his father for not returning to Washington quickly enough, later claimed the episode permanently damaged his mother's already fragile emotional state. Not long after the accident, she left Washington for nearly eight weeks, seeking greater seclusion and rest in Vermont. Meanwhile, her husband remained in the capital, continuing his daily commute and focusing more effectively than ever before on the business of leading his administration.

The book's third section examines how Lincoln used the Soldiers' Home in 1864 when his concerns turned to the challenge of his reelection. It was here in August of that year, for example, that he vigorously defended his policies to politicians such as Carl Schurz, Alexander W. Randall, and Joseph T. Mills. These meetings illustrate, in the words of one participant, Lincoln's remarkable "elasticity of spirits" and document with surprising clarity his hardheaded strategy during a summer of discontent. Nothing better demonstrates Lincoln's willingness to play hardball, however, than a secret meeting he conducted at the Soldiers' Home in September 1864 with Copperhead political leader Fernando Wood. This was an encounter that has generally escaped Lincoln scholars but offers provocative insight into how far the president was willing to consider going to secure his reelection.

Lincoln's final season at the Soldiers' Home literally began and ended under siege. The family ventured out to the cottage in early July 1864 only to be ordered back to the White House in the middle of the night by Secretary of War Edwin Stanton when Confederate troops threatened the city's defenses on July 10. President Lincoln then risked his own life on two separate occasions as he tried to view the Rebel assaults against Fort Stevens. The family soon returned to the cottage, but as the summer wore on, there were reports in increasing numbers from soldiers, servants, and neighbors around the Soldiers' Home indicating threats against the president's life, specifically those targeting him as he made his daily commute. By the time he returned to the White House in late autumn, the War Department had ratcheted up his personal security by several degrees. In addition to an infantry company and a cavalry escort—both now on full alert—the president also received for the first time a personal bodyguard made up of former Washington police detectives. They would remain on a high state of alert until the following spring when the Confederacy collapsed and the war finally appeared to be ending.

The evolution of the president's security arrangements constitutes a critical element of this narrative. Lincoln had arrived in Washington in 1861 amid fears of an assassination plot against him. Under pressure from concerned advisers, he had been persuaded to enter the city secretly and in partial disguise. This was new terrain since no American president had ever been murdered in office. Given that history and the heated political spirit of the times, president-elect Lincoln received some fierce criticism and ridicule for his "cowardly" entry into office.[29] As a result, he generally declined further security precautions on his behalf during the war's first year. But once his family was living outside the city at the Soldiers' Home in the fall of 1862, he had no choice. The Confederate movement across the Potomac in September demanded extra security around the cottage. Only at this time did Lincoln finally accept the assignment of both a cavalry and an infantry company to help protect the first family.

This turned out to be a decision that changed the nature of the war for President Lincoln in an unexpected way. Obviously the military guards did not succeed in saving the president's life. They did, however, improve it. Despite his initial objections, Lincoln grew to appreciate the presence of soldiers around him. They helped distract him from his concerns and helped him recreate some of the spirit of fraternity that he had once enjoyed as a younger politician and circuit-riding attorney in Illinois.

During the many weeks when his family was away, Lincoln seemed to crave such company, in particular reaching out not only to the soldiers but also to a shifting handful of aides and colleagues who became close friends and helped alleviate some of his loneliness. Many of these friendships were temporary or superficial, but one in particular had lasting consequences for the Union cause. Lincoln's second secretary of war, Edwin Stanton, also maintained a cottage at the Soldiers' Home. Here, he and his children interacted with the president and his family and helped cement a partnership that contributed mightily to the Union victory. All of these bonds ultimately proved to be a great irony of Lincoln's life at the Soldiers' Home. What began as an attempt to find seclusion for his family became a rare opportunity for an overburdened president to experience moments of intimate camaraderie.

This raises a final but essential point. To see Lincoln with a new lens inevitably means to hear new voices. Like all books on the Lincoln presidency, this

one rounds up many of the usual suspects among Civil War diarists and memoir writers. White House staffers John Hay and John Nicolay are frequent con-
tributors. The journals of cabinet members such as Salmon Chase and Gideon
Welles provide important material. Recollections from various secondary figures, like painter Francis Carpenter or journalist Noah Brooks, have been mined
extensively for references to the Soldiers' Home. But the heart of this narrative
comes from testimony not generally reported in Lincoln biographies.

Readers will discover figures such as David V. Derickson and Willard Cutter. Captain Derickson led the infantry unit assigned to the Soldiers' Home, a
company that included his eighteen-year-old son Charles. The politically minded
businessman from Meadville, Pennsylvania, quickly established himself as a
regular presence in President Lincoln's life. He forged a remarkable friendship
with the president that quickly became the object of jealous gossip. His recollections, and those of his son, offer important new details about the first family.

Willard Cutter was a private in Derickson's company, also from Meadville.
Like the president, he escaped private tragedy himself in 1862 by coming to
the Soldiers' Home. Cutter had left behind in Pennsylvania a recently widowed
mother who naturally feared for the life of her young son. The result was a
blessing for historians even though it was an occasional annoyance to the soldier. "You seem to be awful tender-hearted," he wrote to his mother in 1864, "I
hope you don't think you are the only woman that has a son in the army."[30]
Nonetheless, the dutiful young man wrote to his family about once each week,
detailing his adventures in Company K, the infantry unit assigned to guard the
Lincoln family from September 1862 until the end of the war. Though not a
good speller or an especially imaginative observer, Cutter was nonetheless a
faithful chronicler. What makes his particular bundle of approximately 150
letters so extraordinary, however, is its provenance. For years, the Cutter letters
were passed along from one generation of his family to the next, until they
were donated to Allegheny College in the 1970s. They have been used by local
Civil War reenactors, but never before by scholars.

There are many more secondary figures like Derickson and Cutter whose
names almost never appear in Lincoln biographies but whose stories enhance
this narrative. "Aunt" Mary Dines, a runaway slave who served as the family's
cook at the Soldiers' Home cottage, shares recollections of Lincoln visiting her
"contraband" or runaway camp in Washington. There are rare documents from
other soldiers, such as the court-martial transcript of Captain George A. Bennett,
who led the Ohio cavalry escort assigned to the president near the war's end.
The unpopular officer endured a revolt from within his company by troops
who accused him of embezzling government rations. Although no letters or
diaries have emerged from the residents of the Soldiers' Home itself, the

institution's quarterly rolls nevertheless reveal dramatic details about the troubled lives of the crippled veterans who lived right next to the president.

If this sounds like the beginnings of a novel, then that is not entirely unexpected. Narrative histories can often read like novels, aspiring to engage readers with compelling characters and intimate detail. Yet historians, unlike novelists, cannot transcend the sometimes frustrating limits of their evidence. When taken together, the new images of Lincoln culled from sources as diverse as Walt Whitman or Willard Cutter are fresh and, at times, even extraordinary. But they are also mere snapshots. There were over a hundred members of Cutter's infantry company. Testimony of one sort or another is currently available from only about a dozen of them. Lincoln's general movements can literally be traced day by day during the Civil War, but the exact location of his bedroom at the Soldiers' Home is still something of a mystery. Historians can always find a memorable journal entry from a poet like Whitman to open a book, but there are never enough of these types of entries to answer all questions of interpretation or even to create a fully realized narrative. Too many past moments are simply left unobserved. "I see the President," Whitman wrote. That is something a good historian can only dream about.

Part One

1862

☙

1

"Gone to the country"

ON A FRIDAY AFTERNOON NEAR THE END OF MAY 1862, MARY LINCOLN RECEIVED a note from a young White House aide that she considered inappropriate. John Hay, a twenty-three-year-old presidential assistant, was casually inquiring if the Marine Band might once again begin its summer concerts on the White House lawn. It was just a few months after the death of her second son, and the first lady was emphatic in response. "It is our *especial* desire," she wrote, "that the Band, does not play in these grounds, this Summer," adding firmly, "We expect our wishes to be complied with."[1]

Hay had clashed with the president's wife before. Not far removed from his college days at Brown University, the handsome Illinois native had a bachelor's impatience with assertive women. Meanwhile, Mary Lincoln had been determined in the first year of her husband's administration to establish herself as mistress of the nation's house. Their competing interests and insecurities made for some explosive moments. Although the two figures eventually forged a workable truce, during this period the sniping was fairly constant. "The Hellcat is getting more Hell-cattical day by day," the young attorney had confided to a fellow aide only a month earlier.[2]

The tension over the exclusion of the popular Marine Band did not dissipate easily. There was yet another stiff exchange of notes as Hay proceeded to probe the first lady's resolve. He next questioned whether the band might be allowed to perform across the street in Lafayette Park. For Mary Lincoln, still in the process of formal grieving, it was simply too much. "It is hard that in this time of our sorrow," she complained, "we should be thus harassed."[3]

The solution was evident. The first family needed some time away from the White House. Near the outset of his term, the president and Mary Lincoln had discussed the possibility of establishing a summer residence on the city's out-skirts. They knew that former president James Buchanan had enjoyed his time at a place called the Soldiers' Home, a government-run retirement community for crippled or disabled veterans. The relatively new institution had been built on the grounds of local banker George W. Riggs's country estate and contained several suitable cottages amid its shaded hills. But the war intervened, and the surprising Union defeat at Bull Run on July 22, 1861, had derailed their sum-mer plans.

A year later, the fighting continued, but the private tragedy of Willie Lincoln's death had affected the calculus of the first family's public business. President Lincoln had resumed his regular schedule within a week of his son's demise, but Mary Lincoln found it more difficult to emerge from her mourning. This was partly a "cultural" problem, in the words of biographer Jean H. Baker, since it was "a romantic age of exaggerated postures" that demanded from women repeated displays of formalized grief.[4] Under constant scrutiny from Washington society and the national press, Mary Lincoln attempted to meet expectations as a grieving mother while still performing her role as first lady. The flap over the Marine Band simply illustrated the conflicting pressures on a family that was supposed to be both normal and extraordinary at the same time.

"Our home [at the White House] is very beautiful," Mary Lincoln admitted a few days following her eruption over the summer concerts. But she reflected in a letter to a friend that while "the grounds around us are enchanting, [and] the world still smiles & pays homage . . . the charm is dispelled—everything appears a mockery, [because] the idolised one, is not with us, he has fulfilled his mission and we are left desolate." She predicted that the family would be resid-ing in the Soldiers' Home by July 1. "I dread that it will be a greater resort than here, if possible," she wrote, "when we are in sorrow, quiet is very necessary to us."[5] The Lincolns, including husband, wife, and youngest son Tad, left for the Soldiers' Home during the second week of June. Their eldest son, Robert, re-turning from college at Harvard, joined them a few weeks later.

With the decision to establish a presidential retreat came almost immediate relief. After a busy first year the White House office staff, consisting mainly of Hay and his colleague, John G. Nicolay, relished the extra space that the ab-sence of the family afforded them. "Mrs. Lincoln moved out to the 'Soldiers Home,' about a mile and a half from the city this past week," senior aide Nicolay wrote to his fiancée on Sunday, June 15, "so that John and I are left almost alone in the house here." The gruff former journalist added, "I am very glad of the change for several reasons, particularly that it gives us more time to our-selves, the crowd only coming when they know the President to be about."[6]

Mary Lincoln also appreciated an escape from the dreaded White House crowd. Benjamin B. French, the commissioner of public buildings, reported in his journal that he had seen the first lady on Monday heading out to her "summer home." "She seemed to be in excellent spirits," he observed, "and delighted at getting out of the city."[7] The president's immediate reaction to the change in scenery has gone unrecorded, but he took quick advantage of the opportunity by noticeably reducing his workload. Nicolay reported to his fiancée that Lincoln was not arriving in the mornings until about ten and was leaving by four o'clock in the afternoon—a relatively light schedule for the hardworking executive.

The president certainly seemed eager to show off his new country lodgings. On Wednesday, June 18, he sent a carriage to the local residence of Senator Orville H. Browning, a Republican from Illinois, inviting him to the cottage for breakfast. Browning, an old friend from Lincoln's days as a lawyer and state legislator, had been appointed to fill the unexpired term of Stephen A. Douglas upon the latter's death in mid-1861. The new senator decided to bring along some important government contractors for this unexpected private meeting with the president. Before heading out to the country, he stopped at Willard's Hotel and convinced New York retail giant Alexander T. Stewart and his close friend Judge Henry Hilton to join him. Stewart, a Scots-Irish immigrant with flaming red hair, had become one of the wealthiest businessmen in America and the principal supplier of uniforms to the Federal army. Hilton was a Democratic party functionary in New York and a trusted business associate of Stewart's.

"The conversation at the Presidents was chiefly on public affairs," Browning noted in his diary. "Mr. Stewart is very earnest in his support of the Union cause, and urged that [George B.] McClelland [sic] should be superceded and Genl [John] Pope given the command of the Army of the Potomac. He has no confidence in McClellan." This conversation took place nearly a year after thirty-four-year-old George B. McClellan had been given command of the Army of the Potomac and about three months after the young general had launched his much delayed initial campaign on the Virginia peninsula. Such criticism from a leading government contractor was revealing, although by no means surprising. There had been little progress in the eastern theater of the conflict and many observers were questioning both the strategy and the new commander. After enjoying a honeymoon with the press and public through his first six months on the job, the "Young Napoleon," as McClellan was first called, had been steadily losing support, especially from more restless members of Congress and the cabinet who questioned his fighting spirit.

Even the president had become frustrated. He had wanted McClellan to attack directly along the ninety-mile corridor from Washington to Richmond. The first battle of the war had occurred in that region at a small northern Virginia town called Manassas (near Bull Run Creek) and the area remained a focal point of public attention. "Forward to Richmond" had been the cry in July 1861 and ever since, at least with large segments of the northern homefront. For the president, however, the issue was not so much about satisfying public opinion as it was about attacking the principal Confederate force on the outskirts of Richmond. A direct land campaign also offered the advantage of maintaining a Federal army in front of the nation's besieged capital. Lincoln, who had no military experience beyond a few months' service in the militia, considered the strategic issue to be straightforward. The war was a rebellion, in his opinion, organized and executed by a handful of traitors, whose armies needed to be hunted down and destroyed as quickly as possible in order to restore normal civil relations among the various states. He wanted his generals to attack promptly and relentlessly.

McClellan saw the situation differently, finding his task far more complicated, almost overwhelmed by the logistical challenge of subduing over 750,000 square miles of southern territory while protecting his own troops, an exposed capital city, and the extended northern border. Ultimately, he came to believe that by flanking the Rebel troops in northern Virginia with the Union's largest and best-trained fighting force—his custom-built Army of the Potomac—he would achieve a strategic advantage. Thus, in the spring of 1862, after months of delay, he had transported a large body of his troops through the Chesapeake Bay down to the Virginia peninsula, eventually landing near the sites of the original Jamestown settlement and Yorktown battlefield. The president never reconciled himself to this decision and repeated his objections to the strategy on the morning of June 18. According to Browning, Lincoln told his breakfast companions that this was against his better judgment and that he had allowed himself to be overruled by a consensus of his generals.

> During the conversation the president stated, what he on several previous occasions communicated to me, that his opinion always had been that the great fight should have been at Manasses [*sic*]—that he had urged it upon McClellan that if the enemy left Manasses [*sic*] he would entrench at York Town, and we would have the same difficulties to encounter there—that McClellan was opposed to fighting at Manassas, and he, the president, then called a Council of twelve generals, and submitted his proposition for fighting at Manasses [*sic*] to them, and that eight of them decided against him, and four concurred with him, of whom [Samuel P.] Heintzelman was one. The majority being so great against him he yielded, but subsequent events had satisfied him he was right.[8]

Both the tone and content of Lincoln's remarks that morning were revealing. At ease within the quiet confines of the Soldiers' Home, he spoke freely about his doubts and about internal dissension within the military high command. After an often-frustrating year of stalemate, he was no longer planning to defer to his so-called military experts. It was interesting that he claimed credit for convening the controversial March council of war. In his memoirs, McClellan insisted that he was the one who had been responsible for submitting the plan to a vote of the twelve generals, mainly as a vehicle for embarrassing his skeptical commander in chief.[9] Browning recalled that their heated breakfast conversation lasted until half past ten in the morning. The small group then rode into the city, joined by Lincoln's youngest son Tad, who wanted to play with the senator's daughter Emma.

About the time that the president's small party was making its way toward the White House, General McClellan telegraphed the War Department that he had just received reports of a significant number of Confederate troops leaving Richmond to reinforce General Thomas "Stonewall" Jackson's army in the Shenandoah Valley. Since the beginning of the peninsula campaign, Jackson and his men had been complicating Union military plans, and causing tension between the president and his principal general, by harassing Federal forces in the northwestern valley region of Virginia and threatening to advance on nearby Washington. Lincoln considered the intelligence to be good news, indicating new vulnerabilities in the defenses around the Confederate capital. Not surprisingly, McClellan disagreed, believing that the move "illustrates their strength and confidence." With Stewart's criticism still ringing in his ears, the president responded to the report by informing his commander bluntly in a coded telegram that he could "better dispose of things" if he could finally "know about what day you can attack Richmond."[10]

Later on June 18, the president had another important conversation on "public affairs" at the Soldiers' Home, although this meeting concerned the fate of slavery, not the progress of the Union armies. According to the recollection of Vice President Hannibal Hamlin, he stopped by the White House that afternoon just prior to taking a planned vacation. The president requested that Hamlin delay his journey temporarily and that evening the two men went to the Lincoln cottage, shared dinner, and then went upstairs into a "library." At that point, according to Hamlin's account, Lincoln "opened a drawer in his desk and took therefrom the first draft of a military proclamation freeing four millions of slaves."[11]

If true, this discussion at the Soldiers' Home cottage would indeed represent a pivotal moment, offering the very first evidence concerning Lincoln's endorsement of emancipation as a Union war aim. Since the beginning of his political career, Lincoln had been antislavery, but with firm boundaries to the scope of his opposition. Like many northerners during the 1850s, the future president had become agitated by what he considered the arrogance of the southern slave states and their political allies in the North. He was most aroused by the 1854 repeal of the Missouri Compromise. The famous sectional deal over the admission of Maine and Missouri as states had prevented the introduction of slavery into the former Louisiana Purchase territories since 1820. What made the insult of this repeal almost personal for Lincoln was knowing that his longtime rival, Senator Stephen Douglas, had sponsored the action. Lincoln quickly emerged as a leading figure in the new Republican party, an organization that made opposition to the extension of slavery the cornerstone of its political platform. Subsequently, the Republicans became the only antislavery political movement of that era to achieve a national majority—a feat made even more unlikely since they had practically no support whatsoever south of the Mason-Dixon line. Yet even though Lincoln had been elected as the representative of this great antislavery groundswell, he did not consider his victory in 1860 a mandate to dismantle the peculiar institution in states where it already existed. Instead, he entered office focused on the goal of preventing any further extension of slavery while still preserving the Union, essentially what Republicans had been arguing for since Douglas's controversial Kansas-Nebraska Act of 1854.

But the secession of southern states and the outbreak of war soon changed everything. In the first place, slaves had little interest in the details of the Constitution or the Republican party platform. As news of the war spread, the number of fugitives grew exponentially. Their mass exodus inevitably forced a response. Before long, Union general Benjamin Butler had labeled the runaways who made it safely into his camp "contraband of war," equating the ex-slaves with seized Rebel property and thus indicating that he had no intention of returning them to slavery. The phrase delighted members of the northern press who soon dubbed wartime fugitives "contrabands." Some Union generals, men such as John Frémont and David Hunter, went further and attempted to issue emancipation proclamations in the field to encourage even more runaway slaves. Yet President Lincoln, concerned about the constitutionality of such actions and the politics of his rickety coalition, immediately revoked these orders. He also resisted similar calls to action from some members of Congress and his cabinet.

By the spring of 1862, Lincoln had defined his position on the abolition of slavery according to a set of three guiding principles, and a fourth, usually unspoken, assumption. The president believed that emancipation must be gradual, compensated, and voluntary. These were not philosophical issues with him as much as political and legal ones. Out of the nation's fifteen slave states, four still remained within the Union—Delaware, Kentucky, Maryland, and Missouri. Lincoln repeatedly claimed that the fate of the war hinged on their continued allegiance. In a special message to Congress delivered on March 6,

1862, he asserted that to deprive Confederate leaders of the "hope" that they might win over the remaining slave states "substantially ends the rebellion."[12] Conservative by nature, he was also uncomfortable with abolitionist strategies that ignored property rights and legal precedents that had protected slavery in established states. The unspoken assumption of Lincoln's plan to end slavery concerned its aftermath. He was not yet in favor of full equality for blacks, arguing instead, whenever the topic arose, that freed slaves might be sent abroad or colonized voluntarily, preferably somewhere in Central America.

Lincoln was quite adamant about these principles. In April 1862, for instance, the Congress passed a bill abolishing slavery in the District of Columbia immediately but with compensation for loyal slave owners. Senator Browning noted in his private diary that the president said he "regretted" the legislation, even though he signed it, because it did not provide for the gradual strategy that he preferred. According to the Illinois senator, Lincoln told him that he was worried that white families in the city "would at once be deprived of cooks, stable boys &c." He also claimed that the president informed him "in the strictest confidence" that he had secretly delayed signing the bill into law long enough to allow an important figure in the capital to remove his "sickly" slaves because they "would not be benefitted [sic] by freedom."[13]

The president's desire to move cautiously against slavery collided with the plans of the more aggressive Republican-controlled Congress. In June and July 1862, both House and Senate engaged in an intensive debate over general emancipation for Rebel-owned slaves—what legislators termed "confiscation." They soon passed what became known as the Second Confiscation Act (July 17, 1862) that vowed to free slaves of disloyal owners. This mounting pressure compelled Lincoln to reconsider his entire position on abolition. By the close of the year he became committed to the idea that emancipation of Rebel-owned slaves was a necessary war measure and that it must be immediate and uncompensated. He also accepted the idea that freed slaves should be allowed to remain in the country and serve in the Union's armed forces along with other northern free blacks.

The challenge for historians is to pinpoint exactly when the president came around to these new, more far-reaching policies on emancipation and citizenship for African Americans. That is why Hamlin's claim that he listened to an early draft of Lincoln's "military proclamation" at the Soldiers' Home on the evening of June 18 is so provocative. It would be the earliest date available suggesting a change of views on the first part of this critical matter.

There are several reasons, however, for doubting a story that historian David Donald has dismissed as "rather too circumstantial."[14] It comes from a biography written by an adoring grandson who was relying on materials originally put together by his father (and the vice president's son). The vice president was not intimate with the president and because he was closely identified with the radical antislavery wing of the Republican party, it is especially unlikely that Lincoln would have shared such sensitive information, especially at this stage. The vice president's grandson was also openly defensive about his grandfather's ineffectual role in the administration. But most significantly, other evidence appears to contradict the gist of the recollection. On June 20, 1862, just two days after Lincoln had supposedly outlined his new direction at the cottage, he responded to a delegation of Quakers lobbying for emancipation by denying any interest in such policies. "If a decree of emancipation could abolish Slavery, John Brown would have done the work effectually," he wrote, referring to the prewar abolitionist martyr. "Such a decree surely could not be more binding upon the South than the Constitution, and that cannot be enforced in that part of the country now." He added grimly, "Would a proclamation of freedom be any more effective?"[15]

There is an important lesson about the writing of history in the juxtaposition of the two conversations that reportedly took place on June 18 at the Soldiers' Home cottage. One discussion is recorded in a participant's diary, and while not infallible, it provides nineteenth-century historians with a gold standard in terms of evidence quality. The other source is a third-hand recollection offered years after the fact and contradicted by some contemporary information. This does not mean that the second story is necessarily false, but only that it is unreliable and unlikely. Yet one must remember that even this flawed recollected source is a rare gem. Meetings at the Soldiers' Home were informal and ad hoc, without roll calls, minutes, or transcripts. Many of the president's visitors left no record of their encounters at all. To ignore the handful of remaining recollections—whether entered hours later in diaries or years later in published memoirs—is therefore to lose an entire layer of political and social interactions.

There is also another, more subtle lesson lurking in the meetings of June 18. The narrative appeal of combining the two incidents is almost irresistible. Taken together, the conversations about McClellan and emancipation illustrate how the war evolved from a limited conflict about enforcing the Constitution to a bloody, revolutionary struggle that redefined the national purpose. The president was steadily moving toward a realization that the scope of the rebellion had permanently altered the terms of the political debate. He might not have realized all this in a single day in June 1862, but that day was coming nonetheless. The story of this awakening has become a standard interpretation of the Civil War. It is easy to understand why a scholar might be tempted to rationalize including the Hamlin recollection for the sake of making the larger story more dramatic. Examine the guts of any narrative history carefully enough and you will find problematic recollected sources such as this one that were simply too useful to pass by. The lesson is to be vigilant about how sources and stories influence each other. In the struggle to evaluate evidence, the rhythms of narrative invariably color perceptions of what constitutes truth.

With those warnings in mind, it is worth pointing out that the Browning diary is without question the best available source for Lincoln's first weeks at the Soldiers' Home. The old acquaintance from Illinois visited the cottage five times in little more than a month, carefully noting on each occasion the various guests he brought along for the social enjoyment of the president and his family. Square-jawed, with an unruly mat of short hair and piercing eyes, Browning's almost Roman aura offered a striking contrast to Lincoln's earthy demeanor and gangly appearance. Like the president, however, Browning was a self-made man, also born in Kentucky and also devoted to politics and the law. Back in Illinois, Lincoln and Browning had been colleagues on friendly terms but did not regard each other as intimate friends. The future president had actually seemed more at ease with his friend's wife, Eliza Caldwell Browning, turning to her occasionally in his bachelor days for advice about women. For many years, Browning seemed to regard Lincoln with polite indifference, hardly referring to him in the pages of his journal until they reconnected in Washington during the winter of 1861–1862. Only in that season of private grief and national tragedy did Lincoln and Browning draw closer together. The Illinois senator emerged as one of the few people in the president's life who could bridge his public and private worlds.[16]

An example of how Browning's multifaceted friendship served the president occurred on Sunday, June 22. They attended services together at the New York Avenue Presbyterian Church and then spent part of the morning in quiet discussion at the White House. Lincoln pulled his friend into the mansion's library and showed him "some memoranda of important events" that had been put together "by his little son Willie," and which he had only just recently discovered. Reviewing the list of battles and other occasions noted in the precocious scrawl of his favored child, the president indulged in a rare moment of poignant reflection. Earlier in his life, Lincoln's closest friends considered him to be almost too sensitive, prone to bouts of melancholy and blessed (or cursed) with a poetic nature. But there was no longer much time for poetry, and Lincoln quickly snapped out of his reverie and began showing the senator several maps of Vicksburg, a Confederate stronghold on the Mississippi River that was the target of an ongoing Union military operation. This brief scene, recorded in the Browning diary, presents one of the few direct observations of the grieving father seeking solace in his work.[17]

The fact that the president was not using summertime as an excuse to skip Sunday services testified at least in part to the transformation brought on by Willie Lincoln's death. Lincoln had been an occasional churchgoer in Spring-field, but he became a more frequent one in Washington. A number of con-temporaries later claimed to have detected a newfound faith in the president by mid-1862. Historians have since questioned many of these recollected impres-sions, and it is true that Lincoln never formally joined a congregation nor announced a conversion to Christ. Still, it is clear that in the aftermath of his son's death and amid the ever-increasing casualties of war, Lincoln turned in-ward, seeking greater faith—though always with his native skepticism. "Some-times in my difficulties I have been driven to the last resort to say God is still my only hope," he told a delegation of ministers in 1863, even while admitting that he wished he was " a more devoted man than I am." Several scholars have also noted that in his wartime writings and conversations, the president began invoking the divinity more frequently and more emphatically.[18]

As President Lincoln became more spiritual, Mary Lincoln became more interested in spiritualism. Following Willie Lincoln's death, she suspended all White House entertainment, ordered stationery with thick black borders, and wore black for over a year. Nevertheless, she still found these traditional mourn-ing customs inadequate. "How often, I feel rebellious, and almost believe that our Heavenly Father, has forsaken us," she confessed in July, "in removing, so lovely a child from us!"[19] Guests to the cottage in the summer of 1862 some-times found Mary Lincoln inconsolable. "It was months after Willie's death," reported journalist Laura Redden who visited the cottage on horseback, "but she was in deep black and her affliction seemed as fresh as ever."

> She entered the room where I awaited her, evidently striving for some composure of manner; but, as I took the hand which she extended to me, she burst into a passion of tears and gave up all effort at self-control. For a moment my feeling of respect for the wife of the President was uppermost; then my sympathies for the bereaved mother got the better of conventionalities, and I put my arm around her and led her to a seat, saying everything I could think of to calm her; but she could neither think nor talk of anything but Willie.[20]

Like many grieving contemporaries, the first lady subsequently turned to me-diums or spiritualists in an attempt to reach into the afterlife and contact her missing loved ones.

Spiritualism was one of the great fads of the age, especially among educated, middle-class northerners. It was unorthodox but not unusual. According to the historian Jean H. Baker, by the middle of the 1850s "there were more spiritual-ists than abolitionists" in northern cities like Boston and New York, where not coincidentally, the first lady often traveled.[21] Exposed to these spiritualists dur-

Mary Lincoln, with youngest sons Willie (left) and Tad (right), in 1860. CHICAGO HISTORICAL SOCIETY.

ing her visits, and encouraged by friends like Elizabeth Keckley, her seamstress, and Secretary of Navy Gideon Welles and his wife Mary Jane, the first lady began participating in circles or seances soon after Willie Lincoln's death.

According to journalist Noah Brooks, Mary Lincoln held at least one circle at the Soldiers' Home cottage with a medium named Charles J. Colchester, whose suspicious character soon alarmed her husband. Like many spiritualists, Colchester relied principally on "tapping" to raise the dead. Brooks described how "in a darkened room" at the family's country home, Colchester "pretended to produce messages from the lost boy by means of scratches on the wainscoting and taps on the walls and furniture."[22] The president subsequently asked Dr. Joseph Henry, head of the Smithsonian Institute, to investigate the man who portrayed himself as an illegitimate son of an English aristocrat. Henry met with the spiritualist at his office but was unable to identify the source of the mysterious sounds. Brooks then participated in a seance with "Lord" Colchester for the purpose of exposing him, a goal he ultimately achieved, but not before the spiritualist tried unsuccessfully to blackmail an embarrassed first lady.[23] Mary Lincoln continued to engage psychics, even pressing her husband into attendance at one of the eight seances it appears that she held in the White House during the war.[24] There is no way to calculate a total for such occult events at the Soldiers' Home, but it seems likely that Lord Colchester was not the only medium to visit their wartime retreat.

In their respective struggles to cope with tragedy, Abraham and Mary Lincoln embodied a larger cultural obsession with the precariousness of life. Death was a familiar shadow over nineteenth-century American families, even before the war began and only more so in its wake. As children, both the president and the first lady had endured the deaths of their own mothers. Now they had lost two of their four children. Most of those around them—members of the cabinet, family friends, and servants—had similar stories. Edwin Stanton had lost his first wife and a child to illness and his brother to suicide in the 1840s. He lost another infant son six months after Willie Lincoln died. Gideon Welles had a son who died as a child. Rebecca Pomroy, the family nurse, had lost a husband and three sons during the early years of the war. Elizabeth Keckley, Mary Lincoln's closest confidant among the family's servants, had also lost her only son in the war. During a time of larger families and primitive medical technology, death came frequently to almost every household. During the 1850s, average life expectancy was in the forties, owing largely to child mortality rates that exceeded 30 percent. Thus, the war, as terrible as it was, only intensified a reality that already existed. Nevertheless, the figures are unsettling to contemplate. There were over five million households and 31 million people in the nation on the eve of the Civil War. With over 620,000 combatant deaths and an estimated 50,000 civilian deaths, in addition to the standard mortality rates, it seems likely that about one out of every four American families experienced the loss of a household member at some point during the conflict.[25]

The shadow of death followed the Lincolns to the Soldiers' Home. The main institution just beside their cottage was refuge for more than a hundred aging or crippled veterans. Across the road over five thousand Union soldiers rested at a somber national cemetery that was the precursor to Arlington. And then, near the end of June, Lincoln saw his grief as father of a dying child repeated in a neighboring cottage. The Board of Commissioners of the Soldiers' Home customarily invited both the president and secretary of war to occupy cottages in the summer season. In 1862, Edwin Stanton had apparently taken advantage of the invitation. Sharing an adjacent cottage to the president's presumably allowed the intense, ambitious War Department head to enjoy breakfast with Lincoln and then ride with him into town, discussing military and political matters. There are no records testifying to this occasional arrangement other than a poignant note written by Stanton at 6:30 A.M. on Sunday, June 29, canceling their impending morning's plans. The cabinet officer wrote in rushed script that his wife had called him "home" because of the "increased illness of my child." "You will please get your breakfast at my house," he urged the president, noting that it was ordered for 9 A.M. Always efficient, Stanton claimed, "If my child is not dying I will be in town as early as possible."[26] It was a resolution that must have touched Lincoln deeply. Young James Stanton died in early July.

Before the war, Edwin Stanton had been a prominent lawyer, who once removed fellow attorney Abraham Lincoln from a case on which they were supposed to act as co-counsel because he considered his Springfield counterpart too unsophisticated. Stanton then served in James Buchanan's cabinet as attorney general and, along with his wife Ellen, emerged as a fixture in the Washington social scene. He was not part of the original Lincoln circle of advisers, but soon replaced Secretary of War Simon Cameron after the latter became embroiled in a series of scandals near the end of the administration's first year. Very quickly, Stanton gained a reputation for being rude and domineering—but also brutally effective. One of his employees in the War Department later described the bearded, bespectacled figure as "grand, gloomy and peculiar," and a leading Union general said that he had "a shaggy, belligerent sort of look" that scared away most politicians and favor-seekers.[27] Yet it was precisely Stanton's hard-edged demeanor that complemented and arguably made possible Lincoln's legendary compassion. Together, they made a fascinating team.

In late June 1862, the Lincoln-Stanton partnership was facing its first grave crisis of leadership, as General McClellan's forces engaged in what was called the Seven Days' battles (June 25–July 1). The president and the secretary of the War Department had pushed their reluctant general into combat and now the controversial peninsula campaign that McClellan had launched earlier in the spring was reaching its climax. Confederate resistance proved fiercer than expected and the president nervously considered his options. The day before Stanton was forced to skip their breakfast meeting to attend to his dying son, Lincoln had noted in a confidential memo that if he could only find 100,000 more troops for his embattled general, it would "substantially end the war."[28] The problem was that the Union army—now more than a half million men strong—was already overextended. Federal troops were attempting to advance along several fronts in the Mississippi Valley while still protecting Washington and simultaneously attacking Richmond. The only option was to find new soldiers, but the president and his advisers feared that the government could not "publicly appeal" for more volunteers because "a general panic and stampede would follow."[29] Most northerners still believed the war should have been successfully concluded months earlier and reports of widespread dissatisfaction lingered.

While Lincoln and Stanton remained in Washington, Secretary of State William Seward had slipped up to New York City for a hastily arranged meeting of northern governors. The politics of recruitment was tricky in this era before a compulsory national draft. The execution of raising troops largely fell to the states. Apparently, Seward had ventured to New York in the hopes of convincing the state executives to issue a joint statement encouraging the president to call on them for additional men. Instead, the governors persuaded the New York politician to draft a statement from the president touting the "energy and success" of the recent campaigns and vowing that only 150,000 more men would finally enable the "hopes and expectations" of the people to be realized. The secretary of state telegraphed this draft "Call for Troops" to Washington on June 30, 1862, but Stanton replied from the War Department at 9 P.M. that Lincoln had already "gone to the country very tired" and would not reach a decision on his course of action until morning.[30]

The exhausted president arrived at the Soldiers' Home to find his friend Orville Browning waiting for him, along with Orloff M. Dorman, a politician from Florida, and his wife, Margarette Dorman. A former Chicago resident, Dorman had once helped launch the sales office for the famous McCormick reapers and now hoped to be appointed the provisional governor of Union-occupied Florida.[31] Lincoln quickly excused himself from his unexpected visitors and pulled Browning outside to the porch. There the two men sat on the stone steps and discussed the military situation on the peninsula. Lincoln had a map in his pocket and showed Browning how agonizingly close McClellan's army was to Richmond. The president poured out the information he had, releasing all the tension of the previous few days.

When he had finished relating the various developments to Browning, Lincoln seemed unwilling to return inside to face the office-seeker resting impatiently in his cottage parlor. So he pulled out of his pocket a volume of poetry by Fitz-Greene Halleck and recited "about a dozen stanzas" from the book's longest poem, "Fanny" (1819). "The song at the end of the poem he read with great pathos," Browning wrote, "pausing to comment upon them, and then laughed immoderately at the ludicrous conclusion."[32] The stanzas Lincoln read that evening certainly had bittersweet meaning for him.

And childhood's frolic hours are brief,
And oft in after years
Their memory comes to chill the heart,
And dim the eye with tears.

The "ludicrous conclusion" that made him laugh so "immoderately" read:

And the mariner's song of home has ceased,
His corse is on the sea—
And music ceases when it rains
In Scudder's balcony.

The poem was intended to be a parody of the style of the famous English poet Lord Byron. The verses described the fate of a spoiled young woman contemplating marriage. The final line of the 10,000 word comic epic, "In Scudder's balcony," invoked a nineteenth-century term for a public display designed to turn out crowds, such as a band playing outside of a theater or music hall. The absurdity of the parting image tickled the president but infuriated many contemporary critics. The erudite *North American Review* dismissed the reference as "tasteless and unmeaning mockery." Halleck, who had been a private secretary to John Jacob Astor, was a well-known satirist whose work had been introduced to Lincoln by a Chicago literary editor in 1860.[33]

It must have been growing dark that early summer evening as Lincoln sat on the cottage steps chuckling over the strange conclusion to the brooding poem. It had been a long, tense week and this was obviously the release he needed. According to Secretary of War Stanton, the president had left for the country "very tired," feeling overburdened by the pressures of his looming decisions and anxious about the impending outcome of the pivotal Seven Days' battles in Virginia. Browning, with a greater sense of decorum and less responsibility than his old friend, disapproved slightly of the impromptu performance, but did so in silence, confining his comments to the pages of his private journal later that night. At least for the time being, the president was on friendly ground at the Soldiers' Home, blessed above all else with a distant view of his critics and rivals in the hot, embattled city below.

The brief respite was all Lincoln needed. The next morning, on Tuesday July 1, 1862, he called Browning into his office at the White House to read a "paper" he had composed "embodying his views of the objects of the war, and the proper mode of conducting it in its relations to slavery." The president said that the document had been "sketched hastily with the intention of laying it before the Cabinet." He must have written it the night before once his guests at the cottage had gone. The first principle of the president's draft memo was that "no" captured or escaped slaves—the celebrated contrabands—"are ever to be returned to slavery." This was confirmation of the existing reality, but it was also a major step toward the president's eventual emancipation doctrine. Lincoln was still opposed, however, to "inducements" for runaways, or for arming ex-slaves, out of concern, according to Browning's notes, over the army's morale and for other practical considerations. The senator also reported that the president was convinced that "Congress has no power over slavery in the states." Lincoln still claimed to believe that slavery in some places might survive the conflict and would be "in precisely the same condition that it was before the war began."[34] This "paper" on emancipation policy might have been a version of the document that Lincoln read to Hamlin on June 18, but its contents, if Browning's diary is accurate, did not yet constitute a full-fledged commitment to black freedom. Nevertheless, it was a striking sign of the president's continued evolution on the topic, demonstrating that his focus was shifting away from loyal slave states toward the more pressing question of how to use the prospect of emancipation as a military tool for subduing the rebellion.

Finding new tools for wartime success was clearly on Lincoln's mind that morning. After meeting with Browning, he went ahead and issued a call for 300,000 additional volunteers. "It was thought safest to mark high enough," he later wrote to one governor, explaining why he went beyond the expected request for 150,000 men. The proclamation was published with a communication from the governors, drafted by Seward and dated for June 28, that conveniently urged the president to adopt "prompt and vigorous measures" on behalf of the Union cause. The governors' document concluded with a dangerous burst of optimism: "All believe that the decisive moment is near at hand."[35]

2

"Am I to have no rest?"

THE DECISIVE SEVEN DAYS' BATTLES WERE THE BLOODIEST OF THE WAR TO THAT point. In a single week the Union lost more men—over 16,000—than had been in uniform at the outset of the conflict. Confederate losses were even ghastlier, but the inability of Federal troops to dislodge Rebel positions around Richmond signaled strategic failure for the Union cause. The springtime had been a hopeful period for the North, as Federal troops had scored a series of victories in the Mississippi Valley and as McClellan's Army of the Potomac had finally maneuvered into fighting position. Consequently, the impact of the bitter news from the Virginia peninsula threatened to devastate what had been rising northern morale. In this period of renewed crisis, President Lincoln grasped nervously for solutions.

A brief but revealing glimpse of Lincoln's concern appeared in the *New York Tribune* on July 8, 1862, under the heading, "THE PRESIDENT AND THE WOUNDED":

> The President on the Fourth, while on his way to his Summer Residence at Soldiers Home, meeting a train of ambulances conveying wounded men from the late battles to the hospitals, just beyond the city limits, rode beside them for a considerable distance, conversing freely with the men, and seeming anxious to secure all the information possible with regard to the real condition of affairs on the Peninsula and the feeling among the troops from those who had borne the brunt of the fight.[1]

Earlier, on Independence Day, the president had told a delegation of veterans, "I am indeed surrounded, as is the whole country, by very trying circumstances."[2] Now here was the nation's wartime president trailing forlornly along the ambulance trains heading out to the several temporary hospitals that were located near his summer residence, "seeming anxious" to uncover the "real condition of affairs" in the field. On the eighty-sixth anniversary of the nation's birth, the head of the government appeared almost lost.

And yet behind the pathos of this scene lay one secret to Lincoln's enduring popularity. However bewildered the president might have appeared to the *Tribune's* Washington correspondent, he was nonetheless at ease with the nation's ordinary people, someone capable of "conversing freely with the men" and willing to listen to "those who had borne the brunt of the fight." Lincoln's genuine accessibility often helped win over skeptics who felt empowered by his apparent interest in them. Many leaders in similar circumstances would have locked themselves away in the White House, attempting to escape from the constant criticism. In this fashion, the president's decision to relocate to the Soldiers' Home takes on a broader meaning, serving not just as his family's private retreat but also as a striking example of his outreach efforts. The daily commute promised regular, unstructured interaction with the people, which sometimes had value beyond calculation, as the clipping from the *Tribune* attests.

Lincoln was eager for accurate information about conditions along the peninsula because several of his wartime policies hinged on the outcome of this critical campaign. He had invested an enormous amount of personal political capital in the fate of George McClellan, his controversial field commander. The president was also heavily in debt to northern governors who had just recently announced their support for his call to have additional troops—an endorsement contingent on the "decisive" outcome they expected from McClellan's assault on Richmond. But perhaps most significant, Lincoln had based much of his cautious emancipation policy up to this date on the question of military necessity. He had argued that as long as the war was "substantially" near a conclusion, there was no need to upset the fragile Union political coalition by injecting the contentious issue of slavery. If there was real stalemate on the road toward Richmond, the president knew that the center of this argument could not hold much longer.

The uncertainty that followed the Seven Days was not unusual. Conducting a war in the telegraph age did not alleviate the problems of nineteenth-century communications. News still came slowly and often with troubling inaccuracies. Commanders in the field, naturally, offered biased reports of their progress. Newspapers of that era were equally unreliable as they were bitterly partisan and used their correspondents to promote political agendas. Most important, the absence of direct visual confirmation—the public's inability to see the news—created a climate in which wild rumors were common and a degree of skepticism was understandable.

On the evening of July 4, for example, an emotionally drained Lincoln was apparently pulled out of bed at his Soldiers' Home cottage by Union quartermaster Montgomery C. Meigs and former Minnesota governor Henry H. Sibley to hear disturbing and exaggerated reports about the situation on the peninsula. Meigs, almost in a state of panic, urged the President to order "the immediate flight of the Army," going so far as to suggest that their horses would have to be killed since the transports could not carry them. Lincoln was not impressed. Two years later he recalled the incident to an assistant, noting coldly that "I who am not a specially brave man have had to sustain the sinking courage of these professional fighters in critical times."[3]

Senator Browning reported that for a week after the final battle Lincoln was still inclined to believe that the result of the Seven Days' fighting was "much more satisfactory . . . than was previously supposed." The president had received dispatches from McClellan offering a positive account of the army's condition. He showed them to his friend on Saturday night, July 5, at the Soldiers' Home cottage. "The spirit of the army is excellent," McClellan had reported, ". . . all things looking bright." Lincoln offered "a thousand thanks" for the promising words, vowing they would "'hive' the enemy yet," but he remained wary since McClellan's tone contrasted so sharply with the reports of the President's other informants.[4] Deciding that he must view the situation for himself, Lincoln left for the Virginia peninsula on Monday.

On July 7, 1862, the president and a small party traveled down toward McClellan's headquarters at Harrison's Landing, Virginia, for two days of high-level meetings. The general had been requesting an opportunity to present his observations on the state of the conflict and used the visit to deliver a provocative written statement that summarized his impressions. Known as the Harrison's Landing letter, this document offered a strictly conservative view of the war. "A declaration of radical views, especially upon slavery," McClellan warned, "will rapidly disintegrate our present Armies." Still, the general acknowledged that "contraband" slaves should receive protection from Federal authorities. He also admitted that it was "only a question of time" before "military necessity" might justify compensated emancipation for slaves held in Union states such as Missouri, or "possibly even in Maryland." But the tone of the letter was decidedly against any further escalation of the war's stakes. McClellan urged his commander in chief to conduct the fighting only "upon the highest principles known to Christian Civilization," as he vehemently disparaged "a War upon population."[5] Given the president's long-standing frustration with McClellan, the note represented a dismal sign of more stalemate to come. Interviews with McClellan's corps commanders only underscored the hopelessness of their situation. Most felt that they could neither advance nor retreat without creating another catastrophe. Lincoln made no comment at that time but immediately began contemplating important changes in policy and personnel.

During this period of great strain on the president, it might be assumed that he found at least some relief with his family at the Soldiers' Home cottage. Mary Lincoln was certainly aware of her husband's difficulties. A few days before the trip to Harrison's Landing, she had informed an acquaintance while riding out to the summer residence that the president was hardly sleeping at night.[6] Yet the first lady was restless in Washington and by the time the president and his entourage returned from the peninsula, she and Tad Lincoln were already on their way for an extended excursion to New York City. They would not return until July 17.

If the President had trouble sleeping before his meetings with McClellan, his insomnia must have only worsened in the days following his return. Over the span of about two weeks, while he was left alone at the cottage, he made a series of decisions that prepared the way for a complete overhaul of the Union war effort.

The first major policy shift that Lincoln executed was one that had been in the works for some time. He named the scholarly Henry W. Halleck, called "Old Brains" by his ex-students, as general in chief of the Union armies. The former West Point instructor had served with distinction during the first year of the conflict, heading the Union military departments of Missouri and Mississippi. He was the third general-in-chief under President Lincoln, succeeding McClellan, who had lost the position in March when he left with his troops for the peninsula, and the aging war hero and former presidential candidate, General Winfield Scott, who had organized the Federal forces at the outset of the conflict. Lincoln had actually visited General Scott in West Point on June 23 and 24 to get a second opinion on McClellan's strategy. Whether they talked about replacements for the controversial general is unclear, but immediately on his return from New York, Lincoln had named General John Pope commander of a new force to be called the Army of Virginia. Pope, who had been part of the Union military's successes in the western theater, was the new favorite of Union advocates like businessman Alexander Stewart. By mid-July, the young general was preparing to join his new army in the field, ready to launch another overland assault against the Confederate forces near Richmond.

Emancipation was the other leading topic that occupied Lincoln's mind following his visit to Harrison's Landing. McClellan had specifically warned him against "radical" statements, but Lincoln had been cautious to this point in the vain hope that the peninsula campaign would be the war's decisive blow. Clearly, it was not. This disappointment compelled him to reconsider more daring alternatives. One source suggested to an early Lincoln biographer that it was on the boat ride back to Washington that the angry and disheartened president first began drafting an emancipation proclamation.[7] Secretary of Navy Gideon

Welles claimed that it was not a proclamation that Lincoln began crafting on the return trip but rather a "carefully written speech" aimed at convincing border state representatives to finally accept his plan for gradual, compensated emancipation.[8]

The most widely accepted account of Lincoln's new thinking on emancipation during this period comes from Major Thomas T. Eckert, who ran the War Department's telegraph office. He claimed that the president began laboriously pulling together his thoughts in the days and weeks following the Seven Days' battles while waiting for wire reports from other fronts. The story appeared in a recollection by David Bates, one of the junior staffers in the office. Eckert claimed that the president "would look out of the window a while and then put his pen to paper, but he did not write much at once." He added that Lincoln "would study between times and when he had made up his mind he would put down a line or two, and then sit quiet for a few minutes." In this fashion, according to the officer, the president slowly crafted his new policy. He recalled that Lincoln left him in charge of the documents, even offering to let him read the draft in progress.[9]

As with several other key wartime recollections, if true, this would be a remarkable story. The president, besieged by critics and favor-seekers, slipped away from the White House to find a few stolen moments of peaceful reflection at an isolated War Department office where he could thus change the course of history. But as historian Mark E. Neely, Jr., has pointed out, this anecdote is especially "dubious" since the first draft of the Emancipation Proclamation, which was read to the Cabinet on July 22, 1862, contained only two sentences and about two hundred words.[10] It was presumably not something that would be hammered out line-by-line over a period of weeks. The details do not add up either. The recollection begins by confusing the dates of the Seven Days' battles. Eckert reported that the president occasionally left "question-marks on the margin of what he had written," a practice that Lincoln never appeared to employ in any of the other manuscripts of his that have survived. The officer also claimed that the president said he could find no solitude at the White House, but Lincoln wrote most of his great wartime speeches there. When he was drafting such documents, top aides Nicolay and Hay were quite diligent, even enthusiastic, about barring visitors. Many historians consider Eckert, who later became president of Western Union, a credible source, but the story is difficult to accept at face value.[11]

An underlying problem with Eckert's account is that it fails to mesh with how quickly events were moving by mid-July. The president returned from Harrison's Landing on Thursday, July 10. He appointed Halleck the next day. On Saturday, he met with border state congressmen at the White House in order to make one last-ditch appeal for gradual, compensated emancipation before the Congress adjourned. The majority of them appeared utterly uninterested. The next day, while heading to a funeral for Secretary of War Stanton's infant son, the president revealed to cabinet officers Seward and Welles that he planned to issue a military proclamation freeing Rebel-owned slaves. By Monday morning, July 14, he received a formal rejection of his compensated emancipation proposal from the border state representatives. In the afternoon, he learned that the House and Senate had finally reached agreement on a bill that promised to free Confederate slaves by legislative action. For the next two days, he negotiated with congressional leaders over changes in the proposed legislation, which he considered unconstitutional. They finally came to terms, he signed the act, and Congress adjourned on Thursday, July 17. Mary Lincoln and the Lincoln boys returned in the evening. Over the next few days, Lincoln contemplated his choices, called a special meeting of his cabinet, and then on Tuesday, July 22, 1862, read a first draft of the Emancipation Proclamation to his six department heads and the vice president.

Welles believed that the pivotal moment came at the meeting with border state politicians on Saturday, July 12. Originally from Kentucky, Lincoln thought he understood these men and was confident that he could persuade them to accept a reasonable emancipation plan grounded, as always, in his three guiding principles—that abolition must be voluntary, gradual, and compensated. "How much better for you, and for your people," he argued, "to take the step which, at once, shortens the war, and secures substantial compensation for that which is sure to be wholly lost in any other event." He emphasized that the process would be deliberate and fair to them. "I do not speak of emancipation *at once*, but of a decision at once to emancipate *gradually*." And then he warned them that if they rejected his plea, events might make emancipation by decree inevitable. "The pressure, in this direction, is still upon me," the president noted ominously, "and is increasing." He could not resist the self-serving claim that if they had only adopted the plan he had introduced in March, "the war would now be substantially ended."[12] He still clung to the idea that if southerners realized that the four remaining loyal slave states were voluntarily abandoning slavery, they might reconsider their support for the rebellion. This would obviate the need for an unenforceable—and controversial—military decree abolishing the institution by fiat. Once again, however, Lincoln was sorely disappointed. Twenty out of twenty-eight participants in the meeting declined to accept his offer. Although the president did not receive official word of their response until Monday, the mood of the Saturday meeting was clearly strained.

Recognizing that his approach on emancipation was at a standstill no less deadlocked than McClellan's position in Virginia, Lincoln determined to strike boldly. The next day, Sunday, July 13, while riding in a carriage with William Seward, the secretary's son Frederick Seward, and Gideon Welles, the president confided that he had finally decided to issue a military proclamation freeing southern slaves. This represented a significant leap forward from the memo he had read to Senator Browning just two weeks earlier, a proposal limited to the protection of contrabands. Now the president was vowing to make the Union army a general conduit for black freedom. According to the account in Welles's diary, Lincoln was surprisingly adamant about his new position.

> He dwelt earnestly on the gravity, importance, and delicacy of the movement, said he had given it much thought and had about come to the conclusion that it was a military necessity absolutely essential for the salvation of the Union, that we must free the slaves or be ourselves subdued, etc., etc.

The president assured his colleagues that this was "the first occasion when he had mentioned the subject to any one" and that he wanted their opinions. Interestingly, none were immediately forthcoming. Seward said that the issue was "so vast and momentous" that he wanted time to consider a response. Welles concurred.[13]

Lincoln's leap forward on emancipation was not exactly a leap in the dark. Pressure to "free the slaves" had been building for months on Capitol Hill among congressmen increasingly frustrated by the staying power of the rebellion. The day after the president had floated his plans in the carriage ride through Georgetown, a House-Senate conference reported its agreement on a piece of legislation that proposed to accomplish largely the same purpose. Months in the making, the second confiscation bill in its final form offered a sweeping promise to make "forever free" any slaves owned by masters who supported the rebellion. The First Confiscation Act, passed in August 1861, had authorized the seizure of certain slaves—those actually employed on behalf of the Confederate cause—but treated them like any other confiscated property, offering no explicit promise of freedom. The new law went much further by covering a greater number of slaves and offering them, for the first time, the real hope of freedom.

The legislation was actually more complicated than it appeared. The bill provided access to the federal courts and a series of vaguely outlined legal procedures to help resolve contested cases. Yet there were no "personal liberty" safeguards written into the statute—necessary to help freed blacks avoid kidnapping or reenslavement—despite lengthy debates about the need for such measures. Legislators did encourage the president to employ suitable ex-slaves in the Union army, but they also set aside funds for colonization experiments abroad. In this manner, they failed to settle the question of whether slaves were legally defined as people or property, content to leave that fundamental ambiguity unresolved. They also created confusion by establishing a sixty-day window from the date of some unspecified "public warning" by the president before the new law would take full effect.[14]

Lincoln was annoyed by these actions and prepared to veto the legislation. He remained convinced that emancipation by decree could be justified only on the grounds of military necessity and only by the action of the president as commander in chief. Orville Browning visited the White House on Tuesday, July 15, finding the president "weary, care-worn and troubled." With his wife and children still out of town and with the pressures of major military and political decisions converging rapidly, Lincoln appeared thoroughly overwhelmed. He spoke with "a cadence of deep sadness in his voice." Expressing concern for his friend's health, Browning could not revive the sagging spirits of the exhausted president, who said, simply, "I must die sometime." The senator noted in his journal that they parted "with tears in our eyes."[15]

Furiously working behind the scenes, however, several leading Republican legislators arranged a compromise whereby the Congress issued an unprecedented clarification of the law in order to answer some of the president's objections. As the negotiations proceeded, Lincoln asked for, and grudgingly received, an agreement from Congress to remain in session for an extra day. Then finally on Thursday, July 17, 1862, the president signed the new confiscation law, although he delivered with his signature a copy of the veto message that he had prepared in case negotiations fell apart. It was a bittersweet moment that left many legislators perturbed. Within the Republican caucus, according to Indiana congressman George Julian, the president was "arraigned as the deliberate betrayer of the freedmen and poor whites."[16] Exacerbating the tension, Lincoln also vowed to revisit the issue of gradual, compensated emancipation for loyal slave states when Congress returned in December.

As the weary congressmen began filing out of Washington, Lincoln must have contemplated his new carrot-and-stick approach to emancipation with some degree of astonishment at the remarkable course of events. He was pledged to continue to offer the promise of gradual, compensated emancipation to loyal slave states while simultaneously threatening abolition by military decree on areas still under Confederate control. This approach theoretically punished rebels while rewarding moderates. It was not the most practical or consistent set of choices available, but it appeared workable. For the president, the two-track policy also had the advantage of providing a vision for ending slavery that—at least in his opinion—actually passed constitutional muster.

Over the next few days, as the Lincoln family finally reunited and reconnected at the Soldiers' Home cottage, the president prepared to give the sixty-day "public warning" required by the new law. He began (or perhaps finished) a first draft of the Emancipation Proclamation. No matter what the president might have said or written earlier, he had finally made up his mind and now made his intentions unambiguous—at least within the confines of his own administration. He read the following short draft to his Cabinet on Tuesday, July 22, 1862.

> In pursuance of the sixth section of the act of congress entitled 'An act to suppress insurrection and to punish treason and rebellion, to seize and confiscate property of rebels, and for other purposes' Approved July 17. 1862, and which act, and the Joint Resolution explanatory thereof, are herewith published, I, Abraham Lincoln, President of the United States, do hereby proclaim to, and warn all persons within the contemplation of said sixth section to cease participating in, aiding, countenancing, or abetting the existing rebellion, or any rebellion against the government of the United States, and to return to their proper allegiance to the United States, on pain of the forfeitures and seizures, as within and by said sixth section provided.
>
> And I hereby make known that it is my purpose, upon the next meeting of Congress, to again recommend the adoption of a practical measure for tendering pecuniary aid to the free choice or rejection, of any and all States which may then be recognizing and practically sustaining the authority of the United States, and which may then have voluntarily adopted, or thereafter may voluntarily adopt, gradual abolishment of slavery within such State or States—that the object is to practically restore, thenceforward to be maintain[ed], the constitutional relation between the general government, and each, and all the states, wherein that relation is now suspended, or disturbed; and that, for this object, the war, as it has been, will be, prosecuted [sic]. And, as a fit and necessary military measure for effecting this object, I, as Commander-in-Chief of the Army and Navy of the United States, do order and declare that on the first day of January in the year of Our Lord one thousand, eight hundred and sixty three, all persons held as slaves within any state or states, wherein the constitutional authority of the United States shall not then be practically recognized, submitted to, and maintained, shall then, thenceforward, and forever, be free.[17]

The entire proclamation occupied only 325 words and was clearly written in response to the Second Confiscation Act. The first paragraph rested entirely on the sixth section of the new law and the second paragraph is probably best understood in the context of the congressional action. For example, the law signed on July 17 had stated that former slaves of Rebel masters "shall be forever free." Lincoln now seemed to be echoing that language as he concluded that those slaves "shall then, thenceforward, and forever, be free." By choosing January 1, 1863, as the effective date for his new policy, the president seemed to be consciously reaching beyond the sixty-day window in order to provide time for the next session of Congress (which would reconvene in December) to consider the rest of his proposed emancipation legislation.

Reaction from the cabinet members was surprisingly muted, perhaps because at the outset of the meeting Lincoln had coolly informed them that he was not seeking advice, just sharing a decision. Nonetheless, Seward, who had received more time to consider the issue than most of the others, came up with an objection on the timing of the announcement that Lincoln ultimately found persuasive. The secretary of state, keenly aware of growing concern about the war among European governments, suggested that the president should delay releasing any proclamation until after a major battlefield victory. Even though the justification for the emancipation decree was supposed to be military necessity, since Halleck and Pope were already planning a new campaign in northern Virginia, the advice made sense. Rather than a "last shriek on the retreat" as Seward reportedly put it, a proclamation issued during a moment of celebration would instead appear as a calculated strategy designed to help finish off the Confederates.[18] So Lincoln shelved the second paragraph of his draft temporarily, issuing only the first long sentence as his official sixty-day warning on Friday, July 25, 1862.

In the evening after releasing the official notice, Lincoln entertained Senator Browning and his wife and some of their acquaintances at the Soldiers' Home. Browning was preparing to leave for the congressional recess and wanted to say good-bye to his friend. The two men had grown close during the previous session, but they would never again be so intimate. Political differences steadily drove them apart after the summer of 1862. Browning considered emancipation to be ill advised and grew increasingly shrill in opposing it. "I have no faith in proclamations or laws," he wrote in his diary at this time, "unless we follow them by force and actually do the thing."[19] But once Union armies finally began liberating black slaves, Browning suddenly found more reasons to object. At one point, he even lobbied the president to compensate a struggling Mississippi widow whose slaves had been confiscated. Lincoln became visibly irritated, assuring his stunned friend that he would "rather *throw up*, than to do what was asked."[20]

Since Lincoln's shift on emancipation was not yet public knowledge, it is unlikely that he discussed the matter with Browning that evening. The diary entry significantly includes no mention of the topic. Still, the two men had a revealing conversation about General McClellan that sheds light on how the degenerating military situation influenced the president's political thinking. The tired executive bluntly informed the senator that "McClellan would not fight and that he had told Halleck so." He claimed that he gave his new general-in-chief full authority to fire the Young Napoleon. Lincoln then grew sarcastic, mocking the commander's habit of inflating the size of enemy forces arrayed against him. He said that if by magic he could reinforce McClelland [*sic*] with 100,000 men to day he would be in an ecstasy over it, thank him for it, and tell him that he would go to Richmond tomorrow, but that when tomorrow came he would telegraph that he had certain information that the enemy had 400,000 men, and that he could not advance without reinforcements.[21]

Just a month earlier, Lincoln had promised northern governors that 100,000 new men would "substantially end the war." Now, he knew better. His bitter skepticism on the day that he issued at least part of his planned proclamation illustrates why the president came around to his more ambitious approach on emancipation. Within the span of a few weeks, his confidence in the Federal military had plummeted.

The renewed sense of vulnerability on the Union side had a host of unintended consequences beyond simply preparing the way for wartime emancipation. It helped convince Congress to pass a Militia Act at the same time as the Second Confiscation Act—a new law that provided for 300,000 more enlistments and authorized a compulsory draft for the first time in U.S. history. To enforce this controversial step, the War Department in August and then the president himself in September would be compelled to suspend civil liberties across the North for those accused of interfering with the national conscription effort.[22] The relentless quest for new enlistments also forced many in Washington to reconsider the utility of employing ex-slaves as soldiers. Lincoln, for one, pointed out to Browning in the week before the senator left Washington that blacks outnumbered whites by nearly 4:1 in the lower Mississippi Valley. The president vowed to "open" the Mississippi River and "if necessary" to take "all these negroes to open it, and keep it open."[23]

Anxiety over the absence of military progress also rekindled fears of European intervention. Since the beginning of the conflict, Union politicians had been extremely sensitive about the signals coming from London and Paris, in particular. They worried that foreign powers might be tempted to recognize the cotton-rich Confederacy or might be provoked, in some fashion, to interfere in the dispute. President Lincoln had wanted it both ways from the Europeans. He hoped they would agree that the rebellion was an internal matter and not a conflict between two sovereigns. Yet he also expected the international community to honor a blockade that he had imposed on the Confederacy in April 1861—a step that implied sovereignty under the traditions of nineteenth-century diplomacy.

By the summer of 1862, European patience had worn noticeably thin. Great Britain, which received 75 percent of its cotton imports from the South, pressed hard for some accommodation for its economic sacrifices. On the same evening that Lincoln had complained about McClellan's lack of fighting spirit, he also informed Browning that the British government had secretly requested permission to allow at least $50 million worth of cotton to pass through the blockade. The president admitted that "the matter was being considered" but noted sternly that the government "could not let the cotton out without letting its value in."[24]

The Brownings visited the cottage on Friday. Mary Lincoln remained at the Soldiers' Home on Saturday and tried to catch up on her correspondence. During her recent absence, several callers had apparently journeyed out to the summer residence, only to be told that the first lady was in New York. Now she was expected to acknowledge each calling card or *cartes-de-visite* with a gracious note. This turned out to be less of a chore than it might have seemed. In contrast to her overwrought husband, Mary Lincoln found her spirits somewhat revived during this period. She enjoyed her sightseeing excursions in and around Manhattan and relished the return of her eldest son, nineteen-year-old Robert, who had been attending college at Harvard. Writing to another prominent woman from the capital, Fanny Eames, whose family had also drifted to the country during the hot season, she sounded practically joyful upon her return:

> We are truly delighted, with this retreat, the drives & walks around here are delightful, & each day, brings its visitors. Then too, our boy Robert, is with us, whom you may remember. We consider it a "pleasant time" for us, when his vacations, roll around, he is very companionable, and I shall dread when he has to return to Cambridge. I presume, you will not return to W. before cool weather, *thus far*, we have found the country very delightful.[25]

Officially, the Lincolns had been in residence at the Soldiers' Home for about six weeks, but only now, for the past few days, had they been fully together as a family. Mary Lincoln hoped they would remain so much longer.

Robert Lincoln, the family's missing element, had taken up pipe smoking at Harvard and was just then emerging from a period of teenage bashfulness. According to his proud mother, he had "grown & improved more than any one you ever saw."[26] The newspapers, having already dubbed him the "Prince of Rails," tended to concur. Press coverage of the first son was positive, if somewhat condescending. "He does everything very well," commented a correspondent from the *New York Herald*, "but avoids doing anything extraordinary."[27] There was something about Robert that seemed to inspire such backhanded compliments. When he was still a small child, his own father had confided to a close friend that he feared "Bob" was a "rare-ripe sort" who was "smarter at about five than ever after."[28]

The text of Mary Lincoln's letter to Fanny Eames suggests that the family's principal activities together at the Soldiers' Home consisted of entertaining

As a Harvard undergraduate, Robert Lincoln poses with a high hat like his father's.
PICTURE HISTORY, MT. KISCO, N.Y.

guests like the Brownings or the Eameses and in enjoying the grounds around the cottage. The "drives & walks" that so delighted the first lady were actually popular with a wide cross-section of Washington society. Nor does it appear that the presence of the nation's first family deterred local residents from continuing to visit the area. Rebecca Pomroy, who occasionally served the Lincoln family as a nurse, rode through the grounds with some friends in early August in what must have been a typical Washington afternoon outing:

We went first to the Soldiers' Home, a place owned by [the] government, containing three hundred acres, on which are five stone houses, and a larger one for the aged and crippled soldiers who have fought their country's battles, and have settled down quietly till the Great Captain calls them up higher. We rode round the President's country seat, which is one of the five houses, and from there to the graveyard; a more sorrowful sight I have never seen.[29]

In reality, one of the "stone houses" that Pomroy observed, where the Lincolns resided, was made of stuccoed brick. Some of the smaller residences, including the Lincolns' cottage, had been part of the original Riggs estate. The larger marble building, which housed approximately 150 veteran residents, dated from the mid-1850s. The "sorrowful" graveyard, which was not far from the president's home, had been opened as a national cemetery following the First Battle of Bull Run. By the summer of 1862, the graveyard contained more than a few thousand interments.

At this time, anyone could enter the Soldiers' Home grounds, ride around the president's cottage, or even wander up to the door and request a personal interview with the commander in chief. The president and his family had no formal protection of any kind. The question of presidential security had never really existed before the Civil War. A pistol-wielding maniac had once assaulted Andrew Jackson, but the disturbing incident was soon forgotten. Franklin Pierce briefly retained a bodyguard during the 1850s; otherwise nineteenth-century presidents typically traveled without protection. At the outbreak of the rebellion, Senator Jim Lane of Kansas briefly stationed a body of state militia troops he called the "Frontier Guard" in the White House. However once the initial panic subsided, the president spent the rest of the war's first year without taking any other special precautions.

The move to the Soldiers' Home changed nothing at first. Whoever raised concerns about security along the president's new daily commute found his or her fears quickly dismissed. "Assassination is not an American practice or habit," Secretary of State Seward had written in July, responding to one of the more nervous queries. "Every day's experience confirms it," he noted, pointing out that the president went "to and from" the Soldiers' Home "on horseback, night and morning, unguarded." For good measure, the secretary added breezily, " I go there, unattended, at all hours, by daylight and moonlight, by starlight and without any light."[30]

Years later, a handful of Lincoln's associates would claim credit for perceiving the danger of his situation and urging the introduction of a military detail to accompany the president. One such recollection comes from Leonard Swett, an attorney from Illinois who had traveled with Lincoln on the judicial circuit in the 1850s. Swett visited Washington in early August 1862 and recalled that he ventured out to the Soldiers' Home one evening with another Illinois attorney named William H. Hanna. Unlike the secretary of state, who traveled easily "by daylight and moonlight" to the Soldiers' Home, the two newcomers to Washington found themselves at the mercy of an incompetent driver who got them hopelessly lost. They did not return to the city until 2 A.M. But the next day, when they discussed their adventures with the president at the White

House, they raised concerns about the absence of security around the cottage. Swett recalled Lincoln telling them, "I cannot be shut up in an iron cage and guarded." Joined by fellow Illinois attorney Ward H. Lamon, then serving as marshal of the District of Columbia, the guests challenged the president over his "recklessness." According to Swett, Lincoln was shaken by the anxiety of his old friends and finally agreed to allow them to look into the possibility of improved security measures.[31]

From the president's perspective, physical security was the least of his worries. He was increasingly consumed by anxiety as he awaited the outcome of General Pope's preparation for combat. "I am a patient man," he wrote on July 26, "but it may as well be understood, once [and] for all, that I shall not surrender this game leaving any available card unplayed."[32] The more he contemplated the impending assault toward Richmond, the testier he became. As the president ruefully noted to a pro-Union meeting on August 6, 1862, "If the military commanders in the field cannot be successful, not only the Secretary of War, but myself for the time being the master of them both, cannot be but failures."[33]

In several of his political statements during the month of August, Lincoln exhibited moments of uncharacteristic sharpness. On August 14, 1862, he attempted to persuade a delegation of northern free blacks to support his plans for colonization of freed slaves. He asked them to lead the effort in Central America, bluntly reminding them that "on this broad continent, not a single man of your race is made the equal of a single man of ours." This was a "fact," he noted coldly, "with which we have to deal." Although he expressed regret over the great "suffering" of African Americans, he also underlined for his guests the awkward point that "but for your race among us there could not be war," adding heatedly, "although many men engaged on either side do not care for you one way or the other."[34] It was one of his least impressive performances as president.

Just over a week later, Lincoln responded to criticism from newspaper editor Horace Greeley with a powerful but indignant public letter. Greeley's "The Prayer of the Twenty Millions," printed in the *New York Tribune* on August 20, had taken the president to task for failing to execute the emancipation provisions of the Second Confiscation Act more vigorously. Lincoln, who first released his response to a rival newspaper, was not in the mood to be intimidated. "As to the policy I 'seem to be pursuing' as you say," Lincoln wrote, "I have not meant to leave any one in doubt." He stated his position firmly:

> If I could save the Union without freeing *any* slave I would do it, and if I could save it by freeing *all* the slaves I would do it; and if I could save it by freeing some and leaving others alone I would also do that. What I do about slavery, and the colored race, I do because I believe it helps to save the Union; and what I forbear, I forbear because I do *not*

believe it would help to save the Union. I shall do *less* whenever I shall believe what I am doing hurts the cause, and I shall do *more* whenever I shall believe doing more will help the cause.

Lincoln considered Greeley "an old friend, whose heart I have always supposed to be right," but found himself agitated by the "impatient and dictatorial tone" of the latter's public scolding.[35] Nearly everyone, it seemed, was losing patience.

The president responded to Greeley on a Friday, nearing the end of yet another long week, plagued with doubts about the impending assault by General Pope. If Lincoln hoped to gain some rest, however, he was to be sorely mistaken. On Saturday, he spent the entire day at the White House receiving callers. It was a tiring experience, one made even worse by the conduct of an army officer's wife who was lobbying the president over the possibility of a promotion for her husband. In a private memorandum, Lincoln called her a "saucy woman," and complained that "I am afraid she will keep tormenting till I may have to do it."[36]

As the president was attempting to elude his White House tormentor, an employee of the Treasury Department was also laying the groundwork for another special appeal to the president. John R. French, a former New Hampshire journalist working in Treasury, found himself approached on the same day by an Army colonel from his state who was hoping to discuss a personal tragedy with the president. According to French's recollection, Colonel Charles Scott had been wounded during the recent fighting that had occurred along the Virginia peninsula. Upon hearing of his injury, his wife had traveled down from New Hampshire to care for him. Despite the War Department bureaucracy that tried to prevent her from entering a war zone, the determined woman was eventually reunited with her husband. However, the steamer that carried them back to Washington was involved in a collision, and sadly, his wife, along with dozens of others, drowned. Colonel Scott wanted to retrieve her body so that he could bury her at home in New Hampshire, but once again the War Department stood in the way. Secretary Stanton had closed the area due to the impending Second Battle of Bull Run and refused permission to recover her body. Scott rushed to the White House to appeal the decision, but the president had already left for the day. Thus, late in the afternoon on Saturday, August 23, 1862, French agreed to take his desperate friend to see the president at the Soldiers' Home.

"The servant who answered the bell," recalled French, "led the way into the little parlor, where, in the gloaming, entirely alone, sat Mr. Lincoln." There the president relaxed in stocking feet, having "thrown off coat and shoes, and with a large palm-leaf fan in his hand, as he reposed in a broad chair, one leg hanging over its arm, he seemed to be in deep thought, perhaps studying the chances of the impending battle." Without making any interruptions, Lincoln listened to the colonel's long and tragic story. At the end, however, according to French, instead of displaying his legendary generosity, Lincoln reportedly said, "Am I to have no rest? Is there no hour or spot when or where I may escape this constant call? Why do you follow me out here with such business as this? Why do you not go to the War-office, where they have charge of all this matter of papers and transportation?" The embarrassed colonel tried to argue his case with the exhausted president, but to no avail. French claimed that they were dismissed curtly and sent back to the city without any relief. However, all was not lost. The next morning, French reported that Lincoln showed up at Scott's hotel full of apologies. "I was a brute last night," he supposedly admitted, as he agreed to help the officer cut through the red tape in his case.[37]

Such stories are always difficult to accept, dramatic as they are and essentially unverifiable. The extended quotations, culled from memory, are also suspicious and open to question. However, in this case, there are some corroborating details that add special credibility to French's recollection. It turns out that there was a collision of two ships, the *George Peabody* and the *West Point*, carrying wounded soldiers; it occurred along the Potomac on Wednesday, August 13, 1862, and resulted in seventy-three deaths, one of which was Scott's wife. Stanton had closed the area in preparation for the upcoming battle, and French, who later became a congressman, was a figure of enough importance in wartime Washington that he certainly would have approached the president at his retreat. Also, after already expressing his disgust earlier in the day with Mrs. Gabriel Paul, the "saucy woman" who wanted her husband promoted, it seems entirely reasonable that Lincoln would have been ill-disposed to anyone requesting special favors.[38]

On the eve of an impending battle, with so much riding on its outcome, and after an exhausting summer of political and military discontent, President Lincoln was understandably tense by the end of August. His first few months at the Soldiers' Home had offered only occasional moments of relaxation and surprisingly little protection from the torments of his daily public life. The president still needed to find a greater retreat, a place where he could rest and recapture his equilibrium.

3

"Forever free"

THE ANTICIPATION IN WASHINGTON OVER IMPENDING BATTLES FINALLY ENDED IN
late August 1862. General John Pope's Army of Virginia engaged General Robert E. Lee's Confederate forces at the Second Battle of Bull Run on August 29,
1862. The results were devastating for the Federal side, which suffered over 16,000
casualties and yet another terrible blow to public morale. Instead of the victory
that Secretary of State Seward had predicted would pave the way for emancipation, there was now the real possibility that Washington would be surrounded
and overrun. McClellan, who had been reassigned to support Pope, at one point
prepared to demolish the Chain Bridge, a leading point of entry into the city,
in order to prevent what he thought was an imminent invasion by Confederate
forces. He wrote his wife in the midst of the battle, "I am heartsick with the
folly and ignorance I see around me." To his superiors, he was equally blunt,
suggesting in a telegram to the president that the only policy left for the Union
command was to defend the capital and "leave Pope to get out of his scrape."[1]

A number of participants, including the president, subsequently questioned
McClellan's loyalty, even his stability, in the face of this latest crisis. John Hay
reported in his diary that while riding in from the Soldiers' Home on Saturday
morning, August 30, the president "was very outspoken in regard to McClellan's
present conduct. He said it really seemed to him that McC. wanted Pope defeated." On the issue of demolishing the bridge, Lincoln was uncharacteristically harsh. "He spoke also of McC's dreadful cowardice [crossed out and replaced
by "panic"] in the matter of the Chain Bridge," the aide reported. Hay noted
that the president "seemed to think [McClellan] a little crazy," but the young
assistant privately disagreed. "Envy, jealousy, and spite are probably a better
explanation of his present conduct," he speculated in the pages of his journal.[2]

Pope himself was nearly blind with rage, blaming his defeat on insubordination and disloyalty from McClellan and several other generals from the latter's inner circle.

The crushing defeat and the epidemic of finger-pointing created anxiety in Washington as residents prepared for the possibility of a successful Confederate assault. It took a gruff political veteran like Gideon Welles to remain levelheaded. "The military believe a great and decisive battle is to be fought in front of the city," he wrote in his diary, "but I do not anticipate it." Welles accurately concluded that the Confederates would avoid the heavily fortified capital and strike instead at some point in northern Maryland.[3] In his own way, the president also kept his cool, overlooking his suspicions about McClellan's personal character to once again hand control of the dispirited Union forces to the controversial general. On Tuesday, September 2, he went with General Halleck early in the morning to McClellan's home to offer him formal command of the city's defenses.

By mid-afternoon, the once disgraced commander was back in full Napoleonic form. Riding around the capital's fortifications, he fired off orders, energized the troops, and steadily regained control of the chaos. Eager to impress the commander in chief with his newfound fortitude, McClellan paused at three o'clock to scribble an update on his progress. He wrote that his staff was "examining everything" about the city's works and that reinforcements were "rapidly disembarking." He continued to express concern, however, about the potential for a frontal assault on the capital. "I am about riding to the front," he informed the president, "& as I am anxious about the Chain Bridge will return that way," noting that he would "endeavor to pass by the Soldiers Home to report to you the state of affairs unless called elsewhere." "I am still confident," he concluded, "altho' I fully appreciate the magnitude of the task committed to me."[4]

It is unclear whether the suddenly hyperactive commander ever made it to the Soldiers' Home that evening. What is certain is that in the heat of the crisis, Lincoln and McClellan temporarily put aside their differences and worked together. Within a few days, as Rebel forces crossed the Potomac near Leesburg, the president conceded even more authority to McClellan, allowing him to take command of all Union troops in the region. This was not a popular decision among Republican party insiders, but Lincoln was adamant. "We must use what tools we have," he replied in the face of outrage from his cabinet and top aides. The president claimed that McClellan was "working like a beaver" after the "snubbing" he had received in the aftermath of Second Bull Run.[5] Without doubt, the young general did consider his new opportunity as vindication, although not quite in the way Lincoln imagined. "Again I have been called upon to save the country," McClellan wrote smugly to his wife.[6]

Still, the general took his responsibilities seriously and attempted to demonstrate his professionalism by demanding the one step that Lincoln had so far avoided. He ordered a military guard to protect the president and his family at the Soldiers' Home.[7] With Confederate troops moving freely in western Maryland and with Rebel cavalry operating not far from the District, the decision was a necessary one. At the end of the first week in September, General James Wadsworth, the military governor of the District of Columbia, dispatched two companies from a Pennsylvania regiment to guard the cottage. He also ordered members of the 11th New York Cavalry, which had been stationed in Washington, to accompany the president on his daily commute.

The Pennsylvania infantrymen sent to the Soldiers' Home were fresh recruits only just then arriving from their training camp in Harrisburg. They were products of President Lincoln's July call for 300,000 additional troops. Governor Andrew G. Curtin had been one of the first loyal state executives to respond to that request. An ardent unionist, Curtin believed that the northern governors needed to work closer together to support the Federal war effort. The governor endorsed new financial bounties for the latest recruits and authorized the raising of two special "Bucktail Brigades" as a way to encourage compliance with the presidential order. The specially designated regiments had distinctive deer fur or "bucktails" that were attached to the men's hats. "Bucktails" had been made famous by the 1st Pennsylvania Rifles, a unit whose heroism was widely celebrated. Henry S. Huidekoper, a well-connected Harvard graduate from the northwestern corner of the state, received permission to raise four companies in one of the new regiments. He returned to Meadville in his native Crawford County in August 1862 and set about encouraging volunteers. "Enlist Now," the recruiting posters urged the young farmers and tradesmen, "and Receive the Bounty of $25, one month's pay in advance, and $75 at the end of the war, and not wait to be drafted into a poor regiment and receive no bounty."[8] This type of practical appeal proved effective and soon the regiment filled its quota.

The men who enlisted in August were ordered to report in Meadville on September 1, 1862. After some typical delays and last-minute snafus, the new 150th Pennsylvania regiment, composed of companies from Crawford, McKean, and Union counties in western Pennsylvania and Philadelphia county in the eastern portion of the state, organized in Harrisburg on September 4 and proceeded by train to Washington the next day. "We stopped in Bal. 2 hours and then went through to Washington and got there at 5 oclock," wrote Private Willard Cutter, a twenty-five-year-old member of the regiment. One of the regimental officers, Thomas Chamberlin, recalled that the journey was "excessively fatiguing" for the new troops who were frustrated by the long delays.[9]

Things got worse, according to Cutter's contemporary account, once the men arrived in Washington.

> We had orders to leave to go to a fort about 7 1/2 miles and was bout 1/2 mile of there and had orders to go back for [Stonewall] Jackson was in sight so we had to turn and go back to Washington for the night. Next morning we went 2 miles from the City and stopped for the day we thought but at 6 we had to march to where we are.[10]

Charles Derickson, a young sergeant in Cutter's company, recalled that the order to move from their encampment to the Soldiers' Home came suddenly at "about dark." He wrote that "Capt. Lockwood of Gen. [James] Wadsworth's staff rode into camp and ordered Col. Huidekoper to send two companies to the Soldiers' Home immediately. On our arrival there, we first learned that we were to guard the President's House."[11]

What none of the confused, tired troops in Derickson's and Cutter's Company K understood was that the original directive to guard the Soldiers' Home had been delivered on Saturday to Companies C and H. Those troops, however, went by mistake to the Soldiers' Rest, which was a terminal in the city used to provide temporary housing and food for Federal soldiers in transit. So literally by sheer accident and force of circumstance, Company K from Crawford County and Company D from nearby Union County arrived on Saturday evening to become part of President Lincoln's life. The soldiers of Company D would be reassigned in a matter of weeks, but for the rest of the war, the hundred or so men of Company K, 150th Pennsylvania, would follow the president's family, becoming in many ways their trusted friends and most diligent observers.

The president was soon curious about his new neighbors. On Sunday morning, he sent a servant requesting an interview with the officer in charge. "I immediately reported," Captain David V. Derickson of Company K recalled. He was a forty-four-year-old businessman from Meadville whose son Charles was the company sergeant. Derickson was amazed that after a brief and informal introduction, the president asked that he accompany him into Washington for the day. "On our way to the city he made numerous inquiries," the captain noted. Ultimately, they discovered that Lincoln was familiar with Derickson's name because he had previously been under consideration for a local political appointment, one that the president claimed he had just recently approved.[12] Derickson had been active in politics before the war, a founder of the Republican party in Crawford County and a leader of his community in Meadville. He was an early advocate for the Union cause, presiding over a patriotic meeting held in the town after the firing on Fort Sumter where he spoke earnestly for "thinking and acting for the defense of our flag and Constitution."[13] He helped Henry

Huidekoper organize the regiment and when the latter was promoted to colonel, Derickson was named captain of Company K.

According to Derickson's recollection, written years after the war for the
local Meadville newspaper, the president asked his driver to stop at the Union
Army headquarters on the way into the White House so he could check on
developments in Maryland. On this point, at least, Derickson's memory can be
proven reliable since the diary of a leading Union general confirms that the
president did enter the Army building, on the corner of 17th and F Streets,
early that morning.[14] Upon arriving at the headquarters, Derickson happened
to mention to the president that one of General Halleck's top advisers was also
originally from Meadville. Pleased at the serendipity of this personal connection, Lincoln insisted on bringing the generals down to his carriage after their
brief conference. Derickson thought he saw in Halleck "a kind of quizzical
look," as if to say, "isn't this rather a big joke to ask the Commander-in-Chief
of the army down to the street to be introduced to a country captain?" But
Derickson soon found the president's easygoing demeanor to be the rule rather
than the exception, reporting that Lincoln invited him inside the White House
on that first morning for further conversation and ultimately asked him to
accompany him on the commute nearly every day in the fall of 1862.

The president met Henry Crotzer, the captain of Company D, on his return
that evening. Crotzer recalled that the reception his troops received from the
Lincoln family was also quite cordial. But he attributed the warm welcome to
his having organized a church service for the troops on that first Sunday, September 7. He said that afterward the president sent for him and "grasping him
warmly by the hand" assured the officer that he had already informed Mary
Lincoln that with "a praying company of men to guard them and their home,
they need fear neither men nor devils!"[15]

The young Pennsylvanians were impressed by their new surroundings and
their new assignment but anxious about the prospect of a Confederate raid on
their position. Willard Cutter, the young private in Company K, waited until
Wednesday to write to his widowed mother—after the men had nervously
settled into their new camp. He called the Soldiers' Home "the nicest place I
ever seen," noting proudly that it was "where Uncle Abe lives." But he was
clearly worried about the progress of the Confederate invasion, reporting that
the men had heard cannon fire all week long from their positions on the hills
outside Washington. There was concern about Rebel infiltration of the city's
defenses. Cutter claimed that soldiers in his unit had seized a spy on Tuesday
who had been passed through to the president's cottage as an official messenger. The guards apparently found the man on the tower of the main Soldiers'

Private Willard A. Cutter of Company K in the 150th Pennsylvania Volunteers served in Lincoln's military guard and wrote regular letters home to his widowed mother.
ILLINOIS STATE HISTORICAL LIBRARY, SPRINGFIELD, ILL.

Home building, peering suspiciously out toward the network of forts surrounding the capital.[16]

There were other frightening breaches of security reported during this tense period—reports that ultimately convinced Union military officials to further increase protection around the president. The *Cincinnati Gazette* reported that sometime in mid-September "a couple of horsemen" approached the main gate at the Soldiers' Home, "and made some careless inquiry of the sentry as to the time Mr. Lincoln generally came out." According to the correspondent, the aroused guard then reported the incident to Mary Lincoln who "immediately took the alarm." The newspaper credited the agitated first lady with shaming the Union military into providing a full cavalry escort for the president as he traveled to and from the Soldiers' Home.[17]

Apparently bowing to pressure from several sources, General Wadsworth ordered the already overextended 11th New York to provide a company for the presidential commute. At first, various units filled this function, but the daily responsibility of accompanying the president soon fell exclusively to Company A, a group of about eighty horsemen from New York City, the Staten Island suburb of Tompkinsville, and the small Hudson River village of Tarrytown.

The 11th New York was also known as Scott's Nine Hundred, after Thomas A. Scott, the assistant secretary of war and close friend of the regiment's organizer, Colonel James B. Swain. Originally, Swain had approached the War Department in October 1861 about the possibility of forming an elite volunteer cavalry unit. He received permission and began recruiting for what he termed the 1st United States Voluntary Cavalry but what ultimately came to be designated, over his repeated objections, as the 11th New York Cavalry. Most of the twelve companies in the regiment were recruited from New York City. Nearly the entire regiment, about 850 strong, arrived in Washington in May 1862 and formed an encampment at Meridian Hill, an area past the northwest section of the city not far from the Soldiers' Home. The soldiers dubbed their new home "Camp Relief" and quickly established themselves as a loud, unruly presence in Washington. Some wags began calling them "Scott's Blind One Thousand." Various companies in the regiment spent the summer providing escorts for leading military figures and helping to police the city. Camp Relief became a hub of activity, in part because of the organization skill of J. R. Bostwick, the regimental sutler or civilian supplier, who ran such a brisk business in food, tobacco, and miscellaneous sundries that in this era before a common national currency he actually issued his own paper money.[18] Eventually, about half the members of Company A established their own encampment at the Soldiers' Home on the slope near the national cemetery.

President Lincoln was not pleased by this latest addition to his expanding security arrangements. Unlike the infantry soldiers who camped near the residence, the cavalrymen threatened to impair both the president's mobility and his access to the public. He complained loudly at first over what he considered to be an unnecessary intrusion on his independence. "I do not believe that the President was ever more annoyed by anything than by the espionage that was necessarily maintained almost constantly over his movements," recalled one member of the cavalry detail. "Nearly every day we were made aware of his feelings upon this matter."[19] A young drummer in one of the infantry companies assigned to the Soldiers' Home agreed with that assessment. He recalled that during the first few weeks of September he frequently saw the president hurry out in the mornings "as if to escape from the irksome escort of a dozen cavalrymen." The young soldier particularly remembered these episodes because he enjoyed laughing over the spectacle of the embarrassed detail arriving at the appointed hour, discovering the presidential carriage already gone, and then being compelled to dash out of the gate in a furious attempt to catch up with their elusive commander in chief.[20]

The president eventually settled down but still made his objections clear to General in Chief Halleck, whose top aide recalled that Lincoln arrived one evening to protest "half jocularly, half in earnest" about the new cavalry detachment.

The burden of his complaint was that he and Mrs. Lincoln "couldn't hear themselves talk," for the clatter of their sabres and spurs; and that, as many of them appeared new hands and very awkward, he was more afraid of being shot by the accidental discharge of one of their carbines or revolvers, than of any attempt upon his life or for his capture by the roving squads of Jeb Stuart's cavalry, then hovering all round the exterior works of the city.[21]

Halleck politely ignored the president's sarcasm and even expanded the guard's assignment. One member of Company A recalled that they were subsequently directed to post sentries in front of the cottage itself. At midnight after their first posting, the soldiers reported that president walked outside and asked, "What are you two men doing here?" After being assured that they had been ordered to guard the home by their superiors, Lincoln invoked his rank as commander in chief and dismissed them. The next night the soldiers returned, on orders, but this time they crouched behind "a large oak tree" that grew directly in front of the house, hoping the president would not see them. Again, about midnight he peered outside from the porch and "sent them to their quarters."[22]

To a degree, the president's growing impatience reflected his view of the war. He invariably focused on the need for the Union to take the offensive. Instead, the situation by September 1862 had reversed his priorities. Confederates were now actually moving on three fronts. As Lee's Army of Northern Virginia invaded Maryland, Rebel forces had also gone on the attack in Kentucky and Mississippi. Adding to Federal woes, government officials simultaneously faced a massive Sioux uprising in the Minnesota territory. For many northerners, these developments offered abundant cause for despair. By contrast, for the president they represented a long-awaited chance to finally "hive the enemy."[23] Lincoln simply had no interest in playing defense. He wanted his generals to track down and destroy the exposed Confederate armies.

In his intense focus on the escalating military situation, Lincoln brushed aside other concerns. On Saturday, September 13, the distracted president lost control of his horse while riding in from the Soldiers' Home and badly sprained his wrist.[24] Later that day, still nursing his sore arm, he conducted a meeting with two Chicago ministers over the nearly forgotten topic of emancipation. It was not an issue the president wanted to address at that moment, but with the sixty-day clock on the Second Confiscation Act about to expire, he needed to make a final decision on his policy. The president was surprisingly candid with his guests, who brought with them a petition supporting abolition. "What *good* would a proclamation of emancipation from me do, especially as we are now situated?" he asked, echoing an argument that he had made in June to a delegation of Quakers. "I do not want to issue a document that the whole world will see must necessarily be inoperative," he said emphatically, "like the Pope's bull against the comet!" Lincoln conceded that emancipation would "help somewhat" on several domestic and international political fronts, but appeared uneasy, searching almost desperately for guidance. He confessed that it was his "earnest desire to know the will of the Providence in this matter," vowing that if he could determine what it was, "*I will do it!*"[25]

The answer, as always during wartime, came from the battlefield. On the same day that Lincoln met with the Chicago ministers, Union soldiers discovered a copy of Lee's orders for his invasion of Maryland wrapped around some cigars and left behind at an abandoned camp. They quickly delivered their discovery to General McClellan, who now had an intelligence advantage for the first time in his encounters with General Lee. The Army of the Potomac, which had been shadowing Lee's army uncertain of its exact location, began concentrating its forces in western Maryland along the suddenly exposed gaps in the Confederate lines. General Lee soon became aware of his lost orders and responded quickly to the Union movement with his own redeployment. The two sides maneuvered toward a major battle that would culminate in the bloodiest single day in American history.

Nervously, Lincoln watched these critical events unfold. From his residence at the Soldiers' Home, he could actually hear the random skirmishing between the tail ends of the Union and Confederate lines. Private Cutter was on guard duty at the cottage on Sunday night. He wrote to his brother that he heard cannon fire at daybreak—sounds that also woke up the president, who soon appeared at the doorway, asking the surprised sentry where he could find "Captain D." Cutter saluted and watched as Lincoln walked over to the principal Soldiers' Home building and ascended the tower, apparently hoping to catch a glimpse of the action. The president soon returned, however, disappointed, commenting that this skirmish was not yet the "general engagement" they all anticipated.[26]

The climactic battle of Antietam or Sharpsburg occurred on Wednesday, September 17, 1862, resulting in horrific casualties for both sides. Scholars now estimate that over 4,100 soldiers died that day and another 2,500 succumbed shortly after from mortal wounds.[27] On the field itself, there was a strategic stalemate, but the Confederates found themselves in an impossible position, utterly outnumbered and unable to hold their ground in hostile territory. Frustrated, Lee ordered the withdrawal of his army back across the Potomac. By Friday morning, September 19, General McClellan felt confident enough to issue an exultant report that was widely reprinted in northern newspapers. "The enemy is now driven back into Virginia," he proclaimed, "Maryland and Pennsylvania are now safe."[28] For Lincoln, such talk was utterly irritating. "To claim a great victory because Pa & Md were safe," he would later complain to

Hay, "The hearts of 10 million people sank within them when McClellan raised that shout."[29]

And yet as Lincoln initially contemplated the meaning of Antietam, he came to see the withdrawal of Lee's forces—on the eve of his deadline for an emancipation decision—as a sign of divine inspiration. He spoke about his feelings to the cabinet early in the following week. According to Gideon Welles, the president said that he had "made a vow, a covenant, that if God gave us the victory in the approaching battle, he would consider it an indication of Divine will, and that it was his duty to move forward in the cause of emancipation."[30] Secretary of Treasury Salmon P. Chase recalled that the president, unaccustomed to invoking his faith so openly, appeared uneasy as he described his decision-making process. "I made the promise to myself, and (hesitating a little)—to my Maker," Chase remembered him saying. "The rebel army is now driven out, and I am going to fulfil that promise."[31] By this faithful reckoning, Antietam became the battlefield victory that Seward had urged the president to wait for back in July.

With his mind finally made up, Lincoln set about revising the draft proclamation that he had shared with the Cabinet on July 22. Some recollected evidence suggests that he might have been tinkering with the actual wording for weeks prior. George S. Boutwell, the nation's first internal revenue commissioner, claimed that the president afterward told him that he had a second draft of the proclamation essentially completed before the critical battle began. Boutwell recalled Lincoln saying:

> When Lee came over the river [in early September] I made a resolve that when McClellan drove him back—and I expected he would do it sometime or other—I would send the Proclamation after him. I worked upon it and got it pretty much prepared. The battle of Antietam was fought on Wednesday, but I could not find out till Saturday whether we had really won a victory or not. It was then too late to issue the Proclamation that week, and I dressed it over a little on Sunday and on Monday I gave it to them.

Boutwell, a prominent Massachusetts politician who eventually served in both the House and Senate and as the nation's Treasury secretary, later changed his story, however, dropping the line, "I worked upon it and got it pretty much prepared" from an account of the same episode published in a later memoir.[32]

There is a tradition that Lincoln physically wrote the second draft, released on September 22, 1862, and known afterward as the Preliminary Emancipation Proclamation, at the Soldiers' Home cottage. This idea derives mainly from the memoir of artist Francis B. Carpenter, who spent several months at the White House in 1864. Carpenter reported that the president told him during a conversation in that year that he had "finished" the "second draft of

Nineteenth-century artist David Gilmour Blythe's highly symbolic rendering of Lincoln drafting the Emancipation Proclamation. LIBRARY OF CONGRESS.

the preliminary proclamation" while at the summer retreat. According to the painter, Lincoln said that he "added or changed a line, touching it up here and there" during the period from the July meeting to the battle of Antietam, but after hearing the news of Lee's withdrawal, concluded "to wait no longer." He told Carpenter that he "came up" to the White House on Saturday and called the cabinet together to hear his new version. "I was then staying at the Soldiers' Home," Lincoln reportedly said.[33]

There is also a separate connection to the Soldiers' Home offered in a recollection by nurse Rebecca Pomroy, who often helped cared for the Lincoln boys. The nurse claimed in her memoir that one afternoon during the difficult period around Antietam, while she and the president rode out to the Soldiers' Home, he spoke of his anxiety over the emancipation decision. "I am having a hard struggle," he admitted to her, "this Proclamation is weighing heavily upon me night and day. I shall encounter bitter opposition, but I think good will come of it, and God helping me, I will carry it through." According to Pomroy, the next morning as they rode into town, Lincoln seemed much more "cheerful" because he said he had finished the document during the previous night.[34]

Most Civil War historians have ignored Pomroy's account because it comes from a little known book that was ghostwritten years after the conflict and contains some obviously spurious material. And yet the nurse was an important supporting figure in the extended Lincoln household who clearly deserves a hearing in any retelling of his story. In addition, her memoir contains a number of selections from her contemporary letters, which adds to its credibility. Ultimately, however, this particular story rings false because it seems too convenient. It allows an ordinary person to claim ownership of an extraordinary event through the power of eyewitness testimony. There is no formula for offering a definitive judgment, but in the absence of corroborating material, Pomroy's claim probably merits interest, not acceptance.

Assessing the value of Carpenter's story is a more complicated matter. He appears to be a credible witness, a well-known painter who worked for a significant amount of time inside the White House and who wrote his own material not long after Lincoln's death. On the other hand, he offers what purports to be a verbatim transcript of the president's discussion—one that runs well over 700 words—in a piece that is actually a second-hand recollection within yet another recollection. Carpenter first heard Lincoln's description of the events that led to the proclamation in early February 1864 but did not write down his account of that conversation until the following year. And yet he put quotation marks around long passages of Lincoln's dialogue. Conventions were different in that era and Carpenter probably did not intend any fabrication, but nobody has a memory that exceptional.

Nor did Carpenter have the advantage of working from notes. "The truth is I had no idea of writing a book at the time of painting my picture," he explained to William H. Herndon, Lincoln's biographer and law partner. "I did not even keep a record of incidents, but simply a pocket diary of my work from day to day."[35] This would explain why the passage that Carpenter attributes to Lincoln is riddled with minor errors and contains phrases that the president never employed in his own writings.[36]

But regardless of any questionable details in Carpenter's recollection, the gist of the story is accurate. Lincoln was living at the Soldiers' Home throughout the entire period that he developed his emancipation policy, including the critical few days after Antietam when he finally made up his mind to go public with his plans for a presidential decree. Does this matter? The answer, with some caveats, is yes.

As a wartime politician, Lincoln liked to compare himself to western riverboat pilots who steer their vessels from "point to point," and set their courses "no farther than they can see."[37] This practical credo came to embody his pragmatic approach to the office. By establishing his family's residence outside the White House in the summer of 1862, the president literally allowed himself the luxury of traveling from point to point each morning and evening. As his encounter with the wounded soldiers on the Fourth of July demonstrates, this was not just an opportunity rich in metaphorical meaning. Lincoln used his daily excursions to gather real data and to assess the state of the country through his conversations and chance interactions.

Unfortunately, the vast majority of these fleeting encounters are now lost to historians. Still, there are reasons to speculate that Lincoln might have met some free blacks and escaped slaves as he rode to and from the Soldiers' Home, and thus might have gained a richer appreciation for the human rights and aspirations of African Americans. Free blacks owned several of the properties along the Seventh Street Turnpike, just outside the main gate to the Soldiers' Home, and some of the wartime city's most heavily populated black neighborhoods occupied ground not far from the White House.[38]

"I used to see Mr. Lincoln almost every day riding out to the Soldiers' Home that summer [in 1862]," recalled a former fugitive slave named Anna Harrison.[39] During the war, contrabands or runaways like Harrison swelled the capital's population. By October 1862, more than 4,200 fugitives lived at Camp Barker, a makeshift compound of tents and temporary buildings located along one of Lincoln's primary routes into the city. Soon there were other camps, schools, and even a model village for freed people established at locations in and around the city.

Mary Dines preserved this Matthew Brady photograph of her Washington contraband camp as a memento from President Lincoln's visit. NATIONAL ARCHIVES.

Lincoln knew at least one of Washington's contraband camp residents. "Aunt" Mary Dines was an escaped slave from Maryland who served during this period as the Lincoln family's cook at their summer retreat. Aunt Mary was popular with the military guard stationed at the cottage, earning several references in Private Willard Cutter's letters home. She was friendly to the men, almost a maternal figure. Sergeant Charles Derickson of Company K recalled that one morning when he was on guard duty and after the president had departed, she called him inside and gave him a full meal, in his own excited words, "off the very plate & fork & knife the President of the U.S. eats off."[40]

After the war, Mary Dines told an interviewer that "President Lincoln stopped many times" at her contraband camp "to visit and talk" with the former slaves. She remembered one occasion when the president and Mary Lincoln, along with a small entourage of guests, arrived to hear a musical performance arranged especially for them. Dines led the singing of various Negro spirituals such as "Nobody Knows What Trouble I See, but Jesus" and "Every Time I Feel the Spirit." As she finished, the cook was startled to see the president "wiping the tears off his face with his bare hands." Despite the fact that the ex-slaves had been warned beforehand to limit their performance for the busy president, Lincoln refused to leave quickly. Even when "the real old folks forgot about the President being present and began to shout and yell," Dines recalled, "he didn't laugh at them, but stood like a stone and bowed his head." During the last performance, "John Brown's Body," she said that the president even sang along in "a sweet voice."[41]

According to Dines, Lincoln later returned to the camp without a large entourage and asked her to arrange a more informal session of prayer and song. She noted with wonder that he "stood and sang and prayed just like all the rest of the people." She claimed that the president was "so tender-hearted that he filled-up when he went over to bid the real old folks good-by."[42]

Reminiscences such as these are invariably flawed as historical sources. They are subject to the natural erosion of memory and the equally natural inclination toward self-aggrandizement. But these problems are universal in the handling of recollected sources and are not insurmountable. There is no proof that Lincoln visited contraband camps or experienced some epiphany in the summer of 1862 as a result of his interactions with African Americans. But if such developments occurred—and there is reason to believe they might have—then it was on the road to the Soldiers' Home where they most likely would have taken place. That might sound like an unsatisfying interpretation, but it is the only one possible within the limits of the evidence.

It is almost ironic that after all the mystery surrounding the evolution of Lincoln's thinking on emancipation, we know with a surprising degree of certainty exactly when and where he put the finishing touches on his September 22 proclamation. Secretary of Treasury Salmon Chase recorded in his journal on Sunday afternoon, September 21, that earlier in the day a friend of his, a doctor, had gone to the White House but was refused entrance. "Dr. F. spoke of having been to the President's, who, being very busy writing, could not see him," Chase wrote. Well aware of the confiscation law deadline and Lincoln's previously stated intentions to issue a proclamation, Chase immediately figured out what was happening. "Thought to myself," he noted, "'Possibly engaged on Proclamation.'"[43] Another diary entry confirmed the suspicion. "The President wrote the Proclamation on Sunday morning carefully," recorded principal aide Hay in his journal a few days later.[44]

The original document that remains provides some clues that Lincoln was writing from notes or previous drafts. It covers four pages and includes three different styles of handwriting: a formal opening and closing in the hand of a clerk, the bulk of the text written in pen by Lincoln, and a few minor corrections added by William Seward. The president's penmanship appears steady, almost laborious, suggesting that this version of the document was written in one sitting without too many stops and starts. Toward the third and fourth pages, there are some subtle signs of weariness in his script—ink smudges, scattered unevenness—further indicating that he wrote continuously, tiring only as he neared completion. In addition, there are gaps in the handwritten text where clippings from previously printed statutes have been pasted neatly inside, clearly suggesting that the writing and pasting were done simultaneously without much improvisation.[45]

If Lincoln was working from a document other than the July 22 draft, which he had read to his Cabinet, then the notes have long since disappeared. Captain Derickson of the military guard recalled that during this period the president "often carried a small portfolio, containing papers relating to the business of the day" as he returned to the Soldiers' Home in the evening, but he remembered nothing specific about drafts for an emancipation decree.[46] Once again, a recollection from a household servant offers a potential, but provocative, explanation. The daughter of William Slade, who was the presidential valet, reported that her father "had destroyed many old pieces of paper with notes upon them" concerning the Emancipation Proclamation and claimed that by the time of the final drafting, "Slade already knew every word of it."[47]

For the most part, the phrasing of the Preliminary Emancipation Proclamation was not memorable, nor was it intended to be. The document was written in the numbing legalese of a typical executive order. The new version was still brief—containing little more than a thousand words, building directly on the July 22 draft, and including extended selections from the amended Articles of

2

That on the first day of January in the year of our Lord, one thousand eight hundred and sixty-three, all persons held as slaves within any state, or designated part of a state, the people whereof shall then be in rebellion against the United States, shall be then, thenceforward, and forever free; and the executive govern-ment of the United States, including the military and naval authority thereof, will, ~~during~~ ~~continue in office of the present incumbents,~~ re-cognize and maintain the freedom of such persons, ~~or being free,~~ and will do no act or acts to repress such persons, or any of them, in any efforts they may make for their actual freedom.

That the executive will, on the first day of Jan-uary aforesaid, by proclamation, designate the States, and parts of states, if any, in which the people thereof respectively, shall then be in re-bellion against the United States; and the fact that any state, or the people thereof shall, on that day be, in good faith represented in the Congress of the United States, by members chosen thereto, at elections wherein a majority of the

A selection from Lincoln's final handwritten copy of his Preliminary Emancipation Proclamation, issued on September 22, 1862. NEW YORK STATE LIBRARY, ALBANY, N.Y.

War (March 13, 1862) and from the Confiscation Act (July 17, 1862). Once more the president indicated his intention to offer a plan for compensated emancipation, whether gradual or immediate, and again he set January 1, 1863, as the date when slaves in designated Rebel areas would be declared liberated. Nonetheless, there was a sense of majesty in this public paper, which promised that "all persons held as slaves" by traitors to the Federal government would soon be considered "then, thenceforward, and forever free."[48]

Even though the change in emancipation policy had been in development for months, the public announcement hit like a thunderbolt. The proclamation was distributed on Tuesday, September 23, 1862. By Wednesday night, a large crowd formed outside the White House to serenade the president over his great decision. "I can only trust in God," he told them warily, "that I have made no mistake."[49] As a politician, Lincoln knew well that such a turning point might energize advocates in the short run but leave critics seething indefinitely. Amid the cheers, he worried about the future. John Hay, writing anonymously for the *Missouri Republican*, focused instead on the riotous scene at hand. "The portico was filled, the pedestals of the outer columns were crowded," he reported, "eager hands clung to the spikes of the iron railings, and the adventurous crowd clambered over the gates and dropped into the basement area." As the mob celebrated, the president quietly "entered a carriage in waiting at a side door, accompanied by Mr. Hay, his Secretary, and drove through the shouting throng unnoticed to the Soldiers' Home."[50] The young aide tried to discuss the newspaper coverage of the proclamation, but Lincoln cut him off, commenting wearily that "he had studied the matter for so long that he knew more about it than they did."[51] The decisive moment had arrived, but its meaning was not yet clear. Riding out of the city into the darkness of the autumn evening, the tired president must have been straining greatly to see the points that lay ahead.

4

"Capt. D and his company"

WHITE HOUSE AIDE JOHN HAY WAS APPROACHING HIS TWENTY-FOURTH BIRTHDAY in late September 1862, but he had already figured out one of the keys to gaining influence in Washington. He had learned to stay near the president. Riding along on the commute from White House to Soldiers' Home had quietly become one of Hay's more useful daily chores. He found that on the dusty thirty-minute journey, the president could sometimes prove quite expansive and candid. The aide surreptitiously recorded several of their most revealing conversations in his wartime journal.

On Thursday, for example, the day after the emancipation serenade, Lincoln and Hay once again made the early evening ride together out to the Soldiers' Home. On this occasion, their talk focused on some of the darker rumors concerning disloyalty within the Union military. The president claimed "he had heard of an officer who had said [the army] did not mean to gain any decisive victory but to keep things running on so that they . . . might manage things to suit themselves." Lincoln angrily vowed that he would investigate this allegation, and if it were true, the officer's "head should go off." Hay then "talked a great deal about the McClellan conspiracy," but the president was reluctant to comment. After some prodding, Lincoln would only say that the general was "doing nothing to make himself either respected or feared."[1] Both men were referring to gossip that had been rampant since the time of the Harrison's Landing meeting in early July. After the failure of the peninsula campaign, many leading Republican politicians had become convinced that McClellan and his senior staff were intent on undermining the administration's political strategy.

The Machiavellian undertone to the president's conversation on September 25 was not surprising. This was a period of intense political pressure. Midterm elections were approaching. Emancipation threatened to divide northern public opinion. Recruiting efforts had stalled and the dreaded prospect of a military draft was looming as a reality. To help quell dissent, the president had just authorized the suspension of civil liberties across the North. In Lincoln's mind, there was no room anymore for what Tom Paine had once famously called "summer soldiers and sunshine patriots."

What agitated the president more than anything else about the deteriorating situation was that it seemed so unnecessary. He was convinced that Antietam should have been the decisive moment he had been anticipating for months. "The army of the enemy should have been annihilated," Lincoln told Orville Browning, "but it was permitted to recross the Potomac without the loss of a man, and McClellan would not follow." Lincoln claimed bitterly that he "coaxed, urged & ordered him," to no avail because, as always, the general's "great defect" was an "excess of caution."[2]

Lincoln was right about McClellan's fatal reluctance to strike, but in his growing frustration, he sometimes failed to acknowledge the legitimate obstacles that stood in the general's way. At this early stage of the war, most Union troops and their officers were terribly inexperienced at combat. The logistics of executing a battle plan, regrouping after a virtual bloodbath, and then pursuing a fleeing enemy were extraordinarily difficult. Notwithstanding Lincoln's stubborn belief that such problems mattered little because both sides were equally "green," this limitation affected the Federal side more severely.[3]

An embarrassing example of Union inexperience occurred at the Soldiers' Home in the evening following the president's brooding conversation with John Hay. At about midnight on September 25, according to Willard Cutter, the Pennsylvania infantrymen guarding the cottage heard an unexpected "call to arms." The company then received orders to march for the Chain Bridge, presumably to face yet another Confederate invasion. They "flew to arms" and left at "a quick pace," but when Captain Derickson ordered the men to "Bare hard to the left" as they approached the critical crossing point, the young men from Meadville panicked. They broke ranks and were forced to regroup back at the Soldiers' Home, somewhat relieved to hear later that they had responded to a false alarm. The experience was unsettling. "It was the first march to battle," Cutter grumbled to his brother, "and we could not get pluck enough to cross a bridge."[4]

The midnight alarm surely roused the light-sleeping president. Whether or not he ever discovered the humiliating truth of his bodyguard's first foray into combat is unknown, but he certainly returned to the White House the next day full of determination to set an example for the Union military. In the morning, he directed John Hay to deliver a blunt letter to Major John J. Key, the officer he had been complaining about the previous night. The president's note revealed that he had heard how Key, when asked in conversation why the Rebel army had not been "bagged" after Antietam, had responded by saying "That is not the game." In a direct interrogatory, President Lincoln then demanded to know, within twenty-four hours, whether the report was "litterally, or in substance," an accurate one. The next morning Key appeared at the White House, attempting to defend his loyalty but declining to dispute the specifics of the accusation. Unmoved, the president summarily dismissed him from the service, announcing that "if there was a 'game' ever among Union men" not to destroy the enemy, then "it was his object to break up that game."[5]

Firing an arrogant officer might have made Lincoln feel better for the moment, but clearly he understood that the problems lay deeper. Everywhere he turned there seemed to be disappointing news. On Sunday, September 28, he responded almost morosely to a short note of congratulations on his new emancipation policy from Vice President Hamlin, who was then at home in Maine. The president admitted that he was "not as sanguine" as some over the preliminary proclamation's effects. Noting that nearly a week had passed since September 22, he reported glumly that "stocks have declined, and troops come forward more slowly than ever." Lincoln was in no mood to be impressed. "The North responds to the proclamation sufficiently in breath," he wrote, "but breath alone kills no rebels."[6]

What the northern public needed was more battlefield victories. The president still had not abandoned hope that the enemy, now "hived" in his homespun phrase, might still be destroyed before winter. But he needed to know for certain that the Union army and its commanders would continue to fight once they officially became an army of liberation. In particular, he worried about McClellan, who was on record as opposing any "radical" steps against slavery. To some astute observers, the dismissal of Major Key appeared to be a warning shot for McClellan since the officer's brother was on the general's senior staff. Cabinet member Montgomery Blair and his father, the political adviser Francis P. Blair, both quickly urged McClellan to make a public statement that he intended "to give full effect to the proclamation."[7] The stubborn general declined at first to speak out and even briefly considered going public with his opposition to the emancipation doctrine. Frustrated on several fronts, Lincoln decided it was time for another face-to-face meeting with his contentious subordinate.

The president and a small entourage of friends left for McClellan's headquarters in western Maryland on Wednesday, October 1. Significantly, the president asked Captain Derickson, from the Soldiers' Home guard, to join the delegation. The invitation demonstrated Lincoln's trust and comfort level with the officer in charge of his new military detail. Several old Illinois friends also accompanied him on what appeared to be a mission that combined business with an escape from the routine of the White House. Stretched over four days, the much-needed excursion allowed the president to roam freely across the battlefield region, greet the regular troops, visit with wounded Union soldiers, and hold high-level meetings with McClellan and his top generals.

Unlike previous visits with McClellan, this time President Lincoln tried to express himself more forcefully to his stubborn young subordinate. He apparently warned him about "over-cautiousness" and strongly urged his commander to take the offensive. It also appears that he raised the topic of emancipation and its effect on the army. But in typically Lincolnian fashion, the president tempered his tough talk with humor and even effusive praise. McClellan reported to his wife that Lincoln was "very affable" during their discussions and had called him "the best general in the country."[8]

Once again, the results of the discussions were not what Lincoln had hoped. He responded by ordering General Halleck to wire McClellan a new, blunt directive on the Monday morning following his return to Washington. "The President directs that you cross the Potomac," relayed the general-in-chief on October 6, "and give battle to the enemy or drive him south."[9] No longer content with making suggestions or putting major questions to the vote of war councils, Lincoln finally attempted to seize control of the vast war-making machinery for himself. McClellan was predictably outraged and tried to mollify the president without conceding control over the army and the timing of its movements. The next day, the general released a long overdue order to his troops reminding them that the politics of emancipation must not interfere with their military mission. He knew this was something Lincoln had wanted accomplished. In the process, however, he could not resist taking some subtle shots at the Republicans on the eve of the midterm elections. McClellan slyly pointed out in his directive that the "remedy for political Errors if any are Committed" must only be found "in the action of the people at the polls."[10]

Politics was on nearly everyone's mind in early October. The critical northern states of Indiana, Ohio, and Pennsylvania held their state and congressional elections during that month. Republicans feared that widespread discontent over emancipation and martial law in those critical swing areas would destroy their chances of holding majorities in key legislative assemblies and perhaps even in the Congress. Anticipating serious electoral setbacks for their party, a number of Republicans began blaming the Lincoln administration and its policies.

While her husband was away on his trip to Antietam, Mary Lincoln tried to help defend his political record. During those first days of October, she exchanged letters with James Gordon Bennett, a key independent in the political process. Bennett was the legendary owner of the *New York Herald* who had helped introduce the forerunner of the nation's mass media, the celebrated "penny press," of the 1830s. He had a sharp mind and even sharper personality. By the time of the Civil War, he had become a powerful and controversial figure with many enemies, someone John Hay labeled in his journal as "too pitchy to touch."[11]

Bennett's reputation did not appear to frighten Mary Lincoln, who wrote the editor an explicit political note from the Soldiers' Home on Saturday, October 4. The first lady acknowledged that "from all parties, the cry, for a 'change of Cabinet' comes." This was perceptive, but also convenient. It was an insightful comment because it anticipated by more than two months a full-blown cabinet crisis that would erupt in December and would lead to the resignations (later withdrawn) of both Secretary of State Seward and Secretary of Treasury Chase, the two leading men of the group. But for Mary Lincoln, who harbored deep suspicions of the president's former rivals, focusing on their critics was also a convenient way to shift blame away from her husband. She even provided the publisher with the potentially damaging information that Rhode Island governor William Sprague had also written to her complaining about the president's men.

Offering such valuable morsels of information allowed the first lady to suggest that she could serve as a useful back channel to the White House. "Doubtless if my good, patient Husband, were here, instead of being with the Army of the Potomac," she wrote deftly, "both of these missives, would be placed before him, accompanied by my womanly suggestions, proceeding from a heart so deeply interested, for our distracted country." She concluded, without a hint of irony, that she had "a great terror of strong minded Ladies," adding that nonetheless "if a word fitly spoken and in due season, can be urged, in a time like this, we should not withhold it."[12]

Mary Lincoln's behind-the-scenes politicking for her husband was nothing new in their long history together. Politics had always been a factor that helped keep their turbulent relationship intact. Over twenty years before in Springfield, the young couple had first fallen in love during the pivotal 1840 presidential contest. At that time, Mary Todd was a well-educated young woman in her early twenties, and Abraham Lincoln was an awkward, self-made state legislator approaching thirty, but both were Kentucky natives and ardent supporters of the Whig party. They forged a unique bond built on the foundation of mutual political interests and ambitions. By January 1841, however, they had broken off their courtship only to reconcile just over a year later when they became embroiled together in a partisan feud with a leading Democratic politician. The wild episode nearly resulted in a duel and helped rekindle their romance.[13]

During more than two decades of married life, Mary Lincoln had always maintained an active role in her husband's political career. When he entered Congress in the late 1840s, she was one of the few congressional spouses from a western state who followed her husband to Washington. After he was offered the governorship of the Oregon territory following his single term in office, it was Mary Lincoln who reportedly vetoed the idea and kept the family in Illinois. Throughout the 1850s, as Lincoln became a prominent attorney in the state and leader of the new Republican party, his wife contributed to his progress by managing their household, entertaining guests, and occasionally helping out with campaign chores like copying circular letters. She certainly followed his career closely, cultivating local allies for him and bearing grudges against both his rivals and their wives.[14]

She had hoped to become an even greater asset during his presidency, but events conspired against her. Her determination to renovate the White House and entertain lavishly hit a sour note during the solemn wartime period. The president was especially worried about her habit of stretching the White House budget in an era of explosive Federal spending. At one point, an enraged president reportedly told Benjamin B. French, the government official in charge of managing public buildings, that "he would never approve" bills for what he termed "flub dubs for that damned old house!"[15] Subject to intense public scrutiny and newspaper criticism for the first time in her life, Mary Lincoln lashed out. She became an embattled figure, jealous of those she considered enemies and vulnerable to the flattery and manipulation of an opportunistic network of hangers-on. The death of Willie Lincoln in February 1862 and her husband's increasing obsession with the management of the military conflict only added to her private turmoil.

From this perspective, Mary Lincoln's letter to James Gordon Bennett, the newspaper publisher, showed flashes of what she had once hoped to become— a valuable political conduit for the president. It was a role that she did manage to serve occasionally during the war with cosmopolitan figures like Bennett or Senator Charles Sumner, the Republican chairman of the Senate Foreign Relations Committee. Ultimately, however, Mary Lincoln was a peripheral figure in the actual workings of the Lincoln administration and she knew it. There was really no other possibility during this era of fraternal politics and Victorian conventions about gender roles. The president brought along men like Captain Derickson and old friends like Ward Hill Lamon to visit Antietam—not his wife—and would have been criticized if he had done otherwise.

This stifling limitation might suggest another reason that Mary Lincoln had pushed for her family's removal to the Soldiers' Home in the summer of 1862. The White House was not just a private home but was also a public space and working office all rolled into one. There was a place for the president's wife, but it was not an appealing environment for an ambitious nineteenth-century woman. The first lady had to compete for attention with her husband's jealous advisers and aides and with the endless stream of visitors, favor-seekers, and politicians. She had to manage an experienced domestic staff who knew the operation and the city better than she did and on a budget accountable to Congress, not simply her husband. The Soldiers' Home must have promised a return to a more traditional balance of power, with Mary Lincoln once again at the center of her household, choosing her guests, supervising only a handful of servants, and finding many more intimate moments with her elusive husband.

By October 1862, however, after four months in residence at the cottage, it was clear that there would be no such perfect seclusion for the first family. Unexpected visitors appeared at odd hours, seeking favors or some special audience with the president. Armed guards were everywhere. Military transport wagons passed along the road outside their cottage day and night. Peaceful country mornings were sometimes shattered by the distant sound of cannon fire. Even their daily carriage rides were now disturbed by the clatter of cavalry escorts.

The only member of the Lincoln family who seemed to truly appreciate these intrusions on their privacy was nine-year-old Tad. Having lost his favorite playmate, older brother Willie, the rambunctious young boy now found surrogate friends in the soldiers who protected him. The infantry guards at the Soldiers' Home bestowed upon the youngest Lincoln an unofficial title of "3rd Lieutenant," and he became, according to their sergeant, "a great favorite" of the company, appearing "often at drill time on his pony."[16] Tad enjoyed hanging around the camp for other reasons as well. Private Willard Cutter reported to his mother on October 8 that he had encountered the boy looking to share some of the soldiers' food. "If this war lasts much longer," he wrote, "I think old Abe will be on the town for his boy was here yesterday to get something to eat and I gave him Bread and Molasses."[17] Albert N. See, another private in the company, recalled that the hungry boy began appearing at the camp "almost every day," and when the dinner bell rang would simply "get in line and draw his rations the same as the rest of us."[18]

Sometimes Tad, invoking his rights as an officer, commandeered soldiers to assist him on various errands. He soon developed a special relationship with the company's teamster, Private Philip Yokum, a small, thin young man who shared a tent with Cutter. Once Tad and his driver were apparently detained by

Tad Lincoln on his pony. LIBRARY OF CONGRESS.

a patrol for not having an appropriate pass. As the military police prepared to arrest the nervous private, Tad "remonstrated" in the words of Sergeant Charles Derickson, and told the patrol that "he was the President's son and that he would be responsible for the soldier." Informed that such facts made no difference, Tad defiantly marched along with his friend to the Central Guard House. Yokum was quickly released when Tad's identity was confirmed, but the young boy insisted on subsequently obtaining from his father an official pass that read:

Guards & Patrols
Pass Phillip Yocum of the Presidents Guard.
A. Lincoln

Yokum was "so proud of this," recalled Sgt. Derickson after the war, "he won't let it get out of his hand." [19]

Despite his mischievous self-confidence, Tad Lincoln was a slow-developing child, hindered by a speech impediment that made his conversation almost unrecognizable to strangers. He called his father "Papa-Day" which seemed to be an attempt at "Papa Dear." At this stage of his life, he did not yet dress himself. Nor could he read or write much until well into his teenage years. During the war, the family had retained a tutor, a young employee from the Treasury Department, but he could never seem to convince the boy (or his indulgent father) that it was important to apply himself to his lessons. Jean Baker, Mary Lincoln's biographer, goes so far as to suggest that Tad may have been "slightly retarded." [20] Perhaps recognizing his son's disabilities, the president seemed to shower him with special attention. He allowed him to fall asleep in his office, and often kept him throughout the night in his own bed.

Both parents seemed to appreciate the genuine affection that the soldiers demonstrated toward Tad and encouraged their son to spend time with the men. Although Mary Lincoln reportedly complained about the grime that accumulated on her son's face and clothes from the campfires, she never stopped him from going. The president was equally supportive. Albert See remembered seeing Tad and his father playing checkers on the porch of the Soldiers' Home cottage one evening while he was on sentinel duty. Lincoln asked if he wanted to lay down his gun for a moment and "take a game," an offer the young soldier proudly accepted. [21]

For Tad Lincoln, the coming of autumn air to the Soldiers' Home only promised a continuation of the idyllic camp life he was then busy discovering. To his mother, however, the evening chill stirred a desire to find further escape from the troubles of Washington. On October 20, 1862, she departed for a visit to Manhattan, bringing her son along with her and leaving her husband alone at the cottage with the guards and a handful of servants—cook Mary

Dines, probably valet William Slade, and a housekeeper named Mary Ann Cuthbert. She did not return for over a month, traveling through New York and Boston (to see Robert at Harvard) before returning to Washington in late November.[22]

Once again, the president's family was essentially abandoning him in the midst of a difficult period. Electoral results from the October states had been discouraging, with Republicans losing ground nearly across the board. There were reports of scattered resistance to the Militia Act draft. In the western theater of the war, the Confederate advance into Kentucky had been stymied at Perryville, but the slow pace of Union pursuit convinced the president to fire one of his top commanders, General Don C. Buell. Back in the East, Lincoln's battle of wills with McClellan was also erupting into open hostility. On October 25, the general sent a report to the War Department complaining that the Army of Potomac's horses were "absolutely broken down with fatigue." The president instantly snapped back in a telegram that asked sarcastically "what the horses of your army have done since the battle of Antietam that fatigue anything?"[23]

Lincoln was growing short-tempered, but unlike the previous summer he was not as visibly depressed or anxious. The close-mouthed president did not discuss his feelings with anyone, but the reasons for his newfound equilibrium seem readily apparent. He was now publicly committed to some major policy changes—most notably, emancipation and the enforcement of conscription—and so regardless of the uncertainty that remained over the outcome of those shifts, at least his direction was clear. There was still the unresolved question of McClellan's future with the Army of the Potomac and the perennial questions about progress on the battlefields, but the evolution of Union war aims seemed irreversible.

On a personal level, there were other stabilizing factors. Every month was another month further away from the tragedy of Willie Lincoln's death. The pain undoubtedly remained, but both parents were now functioning again. Tad Lincoln had fully recovered from his winter sickness and appeared healthy and happy. Unlike many other young men of his age, Robert Lincoln was safely ensconced within the protective walls of Harvard Yard. The family was apart at present, but they had spent more than two full months together over the summer.

For the president, there was also a new spirit of camaraderie in his life. As a lawyer and politician in Springfield, Lincoln had always been at the center of a small, male-dominated universe. He swapped stories and talked politics at local grocery stores, taverns, and courthouses throughout central Illinois. There were few such relaxed opportunities for a president, especially during wartime.

Charles M. Derickson,
whose father was the unit captain,
served as a sergeant
in Company K.
ILLINOIS STATE HISTORICAL LIBRARY,
SPRINGFIELD, ILL.

Maintaining a cottage at the Soldiers' Home allowed Lincoln to recreate some of the fraternal atmosphere of his frontier past.

Company K sergeant Charles Derickson recalled that President Lincoln, like his son, used to enjoy coming over to camp for a cup of "army coffee" and "a plate of beans."[24] At these moments, the president relished talking with the men and watching their antics. One of the favorite camp-life distractions for the Bucktails was something called the "Trained Elephant," a game introduced by the Kepler brothers—Isaac, James, and Solomon, all members of the company. The idea was to have two men about the same size bend over, with the man in the rear grabbing hold of the one in front, while someone else covered them in a blanket and attached a piece of wood wrapped in a blanket to serve as an impromptu trunk. Then pretending to be an elephant, the men acted out a series of tricks—sitting, standing, standing on a single leg, and so on. Apparently, one day in the autumn of 1862, the president strolled into camp and caught a glimpse of the man-made elephant. Amused, he returned later with a friend, someone Derickson thought was a senator, and the two politicians watched and applauded as the Kepler boys demonstrated their talent.[25]

Members of the cavalry escort who camped near the Soldiers' Home cemetery reported that the president often approached them in the evening as they sat around discussing current events or complaining about life in the Army. "Mr. Lincoln used to leave the house, come down near the edge of the camp and pace up and down as if in deep thought," one soldier remembered. "Whenever he heard loud talking, he would send in and inquire its cause." It was not long before the members of the escort figured out that they had unparalleled access to the Federal court of last resort. "We soon appreciated the situation," claimed the soldier, "and when we had been ill treated we used to make it a point to talk the matter over in loud tones." When the price of clothing increased dramatically, the soldiers balked and the president listened. When some of the troops received defective socks, their curses captured the president's attention. According to one of the members of the cavalry detail, Lincoln took the shoddy stockings and had the contractors sent to prison.[26]

Whether that particular story was true, the soldiers who guarded the president did have legitimate complaints that would have concerned him. Private George W. Flemming of Company K, for example, deserted on October 17, because his wife had fallen ill and there was no money to pay for her care. "I have a family, a wife and three small children," he testified later at his court-martial hearing, "and they are dependent on me for support." He had left his post at the Soldiers' Home to return to Meadville, where he had gathered up his family and helped them relocate to his sister's home in Ohio. He said he tried to return to his company promptly but hurt his leg, developed an infection, and did not make it back until the following summer. Flemming blamed the government for his financial predicament, noting bitterly that the bounties promised to Pennsylvania soldiers who enlisted in 1862 had never arrived, leaving his family "completely destitute."[27]

Openness to the men's complaints was important because, as historian William C. Davis details in his book *Lincoln's Men* (1999), the president became a unique symbol to many of the Federal troops and their families. Northerners honored Lincoln as "Father Abraham," both for his merciful and forgiving nature and for his iron determination on behalf of the Union cause.[28] He was even the inspiration for popular songs:

> We are coming Father Abraham, three hundred thousand more,
> From Mississippi's winding stream and from New England's shore,
> We leave our plows and workshops, our wives and children dear,
> With hearts too full for utterance, with but a silent tear;
> We dare not look behind us, but steadfastly before,
> We are coming Father Abraham, three hundred thousand more.[29]

In his relationships with the soldiers around him, the president demonstrated a capacity to move beyond protocol and create honest interaction. He exhibited his legendary empathetic skills and cultivated loyalty from men who did not always offer their affection freely.

Although Lincoln was accessible to the regular soldiers, he was on even friend-
lier terms with the officers. According to Major Thomas Chamberlin, who
visited the Soldiers' Home during this period to drill the new troops, both
captains David Derickson of Company K and Henry Crotzer of Company D
were regular dinner companions for the president when his wife was out of
town. James B. Mix, the officer in charge of the cavalry escort, reported that he
often shared breakfast with the president in the morning before the day began.
Derickson and Mix both claimed that in the mornings they frequently witnessed Lincoln reading the Bible or other volumes of literature either alone or
to his son. Sometimes they claimed that he engaged them in conversations
about the texts.[30]

Without doubt, it was David Derickson, above all others, who emerged as
the president's favorite new companion. In the good-natured officer from
Meadville, Pennsylania, Lincoln found someone who shared his background as
a former small town resident and Republican politician. Derickson even occasionally spent nights at the cottage, reportedly sharing a bed with the president—a fact that surprised and amused his fellow officers. Major Chamberlin
recalled:

> Captain Derickson, in particular, advanced so far in the President's confidence and es-
> teem that, in Mrs. Lincoln's absence, he frequently spent the night at his cottage, sleep-
> ing in the same bed with him, and—it is said—making use of His Excellency's
> night-shirts![31]

The soldiers were not shocked by the idea of two men sharing a bed together. This was common practice in the nineteenth century. In fact, the men
of Company K engaged, like many other regular soldiers, in what they called
"spooning" during cold nights in order to help keep warm. But the idea of a
president and an officer socializing was a little scandalous. Part of the humor in
this particular situation also derived from its purely physical aspect: Lincoln
and Derickson made a comic pair. The president, at about 6'4" and 180 pounds
was tall and lanky while the captain was much shorter and stockier. Lieutenant
Colonel (later General) Huidekoper, who noted that the portly captain had
"most pleasing manners," remembered hearing Lincoln make jokes about his
unusual friendship with Derickson, claiming "with a twinkle in his eye" that
"[t]he Captain and I are getting quite thick."[32]

In his own brief memoir of his days with Lincoln, Captain Derickson also
emphasized their special rapport. He recalled that he found the president "to
be one of the most kind hearted and pleasant gentleman that I had ever met."
He claimed that from their first memorable morning ride on September 7 until
the return to the White House in early November, he commuted with Lincoln

almost every day from the Soldiers' Home. Derickson recalled that frequently on their rides together the president "discussed points that seemed to trouble him." The captain also noted that the first lady appealed to him with her concerns and sometimes even asked him to serve as intermediary with her husband. Calling her "one of the best rebel haters that I met during my stay in Washington," he wrote that she repeatedly urged him to warn the president about government officials whom she suspected of treason. Although Derickson made no reference to any nights spent at the cottage, he did acknowledge that he was "conscious and proud" of the fact that he was able to call Lincoln "a friend and acquaintance."[33]

The available contemporary evidence fully supports these recollections of a special relationship. As noted earlier, the president had brought Derickson on the four-day trip to Antietam, a fact reported in the newspapers of the day and captured in photographs.[34] Lincoln himself also penned a note during this period indicating his appreciation for his new friend and a desire to keep him nearby. Captain Derickson and the other members of the Bucktail unit, the president wrote on November 1, 1862, "are very agreeable to me; and while it is deemed proper for any guard to remain, none would be more satisfactory to me than Capt. D and his company."[35] What brought on the president's testimonial, according to Willard Cutter, was the arrival on October 31 of another unit from the Army of the Potomac apparently sent to relieve Company K. The nervous private, who shared a meal with some of the new arrivals, called them "a hard looking lot."[36] It appears that the next morning Derickson subsequently secured a letter from the president to protect his unit's status as the "President's Military Guard," a proud caption he had ordered inscribed on special company stationery.[37]

Naturally, the appearance of a new figure around the president generated talk in Washington. Virginia Fox, the wife of the assistant secretary of Navy, noted in her diary in the middle of November that a friend had informed her that "there is a Bucktail Soldier here devoted to the President, drives with him & when Mrs L. is not home, sleeps with him." Surprised, Fox could only exclaim, "What stuff!"[38]

There is something remarkable about the speed with which Derickson became an important part of Lincoln's personal life. More than anything else, their instant friendship seems to testify to the president's deep-seated need for support during a trying period. His family was gone and most of his Illinois friends were either back home or drifting apart from him. He had been facing some tough decisions over emancipation and the enforcement of the draft—and still had to contend with the ever-frustrating General McClellan. It was clear that Lincoln felt lonely. This was surely why secondary figures such as

Captain David V. Derickson (inset) has been identified as the soldier standing with his arms crossed on the far left of this photograph, which was taken at the Antietam battlefield in October 1862. LIBRARY OF CONGRESS; INSET, CRAWFORD COUNTY HISTORICAL SOCIETY, MEADVILLE, PA.

Derickson and aide John Hay increasingly began to fill in as presidential companions during the autumn of 1862.

Mary Lincoln might have performed that role, but she appeared incapable of grasping the scope of her husband's isolation. Instead, she wanted his attention, believing that after their son's death she was the one in greatest need. "My Dear Husband," she wrote from New York the day after he insisted on keeping Derickson's company in place, "I have waited in vain to hear from you, yet as you are not *given* to letter writing, [I] will be charitable enough to impute your silence, to the right cause."[39]

Her rebuke must have been especially jarring to President Lincoln, who was just then on the verge of firing McClellan for the final time. The decision to remove the Army of the Potomac's commander was not entirely unexpected, but it was nevertheless a wrenching, risky call. On this issue, the president moved with extreme caution, waiting until after the last of the midterm elections on November 4 before finally executing the order. In her letter on November 2, Mary Lincoln had reported that "McClellan & his slowness" were being "vehemently discussed" in New York. She informed her husband that the controversial general was uniformly unpopular. "Many say," the first lady reported, "they would almost worship you, if you would put a fighting General, in the place of McClellan."[40]

The president had been listening to a similar chorus of complaints in Washington. Union financier Jay Cooke went out to the Soldiers' Home one evening during this period specifically to discuss the McClellan problem. Arriving at the cottage, he noticed the growing contingent of presidential companions. "I found Mr. Lincoln surrounded by a small army of officers," he recalled, "and civilians, coming and going." Cooke claimed that the president asked him to remain at the cottage until after 10 P.M., "when all this crowd would disperse." He did so and then had what he called "one of the most interesting and important interviews held by me with Mr. Lincoln or his Cabinet during the war." During their conversation, the influential Treasury agent pointed out that bond sales were declining because public confidence had plummeted in the aftermath of Antietam. He warned that "unless McClellan was sent away very soon," there would be a financial catastrophe.[41]

Not everyone was so tough on the general. When Lincoln discussed his plans to relieve McClellan with the cabinet on Wednesday, November 5, 1862, Postmaster General Montgomery Blair objected vehemently. He was concerned about who would replace the commander, convinced that his political rivals within the administration—particularly Secretary of Treasury Chase and Secretary of War Stanton—were behind the precipitous decision. Blair attempted to head off the dismissal by appealing to his father, a respected senior political hand, for help with the president. "I went out to Silver Spring for my father to go that night to the Soldiers' Home," Blair recalled, "to endeavor to prevent the removal." Francis Blair, Sr., subsequently went to the president's cottage on Thursday night, where he found Lincoln, for once, "in his solitude."[42] The two men had a long, intense conversation.

The day after their talk, Blair described the blunt conversation in a letter to his son. The former Democrat wrote that he had warned the president of the political consequences, spoke of the next election, and urged him against yielding to the "ultras," whom Blair believed were destroying the administration. He advised one last overture to the recalcitrant general, through an intermediary who could convey to McClellan exactly "what the President expected him to do & when." Lincoln was unmoved, responding dryly that "he had tried long enough to bore with an augur too dull to take hold."[43]

According to Montgomery Blair, his father then "spent a long time arguing" with the president without effect. His father told him that Lincoln simply rose at the end of the interview, "stretched his long arms almost up to the ceiling above him" and replied sternly, "I said I would remove him if he let Lee's army get away from him, and I must do so. He has got the 'slows,' Mr. Blair."[44]

Union general Ambrose Burnside took command of the Army of the Potomac on Sunday, November 9, 1862. The same day, the president wired his wife, then in Boston, asking for guidance about whether he should continue at the Soldiers' Home. Referring to the family's housekeeper and cook, he asked, "Mrs. [Mary Ann] Cuthbert & Aunt Mary [Dines] want to move to the White House, because it has grown so cold at Soldiers Home. Shall they?"[45] The question was timely in the opinion of Willard Cutter, who wrote his brother on the same day that he did not believe they could remain more than a week because it was "getting too cold for [us] to stay in these tents much longer." He reported that Aunt Mary had already told him that she would be gone in a matter of days. Everybody seemed anxious to leave. In Cutter's words, "as soon as Abe goes we goes and mabe [sic] sooner."[46]

Subsequently, over the next two days the president and his chilly entourage began the process of relocating back to the White House. Lincoln had been in residence at the Soldiers' Home since mid-June, a period of nearly five months. During that time, he cautiously embraced emancipation as a Union war aim, steadily authorized a series of stern measures to increase enlistments, and after much debate, finally decided to fire his leading military commander. These controversial actions were all born from the same predicament—the continued inability of the Union military to subdue the rebellion. And beneath the public events, there was an undercurrent of private tragedy and personal loneliness descending around the president. It was a difficult period, arguably the most wrenching of the entire war for him. Nonetheless, he had survived and seemed, almost remarkably, to be gaining inner strength from his ordeals.

But Lincoln was not superhuman, and thus, it seems fitting that after making one tough decision after another, he looked almost plaintively to his wife for an answer about a simple domestic matter. The episode illustrates the many dimensions of a president's life. The man who fired McClellan and vowed to free the slaves now wanted permission to vacate a summer cottage as winter approached. He received the necessary approval and finally returned to the White House, not with his family, but surrounded instead by his new "band of brothers," the men of his military guard.

Part Two

1863

☙

5

"Mother very slightly hurt"

IN JUNE 1863, THE LINCOLN FAMILY, WITH THE EXCEPTION OF ROBERT, RETURNED together to take up residence at the Soldiers' Home. Commissioner of Public Buildings Benjamin French recalled that he witnessed a revealing standoff just prior to the family's scheduled departure. As the Lincolns were stepping into a carriage that was supposed to take them out to the country for the season, Tad Lincoln suddenly threw a small fit. "I have not got my cat," he screamed. With great patience, according to French, the president reentered the Executive Mansion and after several minutes returned holding the boy's favorite pet in his arms.[1]

The president's tenderness toward his son was not unusual but seems especially memorable since it came during a period of tense concern in the capital. Robert E. Lee and his Army of Northern Virginia had crossed the Potomac and were headed toward some unknown destination in the North. "General excitement has marked the time," Benjamin French noted in his diary on June 22, the actual day of the Lincoln family departure. "The Rebels have been raiding into Maryland and Pa.[,] and there is some prospect of an attempt on Washington."[2] Consequently, the family traveled with full military guard accompanying them, making quite a spectacle in their procession. "We marched to the Soldiers' Home," Bucktail soldier Willard Cutter reported, "followed by 6 horse teams all mules [and] 3 four horse teams come an hour or two afterwards" in addition to "forty cavalry [that] come up with the President." It was, he wrote, "a big thing."[3]

There were some minor changes around the Soldiers' Home that were immediately apparent. The infantry soldiers moved their camp about a quarter of a mile down the hill, perhaps to make room for the expanding national cemetery. A report from the Quartermaster noted the number of interments had

93

reached nearly 8,000 by this point, leaving the graveyard "in miserable condi-tion."[4] Regardless of the reason, Cutter appreciated the decision because it im-proved his view of the city. Near their tents, the soldiers also erected a fifty-foot flagpole, which the private considered the "nicest pole in the town." He noted proudly that Tad had located for them a "brass eagle for the top." If there had been changes or additions to the cottage, the young soldier did not report on them. He did notice, however, that Mary Dines was no longer the cook. "There is a white cook in her place," wrote Cutter, "a nice good looking woman."[5]

What happened that summer to Mary Dines is not clear. Her stories about the Soldiers' Home have not been recorded, at least in writing. She might have run into trouble with Mary Lincoln, perhaps over her habit of providing meals to the soldiers who guarded the cottage. The first lady had always been notori-ously hard on her domestic help, even when the family had lived in Springfield and had only retained one or two part-time servants. Or perhaps the contra-band singer, caught up in the spirit of post-emancipation Washington, might have tried something new in this year of freedom.

African Americans certainly perceived the final Emancipation Proclamation, signed by the president on January 1, 1863, as a life-altering event. Many crit-ics have since questioned the significance of the document and the motivations behind it. But at the time, the overwhelming majority of American blacks un-abashedly celebrated Lincoln in his role as emancipator. "I can remember how we laughed and cried when he set the slaves free," recalled Anna (Harrison) Chase, a contraband from Virginia, in 1936.[6] Chase's Depression-era recollec-tion illustrates the long-lasting impact of the emancipation moment on the African-American community. At the age of ninety-two, the former slave and Washington resident walked out to the Soldiers' Home on her own in a touch-ing pilgrimage to see the place where she had heard that Lincoln had originally drafted the great proclamation.

As Anna Chase's story testifies, the Emancipation Proclamation was a pow-erful document despite its immediate limitations. Numerous critics have pointed out, for example, that the proclamation only freed slaves in Rebel-controlled territories. In fact, the final version signed by the president literally spelled out sections of Rebel states that would be exempted from the order since they were occupied by Union forces and would be, in the dismal words of the text, "left precisely as if this proclamation were not issued." Yet the emancipation decree also spelled out important new opportunities for former slaves or contrabands. The president recommended that ex-slaves be allowed to "labor faithfully for reasonable wages" or that those of "suitable condition" be "received into the armed service of the United States."[7] The Congress had authorized the enlist-ment of black soldiers in the Union army at the same time they had passed the

Second Confiscation Act in July. Now the commander in chief was formally endorsing that decision.

Even more significant than what the document contained was what it omitted. Lincoln was no longer publicly advocating the alternative of colonization or the removal of blacks from U.S. soil—a proposal that had been dangled in almost every previous proclamation or piece of legislation concerning the fate of freed slaves. Even as recently as December 1, 1862, in his Annual Message to Congress, Lincoln had discussed the prospects for colonization in both Latin America and Africa. Prior to 1863, most Republican politicians had believed it was political suicide to promote the end of slavery without providing for colonization, since northern white voters generally feared the prospect of racial integration, or what was often termed "amalgamation." By avoiding what historian Gabor Boritt has labeled the "defense mechanism" of racial separation and removal, the president was making a bold statement through his silence.[8] The other noticeable omission from the final proclamation was a call for gradual, compensated emancipation. Once again, this was a subject that Lincoln had last raised in the 1862 Annual Message, which had outlined a complicated scheme for financing the abolition of slavery in the remaining loyal slave states by 1900. The January 1, 1863, presidential decree contained no mention of this proposal.

The omissions would not have been significant if the president had continued to lobby for the passage of these proposals in the upcoming months. Instead, he largely chose to ignore them. He never again raised either topic in a public speech or official document. By 1864, John Hay reported that Lincoln had entirely "sloughed off" his support for colonization.[9] That same year he also endorsed a constitutional amendment calling for the immediate and uncompensated abolition of slavery across the country.

Northern whites also viewed the emancipation decision as monumental, though their reactions were naturally far more ambivalent and polarized than those of blacks. According to Civil War historian James McPherson, the Emancipation Proclamation at first "intensified a morale crisis" in the army that had been building since the controversial removal of General McClellan and some subsequent defeats suffered by Union forces in the winter of 1862.[10] "I very much doubt the effect of the Proclamation," one officer stationed near the Soldiers' Home had nervously informed his father in October. "I foresee a reaction against the war, and fear that we shall break down, and that before long, from internal dissensions."[11] Beyond the widespread fears that the races could not live together in peace, the essential problem was partisanship. Many Democrats who supported the war effort and some conservative Republicans believed that emancipation would divide the Union coalition. Other so-called

Radical Republicans or "ultras" considered the demise of slavery long overdue and believed the proclamation would finally unleash the full moral energy of the North.

These bitter political divisions had a dramatic impact on the president's own circle of advisers. Republicans had suffered significant setbacks in the 1862 midterm elections, an outcome not unusual for the party in power, but nonetheless discouraging. What followed was an inevitable round of recriminations that came from all directions but was aimed principally at the president and his cabinet. By December, Lincoln had faced open revolt from among Republican leaders on Capitol Hill. Under intense pressure, leading cabinet officers Seward and Chase both subsequently offered their resignations. In the midst of this crisis, Lincoln growled ominously to his friend Orville Browning that the administration was on "the brink of destruction."[12] The president managed to hold his cabinet together for the time being, but it was a tense period.

During the crisis, Browning had only been partly sympathetic. Though he had grown closer to the president in the aftermath of Willie Lincoln's death, the outgoing Illinois senator was convinced that emancipation was a dangerous mistake and repeatedly urged his old friend to reverse course. As late as New Year's Eve, the day before the issuance of the final proclamation, he was feverishly consulting with allies whom he believed might convince the president to change his mind. "There is no hope," Browning finally confessed that night in his diary, recognizing glumly that Lincoln "was fatally bent upon his course."[13] A few weeks later, Supreme Court justice David Davis, another old Illinois friend with conservative tendencies, relayed to Browning his conversation at the White House in mid-January when President Lincoln had announced to him in no uncertain terms that emancipation was now "a fixed thing." Browning reported that he was not alone in his frustration. "The Judge thinks our cause is hopeless," he wrote in his diary.[14]

The result of these political differences among old friends was a rising sense of personal tension and distance. The newly elected and now Democratic-controlled Illinois legislature did not choose Browning, a Republican, to continue as the state's junior senator. He remained in Washington as a lobbyist but never again enjoyed the regular social intercourse with the president that he had during the previous year. Lincoln avoided him on January 1, the day of the proclamation's signing, for example, when Browning showed up at the White House to share an afternoon carriage ride out to the Soldiers' Home. Instead, the senator rode with Mary Lincoln, who regaled him with stories of her latest spiritualist, a woman named Margaret Laurie from Georgetown, who had assured her quite confidently that the cabinet officers "were all enemies of the president" and needed to be dismissed.[15]

Not everyone in Washington was so heavily invested in politics. The soldiers of Company K, who had been guarding the president and his family at the Soldiers' Home and at the White House, seemed largely indifferent at the outset of 1863 to the bitter debate over the war's new direction. Though nominally part of the Army of the Potomac, they identified themselves more directly as the "President's Guard" and gave their loyalty almost entirely to Lincoln. Unlike Senator Browning, Private Andrew B. Hart made it a point to see the president on New Year's Day, using the traditional public reception at the White House as an opportunity to shake hands with the "chief Magistrate of the United States of America." Hart reported proudly in a letter home that the president was "just as friendly a man as you can find." Still, the soldier was not blind to practical issues and urged his widowed mother to see about collecting the local bounty that had been promised but not paid at the time of his enlistment.[16]

Willard Cutter also seemed to have developed a seasoned outlook after little more than four months of military service. The private coolly decided against attending the New Year's Day reception as Hart and others in the company had done, teasing his mother that he did not go "for fear I would jerk old Abe off his legs" in the receiving line. Writing separately to his grandmother, Cutter described his feelings on being enlisted in sober, measured terms. "I am not home sick yet," he wrote, claiming that "as long as the war lasts I am in so let this wide world go as it will."[17]

This emerging dichotomy—the skittishness of Lincoln's political friends versus the fundamental steadfastness of most Union troops—was becoming a perceptible fact of northern life. From 1863 forward, the president continued to endure criticism in the press and public dialogue, but there was a growing sense that he had established himself as a popular favorite among the fighting men and their families. In his study of soldiers' letters, historian James McPherson notes that after an initial period of plunging morale, Federal troops seemed to accept the reality of emancipation, or vow, like Private Cutter, to "let this wide world go as it will" while they completed their duty.[18]

Others in the North, less invested in the outcome of the war, simply wanted the conflict to go away. War weariness on the homefront had become an increasingly serious problem for the Lincoln administration as the year progressed. The main issue, as always, came down to enlistments. The army needed more men. The Militia Act of the previous year had produced only a quarter of its anticipated quotas. In March 1863, the Congress responded to the failures of the state-dominated recruiting system by adopting the Enrollment Act of 1863. This legislation finally consolidated the mobilization effort, creating a new federal authority for conscripting men in the event of state or local failure to meet predetermined enlistment quotas. The action established the nation's first comprehensive wartime draft.

The new federal authority responsible for registering eligible northern men and for organizing the draft was the provost marshal's office. Based out of Washington, the provost marshal established agents across the congressional districts of the North. These marshals had a difficult and politically sensitive mission, especially in communities with significant populations of Democrats or anti-war activists. Recognizing the challenges of imposing conscription on a war-weary public, Congress had simultaneously passed a Habeas Corpus Act, which authorized the president and his agents to place draft resisters and those who encouraged them under military arrest. In many ways, these measures only codified a reality that had existed since the War Department had begun aggressive enforcement of the Militia Act back in August of 1862. Nonetheless, the publicity surrounding the 1863 draft and the open congressional endorsement for the suspension of civil liberties galvanized many northern Democrats who loudly accused the Republicans and the president of embracing tyranny.

David Derickson of Company K had been one of the first provost marshals to take his post during the spring of that year. Although he had quickly become a favorite companion of President Lincoln during the previous autumn, Derickson had since grown disenchanted with his position. He complained afterward that his duties as head of the presidential guard were "very light," but it appears that he was mostly worn down by the jealousy his position had engendered. Other units wanted the honor of guarding the president. Fellow officers gossiped about his relationship with Lincoln. And Henry Huidekoper, his immediate superior and the officer in charge of Derickson's regiment, wanted to remove the Company K from its new post near the White House.[19]

In February, when the rest of the 150th Pennsylvania was finally assigned to join the Army of the Potomac in the field, Colonel Huidekoper seemed determined to bring Derickson's unit along. The soldiers received an order to prepare to leave the White House. According to Willard Cutter, the president saw what was happening from his office window and sent word that he wanted these Bucktail men "to be his guard or else he would have no guard." Naturally, Cutter reported, "we could not leave old Abe when he wanted us so bad." The private also noted that "Mrs. Lincoln said we should not go," and "Tad Lincoln says he is Major of this Com. and he was not a going to let us go."[20] Huidekoper apparently went to the White House himself before he found out that the president had overruled his directives.

When Captain Derickson departed at the end of April, he had boasted to the men that they were considered "the best Com[pany] in service," according to Cutter's weekly letter home, "and was spoke well of by every one but some of the mean class."[21] The question of how effective Company K was in their role as presidential guard is a difficult one to resolve. The soldiers were not bodyguards. Their presence was designed more for intimidation and for possible protection in the event of an organized cavalry raid than for security against assassination or kidnapping. Still, the men seemed to take their jobs seriously, and they occasionally performed an important police function. For instance, about ten days before the 1863 departure for the Soldiers' Home, Cutter claimed that guards from the company had to rush inside the White House to detain a visitor who had become too "unruly."

There were occasional lapses in the unit's vigilance. In June 1863, Sergeant Benjamin F. Ellis discovered Private Augustus Halfast "in a sitting posture, apparently asleep" while on guard duty outside of the White House. This particular case, however, did not seem representative of the company. The soldier later explained in his court-martial that he had been "subject to a species of derangement" which had affected him since childhood with "dizziness" and "partial blindness." "I was under the influence of one of those spells," he asserted under oath. Although the court found him guilty, the ruling recommended commutation for time served and Halfast was returned to the unit.[22]

Halfast's arrest might have been designed to send a message. The strategic situation looked disappointing by June 1863, and the level of tension around Washington was especially high. In the western theater of the war, Ulysses Grant and other Union generals such as William S. Rosecrans were conducting a series of separate campaigns across the trans-Mississippi Valley that finally appeared to have stalled after months of steady, if sometimes bloody, progress. Meanwhile, Lee's second invasion of the North had once again created a degree of panic. Since George McClellan's firing in November 1862, two different commanders had been installed at the head of the Army of the Potomac, and each had been associated with disastrous failure. The Young Napoleon's first successor, General Ambrose E. Burnside, had lasted only about three months before being replaced by one of his loudest critics, General Joseph Hooker. At first, Hooker won praise from the troops and the press for instilling a new fighting spirit in what he boasted was the "finest army on the planet."[23] But Hooker soon met his match in Robert E. Lee, whose forces had dealt the Union army yet another major defeat at the Battle of Chancellorsville (May 2–6, 1863) in northern Virginia. Appearing almost invincible, Lee convinced the Confederate high command to back him in risking their western positions by undertaking a dramatic assault on the North.

A former Union army colonel who had graduated from West Point and fought in the Mexican War, Lee had begun the conflict behind a desk in Richmond. He had taken over for a wounded Confederate field commander during

McClellan's Peninsula campaign and soon demonstrated an uncanny knack for strategic audacity and inspired leadership. He also had the highest casualty rates of any general in either army.[24] On June 16, 1863, about a week before the president arrived at the Soldiers' Home, Lee's Army of Northern Virginia began crossing the Potomac heading for Pennsylvania.

The movement of approximately 75,000 Rebel troops, shadowed by an even larger Federal force, developed quite slowly. More than two weeks would pass before the confrontation between the two armies finally occurred at Gettysburg in the beginning of July. During that tense interval, skirmishes connected to the campaign broke out across hundreds of miles in Maryland, Pennsylvania, and Virginia. Some of those contests could be heard from the Soldiers' Home. "Down the Potomac last Sunday there was a big cavalry fight with some artillery which was heard in the city," Willard Cutter reported to his family once the Bucktail soldiers had established their post near the presidential retreat.[25]

Listening to the sounds of the distant battle and poring over dispatches from General Hooker at the War Department's telegraph office, President Lincoln was becoming increasingly agitated. Hooker sounded uncertain and unwilling to force a confrontation with his formidable Confederate counterpart. No longer bound by the same political considerations that had restricted him in 1862, Lincoln now acted decisively. For the third time in less than a year, he removed the commander of the Army of the Potomac, but in this case only days before a major engagement. It was a switch that stunned military experts, but the president was insistent, naming General George G. Meade, a native Pennsylvanian, to head the army as it moved into southern Pennsylvania. Silas W. Burt, an army officer from New York who was in Washington on a mission from his state's governor, recalled that there was widespread anxiety in the capital during this period. He noted that a bartender at Willard's was offering to bet his customers that "General Lee would eat his Fourth of July dinner" at the hotel.[26]

Burt and another officer named John D. Van Buren, who had been a New York state legislator before the war, had come to Washington on behalf of their governor Horatio Seymour, in part to reassure Lincoln about his underlying loyalty to the Union. A popular Democrat who had been holding office since January, Seymour represented an especially thorny problem for the administration after making a public break with the president in May over the question of civil liberties. In a fiery speech, the governor had denounced the arrest of Ohio Democratic gubernatorial candidate Clement L. Vallandigham, who had been accused of inciting resistance to the impending draft. According to Burt, his mission was to make "a formal representation" to Lincoln that despite this public criticism, Seymour still backed "a more vigorous prosecution of the war."

Not surprisingly, the political emissaries found that they could not gain access to a skeptical White House. After repeatedly failing to see the president, Burt and Colonel Van Buren and the latter's son happened to run into Seymour's cousin, a major in the army, who insisted that he would resolve the impasse by taking all of them to the Soldiers' Home on Friday evening, June 26, 1863.

Burt soon realized that Seymour's relative had been drinking but followed him anyway. "It was a bright night and about nine o'clock when we turned from the highway into the winding roads of the Soldiers' Home," he wrote. "We saw gleaming amid the shrubbery in all directions the bayonets of the soldiers who guarded the President's residence." Although this memorable image sounds as if it had been enhanced for effect, the entry in Benjamin French's diary describing the "general excitement" and Willard Cutter's revealing letters both confirm a level of heightened tension following Lee's crossing of the Potomac.

"We drew up in front of a cottage before which a sentry was walking to and fro," Burt recalled. He claims that the major gave the guard a password and a "man-servant" reluctantly ushered them inside, through a "dimly lighted hall" into an equally "dark parlor," before lighting a chandelier and departing with their calling cards.

> At length we heard slow, shuffling steps come down the uncarpeted stairs, and the President entered the room as we respectfully rose from our seats. That pathetic figure has ever remained indelible in my memory. His tall form was bowed, his hair disheveled; he wore no necktie or collar, and his large feet were partly incased in very loose, heelless slippers.

After brief introductions, Lincoln sat down with them on the "hair-cloth-covered sofa" in the parlor and discussed the rumors about Governor Seymour, all of which he claimed that he had been ignoring religiously. This was important information because Lincoln had only recently hardened his position on the subject of disloyalty, authorizing the banishment of Vallandigham and spelling out an expansive doctrine on the topic of civil liberties in a public letter to a group of Albany Democrats. "Must I shoot a simple-minded soldier boy who deserts," he had asked pointedly on June 12, "while I must not touch a hair of a wiley agitator who induces him to desert?"[27] By dismissing the rumors about Seymour, Lincoln was, for the time being, consciously placing him in a different category from the notorious Copperhead leader Vallandigham.

The visitors that evening generally found Lincoln unperturbed by recent events, although obviously exhausted. According to Burt, the president claimed "he had no fears about the safety of Washington, and was certain that the attempted invasion of the Northern States would be arrested." But his deep fatigue was painfully evident. The New Yorker reported noticing that as the conversation continued, the "gaunt figure of the President had gradually slid lower on the slippery sofa." The officer observed that during a pause in the talk, Lincoln's "long legs were stretch out in front, the loose slippers half-fallen from his feet, while the drowsy eyelids had almost closed over his eyes, and his jaded features had taken on the suggestion of relaxation in sleep."

Just before Lincoln actually drifted off, however, the inebriated army major—according to Burt's recollection—slapped his knee and said "Mr. President, tell us one of your good stories." The others were stunned and Lincoln seemed appropriately insulted. Rising and turning his back on the drunk officer, the president told his other guests that he only told stories to illustrate points or to avoid tedious discussions and never for sheer amusement. The chastened men soon left the cottage and returned to the city.[28]

The Battle of Gettysburg (July 1–3, 1863) lasted for three days and was the bloodiest, most important engagement of the war. Lee lost nearly third of his army and was forced to retreat from Pennsylvania without securing the victory that he had hoped would devastate northern morale and finally convince the European powers to intervene. Further, the gamble eastward had left embattled Rebel troops in the western theater to their own devices and on July 4, 1863, Vicksburg finally surrendered. With the exception of Port Hudson, Louisiana (which fell on July 8), the town of Vicksburg was the last remaining Confederate stronghold on the Mississippi River. According to David H. Bates, a cipher operator at the War Department, the president literally stayed in the telegraph office "hour after hour" awaiting news from Pennsylvania and Mississippi during those critical first few days of July.[29]

Lincoln's anxiety for news was certainly understandable, but his focus on the nation's business came at great personal cost. On Thursday morning, July 2, 1863, Mary Lincoln suffered a frightening spill from her carriage while riding on Rock Creek Road near Mount Pleasant Hospital, not far from the Soldiers' Home estate. According to the news reports, her coachman's seat had somehow become detached and he had fallen to the ground, leaving the first lady alone in the carriage with nervous horses "who dashed along with fearful velocity." Terrified, Mary Lincoln apparently jumped out of the runaway vehicle, landing awkwardly on the road. The local press reported that her many bumps and bruises were not serious, although correspondents did note that she had developed a bleeding wound on the back of her head, which doctors at the hospital had quickly stitched together. The president wired his son on the final day of the Gettysburg battle reporting that his mother seemed fine. "Don't be uneasy," Lincoln stated, "Your mother very slightly hurt by her fall."[30]

Mary Lincoln suffered a carriage accident on the road between the Soldiers' Home and nearby Mount Pleasant hospital, pictured above. LIBRARY OF CONGRESS.

There were two problems with the president's outwardly calm reaction to his wife's injury. First, the positive reports on her condition turned out to be premature. Mary Lincoln's wounds soon became infected, a complication not unexpected during an era before advances in antibiotics or an understanding of the germ theory of disease. Second, the carriage accident appeared suspicious and merited investigation. Yet the president seemed determined to blame the incident on the poor condition of local roads. Shortly afterward, he fired off a terse memo to an unnamed subordinate that read, "The place on the road near Mt. Pleasant Hospital ought to be repaired."[31]

The truth is that even if the coachman's seat had simply bounced off the carriage, and even if Mary Lincoln did seem perfectly fine on July 3, President Lincoln did not appear focused on his wife's problems. He was obsessed with getting General Meade to pursue Lee. As usual, the president considered the recent battle an opportunity to destroy armies—not win possession of ground. Meade, like too many Union generals before him, did not appear to share this viewpoint. On the Fourth of July, the same day that Vicksburg fell, the general issued an order to his officers that compared the Rebels to foreigners but offered no plans for pursuit beyond the Potomac. "Our task is not yet accomplished, " he wrote, "and the commanding general looks to the army for greater efforts to drive from our soil every vestige of the presence of the invader." To the president's ears, this comparison sounded defeatist. "Will our Generals never get that idea out of their heads?" he complained to John Hay. "The whole country is *our* soil."[32]

Two days after Meade's directive, Lincoln's frustration boiled over. On Monday evening, July 6, he left the War Department and headed out to the Soldiers' Home for the evening. He had just received word that Lee's army was beginning to cross the Potomac River. This time, however, he could not restrain himself and at 7 P.M. he sent a biting message back to Chief of Staff Halleck at headquarters. "I left the telegraph office a good deal dissatisfied," he began sharply. "You know I did not like the phrase . . . 'Drive the invaders from our soil.' Since that, I see a dispatch from General [Daniel] French, saying the enemy is crossing his wounded over the river in flats, without saying why he does not stop it, or even intimating a thought that it ought to be stopped."[33] The president, who was not a military man, could not understand the absence of a killer instinct in his generals. From his perspective, they seemed to be hampered by inhibitions not suited for the dire challenge at hand. He drafted a memo for Halleck to share with Meade that attempted to spur his new commander to action by underscoring the opportunity created in the twin successes at Gettysburg and Vicksburg. "Now, if General Meade can complete his work, so gloriously prosecuted thus far," Lincoln wrote carefully, "by the literal or substantial destruction of Lee's army, the rebellion will be over."[34]

The next night the president was again inside the War Department monitoring the situation along the upper Potomac when at about 8 o'clock a large group of citizens marched over to the White House for a spontaneous celebration of the recent victories. Lincoln hurried over to the main portico and briefly addressed the crowd, summoning up as much enthusiasm as he could for the unexpected encounter. He earnestly thanked "Almighty God" for the "occasion" that produced their serenade, and then commented, somewhat incoherently, on the symbolism of Independence Day in American history. "How long ago is it?—eighty odd years," he asked about the nation's founding, before detailing other significant events that had occurred on that critical day. He called the story "a glorious theme and the occasion for a speech" but denied that he was prepared to make such an address at that moment.[35]

For the rest of the week, the Union high command watched and waited. They received reports that the river was swollen and that the bulk of the Confederate force had been unable to cross. This was positive news. "The President seemed in especially good humor today," John Hay noted in his diary on Saturday, July 11, "as he had pretty good evidence that the enemy were still on the North side of the Potomac and Meade had announced his intention of attacking them in the morning."

On the personal front, however, the news was not good at all. Mary Lincoln's infection had spread. By July 11, the severity of her situation was too obvious to ignore. "Come to Washington," President Lincoln now urged his son Robert, no longer trying to diminish the extent of her wounds.[36] Rebecca Pomroy, the family nurse, recalled that during this period she kept a "night and day" vigil over the first lady at the Soldiers' Home. The nurse was convinced that the accident had been the by-product of a failed assassination attempt on the president's life. She claimed that she asked Lincoln what additional precautions he was taking for his own safety. "I can do nothing different from what I am doing," she remembered him saying.[37]

By Monday, the absence of news from General Meade disturbed the president, who was growing "anxious and impatient" in Hay's opinion. The report that Lee's army had escaped finally reached Washington on Tuesday afternoon, leaving Lincoln "deeply grieved." "We had them within our grasp," he complained bitterly. "We had only to stretch forth our hands & they were ours. And nothing I could say or do could make the Army move." Meanwhile, Robert Lincoln had yet to respond to his father's request to return to the Soldiers' Home. The sense of powerless made the president's tone sound sharp. "Why do I hear no more of you?" he demanded in a telegram sent that afternoon to the hotel in New York where he supposed Robert was staying.[38] Adding to Lincoln's sense of paternal unease was his knowledge that riots against the impending draft had broken out in sections of Manhattan, leading to hundreds of dead and some of the worst urban violence in American history.

The next day, however, the president's eldest, somewhat prodigal, son finally appeared. He made it to his father's office in time for the afternoon departure to the Soldiers' Home but found his father in "distress," with his head on the writing desk and "evidences of tears upon his face."[39] Out of frustration, Lincoln then unburdened himself in defiant terms. "If I had gone up there," he told Robert, "I could have whipped them myself."[40] According to Robert Lincoln's recollection, his father also informed him that he had sent a secret message up to General Meade, ordering him to attack after Gettysburg and instructing him to destroy the order if he was successful or preserve it for his own "vindication" if the assault failed. This order, if it existed, has never been found, but historian Gabor Boritt notes that Vice President Hannibal Hamlin visited Meade's camp on July 11 and might have carried the secret message.[41]

When father and son returned to the Soldiers' Home that evening, they found a wife and mother who was still struggling to recover her health. The doctors and nurses who treated Mary Lincoln knew practically nothing about infections. They could do nothing but treat her symptoms and hope for the best. Infection was actually the great killer of the war; for every soldier who died on the battlefield, two more succumbed to disease. Moreover, for a woman who had always suffered from migraines, this type of head injury and subsequent infection was especially difficult. Robert Lincoln later confided to one of his aunts that after this episode his mother's headaches came more frequently and, in his opinion, she never entirely recovered from the trauma.[42]

In physical terms though, Mary Lincoln recovered well enough by the end of the next week to endure the discomfort of travel. She was determined to leave Washington and head for New York and Vermont, as she had done at the end of the previous summer. Rebecca Pomroy claimed that the first lady begged her to join the trip, but the nurse insisted on returning to her work at the soldiers' hospital. Robert Lincoln also declined to leave Washington again so soon. But Mary Lincoln was undaunted and she left the Soldiers' Home, with Tad and perhaps also Mary Ann Cuthbert, on July 20. They would not return to the cottage until September 28. One cannot help but speculate that she would have remained at the Soldiers' Home longer if her husband had been more attentive.

Were the Lincolns unhappy with each other? Like any couple, they exhibited traces of almost every emotion, and finding a pattern is difficult given the absence of reliable evidence. Nevertheless, one of the best and most frequently overlooked sources of testimony on the state of their marriage comes from the troops who guarded them at the Soldiers' Home. Charles Derickson, who remained with Company K even after his father had returned to Meadville, reported that one night in the middle of the war he had to enter the cottage and wake the president in order to deliver an important message. He confessed to biographer Ida Tarbell, a fellow Meadville native, that he subsequently discovered Lincoln in bed with the first lady. Jean Baker, among other biographers, has reported on hints of physical intimacy between the aging couple—including rumors that the forty-four-year-old first lady had become pregnant—but this testimony from Derickson appears to be the only eyewitness account from the presidential period placing husband and wife in bed together.[43] On the other hand, Derickson also observed some marital tension. Once, when the president visited the nearby camp and shared coffee and beans with the soldiers, the sergeant saw the beginnings of a small argument. "I remember one evening when his wife was with him," the sergeant recalled, "he turned to her and said, 'Mother, this [is] better coffee than we get at home,' for which remark she did not seem well pleased."[44]

July 1863 marked a turning point in Lincoln's life at two different levels. Union successes at Gettysburg and Vicksburg signaled a new phase of the war. The rebellion was not finally or even substantially over as Lincoln had been predicting now for months, but the momentum had shifted. More important, these victories brought immediate practical benefits. The prospect of major Confederate offensives into Maryland or Pennsylvania was essentially gone. By controlling the Mississippi River, Union forces could choke off an economic lifeline for the Confederacy, divide southern territory, and position themselves for their own major invasion into the Rebel heartland. On a personal level, Lincoln also experienced a new phase in his marriage. His wife's carriage accident eventually threatened her life and damaged her already fragile health even further. Yet the distracted president could not devote himself to his wife's recovery and earnestly sought surrogates—Nurse Pomroy, his son Robert—to represent him. By the end of the month, she decided that her recuperation would proceed more rapidly outside of Washington and away from her husband. Her decision essentially left the president alone at the Soldiers' Home for the next ten weeks, and in the position to focus exclusively on his all-consuming work.

6

"In fine whack"

NOAH BROOKS, A WASHINGTON CORRESPONDENT FOR THE *SACRAMENTO DAILY UNION*, decided in July 1863 that it was time to provide his readers with a glimpse of President Lincoln's daily life at the Soldiers' Home. "The grounds are extensive and beautiful," he reported, "and belong to the Government, which erected the large central building for disabled, homeless soldiers of the regular service." He noted that the president and his family lived in one of "several two-story cottages" built "in the Gothic style" and located near the main hall. "Mr. Lincoln comes in early in the morning and returns about sunset," he informed his readers, "unless he has a press of business—which is often—when he sleeps at the White House and has 'prog' sent up from Willard's." Brooks observed that a cavalry escort and an infantry company protected Lincoln, but he was concerned by the apparent gaps in the security around the president. "[T]o my unsophisticated judgment," he wrote nervously, "nothing seems easier than a sudden cavalry raid from the Maryland side of the fortifications, past the few small forts, to seize the President of the United States."[1]

Others noticed a different type of danger around the country retreat. Shortly after the first lady's departure for Vermont, John Hay observed that the crowds on the nearby roads were not always respectable. "I rode out to Soldiers Home with the Tycoon tonight," John Hay wrote on July 25, 1863. "Had a talk on philology for which the T has a little indulged inclination." After the casual discussion of linguistics with the imperial "Tycoon," the loyal assistant departed and rode back in the dark "amid a party of drunken gamblers & harlots." This reference to the seediness of late-night Washington life was delicately omitted from the first published versions of Hay's diary.[2]

In fact, there was nothing delicate about wartime Washington. The city endured 24,000 arrests in 1863, which was more than three times the total in Brooklyn, with an urban population twice its size.[3] The local newspapers had reported seven murders a week in July, including one member of the 11th New York regiment that provided the president's cavalry escort.[4] William Doster, the District's provost marshal, claimed there were at least 450 whorehouses operating in the city and the *Washington Star* estimated that the total number of working prostitutes in the capital exceeded five thousand.[5] Even more than a cavalry raid, the president and his visitors had reason to fear criminal activity along the roads surrounding the cottage.

It is possible that Mary Lincoln had been unsettled by her suspicious carriage accident and by the reports of rising crime in Washington. Consciously or not, she may have left the city at least partly out of fear, for herself and her youngest son. If so, however, her most likely source of anxiety was disease, not crime. The Washington heat was a breeding ground for mosquito-borne illness. Later in the summer, when President Lincoln tried to entice his wife to return, he emphasized the "clear and cool, and apparantly [*sic*] healthy" air.[6] The extent of Mary Lincoln's troubles after her wounds became infected has not been well documented. Willard Cutter noted in his letters home that the first lady and Tad Lincoln had left the Soldiers' Home on July 20, 1863. But the New York newspapers did not begin reporting on her presence in the city until mid-August.[7] The interval suggests that she was still recuperating and keeping a low profile for weeks after her departure from Washington.

Meanwhile, Robert Lincoln and his father were supposed to be spending some time together at the Soldiers' Home. That did not really happen. What was most revealing about John Hay's visit to the cottage on July 25 was that Robert Lincoln was not present. Hay, who was also on friendly terms with the president's son and shared his bed at the White House when the latter visited from Harvard, noted pointedly in his diary that Robert spent that evening at Secretary of State William Seward's residence. According to Hay, the young Lincoln was more interested in a certain unnamed woman than playing the dutiful son. He suggested playfully in a letter to fellow aide John Nicolay that Robert was "so shattered" by the wedding of this unidentified lady that he soon "rushed madly off" to join his mother and younger brother in Vermont.[8] Regardless of the reasons, Robert spent only a few weeks in Washington that summer and used part of his time to take an excursion to Fort Monroe in Virginia—with the Seward family but not with his father.[9]

Once Robert Lincoln departed on July 29, the president was officially alone at the cottage. His wife and sons were gone. Aunt Mary, the cook, and Captain Derickson were also gone. The other military guards remained to help keep

Lincoln occupied, as well as the acting governor of the Soldiers' Home, Colonel Thomas L. Alexander, who was becoming a friend; but otherwise Lincoln's circle was closing. During the first few days of August, there was also a strange stillness in Washington. Congress was out of session. Cabinet officers were preoccupied with work or absent on their own vacations. John Nicolay, the senior White House aide, was in the West, on a trip to the Rocky Mountains. There was little news to discuss. The Army of the Potomac had finally crossed the Potomac, but Lee's forces had simply withdrawn deeper into Virginia. A stalemate had developed temporarily in Tennessee. Union naval forces were preparing to assault Charleston harbor, but otherwise after a few turbulent months, the whirlwind of tragedies and triumphs had slowed to a more manageable pace. "This town is as dismal now as a defaced tombstone," John Hay complained.[10]

On Friday, August 7, Hay sent an update to John Nicolay—"Nico"—his friend and nominal supervisor at the White House. Hay observed that the president was thriving without the usual distractions of family and favor-seekers. "The Tycoon is in fine whack," he wrote, "I have rarely seen him more serene & busy."

> He is managing this war, the draft, foreign relations, and planning a reconstruction of the Union, all at once. I never knew with what tyrannous authority he rules the Cabinet, till now. The most important things he decides & there is no cavil. I am growing more and more firmly convinced that the good of the country absolutely demands that he should be kept where he is till this thing is over. There is no man in the country, so wise, so gentle and so firm. I believe the hand of God placed him where he is.[11]

Hay's evolution as an admirer of Lincoln was easy to understand. Considering that he was only in his mid-twenties at the time, just a few short years removed from his college days at Brown and still not above noting female conquests in his diary or letters, it was remarkable that he had gained such unparalleled access to the wartime commander in chief. The two men clearly had more than just a typical office relationship. Hay had become almost like a surrogate son to the president.

Originally from Indiana, the young White House aide grew up in Illinois and lived with his uncle, a prominent Springfield lawyer, before the war. He had known John Nicolay for years, and together the two made a tight-knit team as the president's chief private secretaries.[12] As young, smart outsiders, the two assistants also invariably attracted the jealous attention of Washington insiders. "The President is affable and kind," reported Noah Brooks in 1863, "but his immediate subordinates are snobby and unpopular," adding disdainfully, "the least said of them the better."[13] Nicolay, who was older and sterner in

Lincoln with his senior White House aides, John G. Nicolay (seated, left) and John Hay (standing, right), in 1863. ILLINOIS STATE HISTORICAL SOCIETY, SPRINGFIELD, ILL.

appearance, generally managed the office, guarding the door to the president's chamber, and delivering messages to Congress. Hay's principal job was to read and respond to the president's political mail. He later claimed that Lincoln did not read "one in fifty" letters that he received during the war and that "he gave the whole thing over to me," signing the responses Hay drafted usually without even reading them.[14] Over the course of the first term, there were other secretaries occasionally assigned to the office, young men such as Charles H. Philbrick and William O. Stoddard. Invariably, some interoffice sniping developed— Hay once called Stoddard "asinine" and Philbrick complained in letters home that Hay only did "ornamental" work—but for the most part, the group functioned well and appeared to enjoy the president's trust.[15]

The same day that Hay wrote Nicolay, the president answered very different requests from two northern governors. Joseph Gilmore, the governor of New Hampshire, had read in the newspapers that the entire presidential family was coming to the White Mountains of his state. He asked Lincoln for an opportunity to welcome him at Concord. Without specifying that his wife actually planned to stay at the Equinox Hotel in Manchester, Vermont (and not Manchester, New

Hampshire), Lincoln gracefully declined the offer. "I am by no means certain that I can leave Washington at all this summer," he wrote, "*The exacting nature of my official duties renders it exceedingly improbable* [emphasis in original]."[16] More important, the president also responded to a request from New York governor Horatio Seymour on the question of suspending the draft in sections of his state. The violent July riots had shaken the governor's confidence. He was convinced that the quotas were "glaringly unjust" and that the law itself would soon be ruled unconstitutional. Lincoln icily dismissed this plea. "[T]ime is too important," he wrote, pushing aside all arguments for delays or adjustments.[17]

Clearing his desk of this official correspondence allowed the president an opportunity during the next afternoon to send a warm and chatty note to his absent wife. "All as well as usual," he began, "and no particular trouble any way." He updated her on the weather, their finances and some political news from their native state of Kentucky. But the bulk of the letter concerned a goat that Tad Lincoln had kept at the Soldiers' Home. "Tell dear Tad, poor 'Nanny Goat,' is lost," he wrote, "and Mrs. Cuthbert & I are in distress about it."

> The day you left Nanny was found resting herself, and chewing her little cud, on the middle of Tad's bed. But now she's gone! The gardener kept complaining that she destroyed the flowers, till it was concluded to bring her down to the White House. This was done, and the second day she had disappeared, and has not been heard of since. This is the last we know of poor 'Nanny.'[18]

Over the next several days, Lincoln continued to go about his work even as the summer heat became almost unbearable. In his letter to Mary Lincoln the president had described the weather as "excessively warm," but others in Washington were less restrained. On Monday, August 10, General Samuel P. Heintzelman, who commanded the defenses of Washington, noted in his diary that it was "Warm! Warm!" He reported that he rode out to the Soldiers' Home in the afternoon but found it "too dusty to be pleasant." In his weekly letter home, written on Wednesday, Willard Cutter complained to his brother that it was "hot enough to roast eggs."[19]

In the same letter to his brother, Private Cutter expressed concern over Captain Derickson, who had apparently been involved in some sort of incident connected with enforcing the draft in Crawford County, Pennsylvania, where he now served as provost marshall. "I feel sorry for old Capt. Derrickson [*sic*]," wrote Cutter, "but he must look out next time and have his pistols along and ready." Interestingly, the soldier noted that Derickson's replacement, Thomas Getchell, would have handled the situation differently because he was more of "a fighter man." "[I]f it had been Captain Getchell," he speculated, "there would have been some dead Dutchman to show there had been a riot."[20]

The draft and the question of raising more men for the war effort had become the president's overriding concern by the summer of 1863. Concerned about resistance to enrollment in the North and impressed by reports about the fortitude of the new black soldiers, Lincoln began to see the makings of a politically powerful solution. He would alleviate the pressure for more white soldiers by increasing the recruitment of blacks. Meanwhile, a by-product of this action would be a demonstration to the remaining northern skeptics that emancipation had been a wise military decision. On August 9, he wrote General Grant a rare letter proffering advice. He gently urged the commander to increase his efforts to use "colored troops," calling them "a resource which, if vigorously applied now, will soon close the contest."[21] This was a major leap forward for President Lincoln, who had predicted less than a year earlier that African Americans would never fight, stating bluntly, "I am not so sure we could do much with the blacks."[22]

To put into action his plan for increasing black mobilization, Lincoln turned to the famous abolitionist orator and newspaper editor Frederick Douglass. For the former slave, who had mixed feelings about some of the president's policies, it was a revealing encounter. Lincoln treated him like a man. "I felt big there," he boasted afterward to antislavery audiences.[23] They discussed sending Douglass to the Union-occupied sections of the South where he could help in the recruiting effort. After leaving the White House, the editor then eagerly announced the suspension of his newspaper, but when an expected military commission never arrived, he canceled his plans. The two men would meet a few more times, not becoming friends but certainly establishing a respectful political relationship. Sometime that summer or the next, Douglass recalled in his memoir that he was even invited for tea at the Soldiers' Home.[24]

The meeting with Douglass on August 11 might not have produced all the results hoped for by each participant, but the encounter nonetheless yielded important consequences. Lincoln's sensitivity to African Americans was growing. A year earlier in a discussion with free black leaders on the need for colonization, he had coldly informed them that inequality was a fact "with which we have to deal." Now he was asking the nation's most prominent black figure to help him create an army of African Americans. On the same day that he met with Douglass, the president also wrote out a check for five dollars made payable to "A Colored Man with one Leg." It was a small gesture of empathy, but increasingly during the war, the president's ideas and policies on race evolved with such minor steps.[25] He was encountering African Americans more frequently and learning to judge them as people and not abstractions. "In all my interviews with Mr. Lincoln," Douglass later recalled, "I was impressed with his entire freedom from popular prejudice against the colored race."

He was the first great man that I talked with in the United States freely, who in no single instance reminded me of the difference between himself and myself, of the difference in color, and I thought that all the more remarkable because he came from a State where there were black laws. I account partially for his kindness to me because of the similarity with which I had fought my way up, we both starting at the lowest round of the ladder.[26]

What attracted Douglass to the president was the same appealing combination of honesty, humility, and steely determination that had impressed the soldiers and loyal aides around him. Lincoln conveyed respect without appearing phony or awkward.

The next day Walt Whitman recorded his memorable description of President Lincoln, "rusty and dusty," commuting into work with his "unornamental *cortège*." The poet, who had been living in Washington for several months visiting the wounded and working part-time in the Army paymaster's office, occasionally submitted his vivid journal entries to New York newspapers, such as the *Times* or the *Brooklyn Union*. He planned to write a book, tentatively titled *Memorandum of a Year*, that would "have something to say of the great trunk America."[27] By this stage in his career, Whitman, who was in his forties, was already well known as a poet and as the author of *Leaves of Grass* (1854). He was an inveterate reviser whose journal entry on August 12 actually echoed a letter he had written to his mother in June depicting Lincoln riding out to the Soldiers' Home in evening. "He looks even more careworn than usual," Whitman wrote on June 30, "his face with deep cut lines, seams, and his *complexion gray* through very dark skin—a curious looking man, very sad."[28]

A Unionist who also had strong sympathies for southern soldiers, Whitman found Lincoln to be the most compelling figure of the war. He noted on August 12 that the president "looks about as ordinary in attire, &c., as the commonest man," and yet claimed that "one of the great portrait painters of two or three centuries ago is needed" to capture the "indirect expression" and "latent sadness" of his face.[29]

The poet, who was friendly with John Hay, found himself far less impressed by the president's cavalry escort. "The party makes no great show in uniform or horses," he observed. "A lieutenant, with yellow straps, rides at his left, and following behind, two by two, come the cavalry men, in their yellow-striped jackets," he noted. Whitman might have been confused about rank, seeing Captain James Mix, the head of Company A, at President Lincoln's side. Or he might have been correct and more prescient than he could have realized, observing Lieutenant George A. Bennett in the primary post. Bennett certainly aspired to replace Mix. Moreover, the lieutenant soon found an ally in Ohio governor David Tod, who came to the White House on August 13, lobbying the president for authorization to recruit a special cavalry unit from Ohio. The

Abraham Lincoln and Walt Whitman as they appeared in 1863.
LINCOLN: LIBRARY OF CONGRESS; WHITMAN: NATIONAL ARCHIVES.

governor wanted to replace the unimpressive-looking New Yorkers. The president eventually relented and in December 1863 the Union Light Guard from Ohio arrived in Washington to take over all presidential escort responsibilities. George Bennett was their first captain.[30]

The president often dispensed with his cavalry escort altogether during this period, especially in the evenings. On Saturday, August 22, for example, he went with Hay and a woman named Mrs. Long to the Naval Observatory at 23rd and E Streets, examining the moon and Arcturus, the fourth brightest star in the sky. John Mangan, one of the president's regular drivers, was recovering from an injury and his brother Laurence filled in for him that night. Mangan, an immigrant from Ireland, later recalled that the president asked for the carriage after supper, announcing that he "wanted to go out and look at the stars through that big, new telescope they had installed at the naval observatory." According to the coachman, he even took a peek through the telescope himself.[31] Afterward, Mangan drove the president and his assistant to the cottage. "I went with [Lincoln] to the Soldiers' Home," Hay reported, "& he read Shakespeare to me, the end of Henry VI and the beginning of Richard III till my heavy eye-lids caught his considerate notice & he sent me to bed." The next morning, Hay noted that they "ate an egg" and left for the White House "very early."[32]

On their return to the city, Lincoln went straight to the White House library to "write a letter to Conkling," according to Hay's diary. This was a reference to a shrewdly crafted public document sent to James C. Conkling, a friend of the president and a political ally in Springfield, Illinois. Lincoln had written other public letters earlier in the year to both political friends and rivals in key states like New York and Ohio. He addressed controversial topics, like the constitutionality of the draft, in a direct, engaging manner that worked well and earned him praise.

The Conkling letter was arguably the most important of these unusual political documents. In the text, the president addressed himself to critics of his war policy, particularly to those opposed to emancipation. "There are those who are dissatisfied with me," he admitted at the outset. He outlined several types of objections to the thrust of his war policy, but ultimately turned the focus to the all-consuming race question. "But, to be plain," he wrote, "you are dissatisfied with me about the negro." Continuing in the guise of speaking directly to his opponents, Lincoln wrote, "You say you will not fight to free negroes. Some of them seem willing to fight for you; but, no matter. Fight you, then, exclusively to save the Union."

Echoing words he had written a year earlier to Horace Greeley, Lincoln added, "I issued the proclamation on purpose to aid you in saving the Union." Then the president bravely attempted to convince his white audience to consider the issue from a black perspective. African Americans, "like other people," he argued, "act upon motives." He asked, "Why should they do any thing for us, if we will do nothing for them? If they stake their lives for us, they must be prompted by the strongest motive—even the promise of freedom." Then he concluded categorically that the "promise being made, must be kept." Lincoln ended the appeal with a brief summary of the war's progress. "The Father of Waters again goes unvexed to the sea," he reported eloquently on the state of the Mississippi Valley campaign. "Peace does not appear so distant as it did," he wrote, though still urging his audience to "not be over-sanguine." Striking the note of the times, he then closed by exhorting the pro-Union forces in the plainest possible terms to be "quite sober" and have faith in a "just God."[33] The letter was widely reprinted in northern newspapers.

As August drew to a close, the concerns that the president had expressed earlier to the governor of New Hampshire had been realized. He was stuck in Washington. There had been talk that he would visit his family in New England, or journey to Cape May, New Jersey, with friend Ward Hill Lamon, but leaving the capital proved impossible.[34] On August 25, Secretary of War Stanton replied to a letter from his wife Ellen, who had gone to a country cabin in

Bedford, Pennsylvania, and had asked if he and the president might not be able to join her in escaping at least temporarily. "Some thing always turns up to keep him or me in Washington," Stanton wrote by way of explanation. He refused to give up hope, however. "[Lincoln] is so eager for it," he informed his wife, "that I expect we will accomplish it before the season is over."[35]

Stanton was part of the reason that the president was "in fine whack" as autumn approached. Since assuming office in early 1862, the secretary had overhauled the corrupt War Department and turned the Union high command into a much more efficient body. As in the case after Gettysburg, Lincoln was still often frustrated by Union commanders who failed to wage war more aggressively in the field, but he was increasingly comfortable delegating authority to the hyper-competent Stanton. Their level of trust had grown out of both professional and personal respect. According to historians Harold Hyman and Benjamin Thomas, as the two men rode back and forth to their cottages at the Soldiers' Home during the final two years of the war, they developed a special relationship. They often "talked incessantly in low tones so that the drivers and the escorting cavalrymen would not hear," report Hyman and Thomas in their insightful biography of Stanton, "and jotted notes on scraps of paper from the time they left Pennsylvania Avenue" before "visibly relax[ing]as they approached their destination."[36]

At that time, there were only seven department heads: secretaries of state, treasury, war, navy, and interior, the postmaster general, and the attorney general, in addition to a cabinet-level rank for the vice president. None of the men who filled those positions at the beginning of the administration knew Lincoln well before he selected them. In addition, a few had entered office with far more extensive national reputations than the man they served. William Seward, the secretary of state, had been a front-runner for the 1860 Republican nomination and a titanic figure in antebellum political life. Seward was older and much smaller in size, but like Lincoln, a natural storyteller and a true politico. They became close during the war, although the secretary of state emerged as a target for more radical Republicans who suspected him, somewhat unfairly, of being opposed to emancipation. Seward conferred with Lincoln regularly and occasionally brought diplomats out to the Soldiers' Home for a social evening, but he never achieved the day-to-day intimacy with Lincoln that Stanton managed.

Along with Seward and Stanton, Secretary of Treasury Salmon P. Chase emerged as one of the cabinet's three most powerful figures. He was about the same age as Lincoln but had enjoyed a much more distinguished career prior to 1860, having been an accomplished lawyer and a former governor and U.S. senator from Ohio. More important to some contemporaries, Chase looked and acted like a chief executive, in stark contrast to the "Railsplitter" whom the people had actually elected. Much of the political drama inside the administration during Lincoln's first term came from the expectation that Chase would run against him for the Republican nomination in 1864. Although John Hay was convinced that Lincoln " should be kept where he is till this thing is over," not everyone else in the Republican party was so certain. By mid-1863, it was clear that Chase had been employing the patronage power within his department to build a personal political machine. Some presidential advisers urged Lincoln to punish this disloyalty but he insisted that there was little to fear from his cabinet subordinate, comparing the "presidential aspirations" of Chase to a fly at the neck of a horse, useful for keeping him "lively about his work."[37]

The rest of the cabinet played less central political roles but some of them were nevertheless important figures in Lincoln's social world. The president and his wife often entertained Secretary of Navy Gideon Welles and his wife Mary Ann. Nevertheless, journalist Noah Brooks, a favorite of the president, mocked "Father Welles," who had a flowing white beard and a reputation for being old-fashioned, as "slightly fossiliferous." Brooks was even more dismissive of the other secondary cabinet figures. Postmaster General Montgomery Blair, whose extended family also frequently interacted with the president, was, in the reporter's eyes, "awkward, shy, homely and repellent." Brooks described Lincoln's longest serving secretary of interior, John P. Usher, as "fair, fat, fifty and florid." Attorney General Edward Bates, who was in his seventies, appeared to the newspaper correspondent as simply a "nice old gentleman."[38] Vice President Hannibal Hamlin escaped Brooks's notable sarcasm but that was only because he was not perceived as a vital figure in the administration.

At the beginning of August, Hay had described Lincoln's authority over his cabinet as "tyrannous." The power that the president had wielded so firmly during the summer faced greater challenges as autumn approached. In September and October, while still residing at the Soldiers' Home, he faced a series of new headaches over the management of the war and the shifting politics of the Union coalition. Federal forces suffered some temporary reversals in their drive to push the Rebels out of Tennessee. Political tensions escalated as important election contests occurred in states like Ohio and Pennsylvania. The question of how to reincorporate Union-occupied southern territory was becoming complicated and provoked new divisions among conservatives and radicals. Added to the ongoing dissension over conscription and emancipation and the occasional frustrating news from the battlefields, these new problems filled Lincoln's political agenda with turmoil. In response, the president invoked his new powers under the Habeas Corpus Act of 1863 and suspended civil liberties across the nation on September 15 for a wide range of political and military offenses.

Facing his latest set of obstacles, Lincoln exhibited a newfound assertiveness that was rooted in his recent experiences as president and commander in chief.

An example of this new attitude came in Lincoln's approach to the contentious Middle Department. The Union army was organized in regional departments and the Middle Department covering Maryland and nearby border states was especially prone to political problems. The president had a difficult relationship with Robert C. Schenck, a former congressman and the general in charge of the department, as well as with his second in command, Donn Piatt, a former journalist. The department was not typically at the front lines of combat but was subject to much anxiety whenever there were sudden Confederate excursions across the Potomac. Neither Schenck nor Piatt had many allies in the War Department or Army headquarters. According to the president, General Halleck completely discounted Schenck's abilities, claiming he "never had a military idea & never will learn one."[39]

When Lee had invaded the North in June 1863, there had been confusion in the orders issued from Schenck's command that led to an embarrassing surrender of 3,400 Federal soldiers at Winchester, Virginia, by General Robert H. Milroy—who had also been repeatedly criticized by Halleck for incompetence. The subsequent controversy led to a court-martial of Milroy that began in the summer of 1863 and continued through early September. Schenck correctly understood that the trial had the potential to be just as damaging to his reputation as to Milroy's. The question concerned the exact interpretation and timing of his orders. As Lincoln put it bluntly in a letter to Milroy, the case was "inevitably between Gen. Schenck & you." According to John Hay, the president had concluded early on that Schenck was "somewhat to blame for the Winchester business."[40] On September 1, 1863, when Schenck was called to testify at the trial, he initially declined to attend, sending Piatt in his place with a stinging message that he wanted read directly to the president. The document claimed that he had not received the order to testify through proper channels and that moreover the entire inquiry was biased against him even though he was not ostensibly on trial. This was the sort of dispute—with careers at stake—that created permanent political enemies and tended to waste large amounts of time. Lincoln needed to handle the situation with a delicate combination of decisiveness and restraint.

Piatt recalled that he met the president leaving the War Department late in the afternoon as he was preparing to head out to the Soldiers' Home. "Let me see the protest," the president reportedly demanded as they walked toward the White House. "General Schenck ordered me, Mr. President, to read it to you," Piatt claimed he replied. "Well, I can read," Lincoln allegedly snapped, taking the protest from the officer. For Piatt, the scene was indelibly etched into his memory.

Arriving at the entrance to the White House, we found the carriage awaiting to carry him to the Soldiers' Home, where he was then spending the summer, and the guard detailed to escort him drawn up in front. The President sat down upon the steps of the porch, and continued his study of the protest. I have him photographed on my mind, as he sat there, and a strange picture he presented. His long, slender legs were drawn up until his knees were level with his chin, while his long arms held the paper, which he studied regardless of the crowd before him.

Lincoln finally looked up, asking Piatt, "Don't you think that you and Schenck are squealing, like pigs, before you're hurt?" The officer, who had also been a lawyer and a journalist before the war, proceeded to argue the technicalities of the case and implied that the court was "packed." According to his recollection, this phrase drew "an ugly look" from the president who told him to stop implying such slanders. Years afterward, Piatt believed that his efforts had led Lincoln to end the inquiry, but the trial actually proceeded, ultimately exonerating Milroy and only indirectly criticizing Schenck, who later became an ambassador to Great Britain and an internationally recognized expert at the game of poker.[41]

A more significant example of the hard-edged and efficient style that was developing within the Union high command occurred later in September. General Rosecrans ran into trouble during his efforts to force the Confederates out of Tennessee, a critical state in the Upper South. About ten miles outside of Chattanooga, an important railroad center for the region, Federal troops had massed along West Chickamauga Creek. A fierce battle erupted on Saturday, September 19, 1863, and by the next day Union lines had almost completely broken down, sending most Federal troops fleeing back to the nearby city. On Sunday night a messenger roused the president from his sleep at the Soldiers' Home to hand him a dispatch bearing the bad news. Disturbed, Lincoln came into the city, heading straight for the War Department. Shortly after midnight, he telegraphed General Rosecrans some words of encouragement. "Be of good cheer," he stated, "We have unabated confidence in you, and in your soldiers and officers." Yet in the morning the president appeared at John Hay's bedroom, saddened over yet another setback. "Well, Rosecrans has been whipped," he remarked, "as I feared."[42]

Perhaps feeling the burdens of his office for the first time in weeks, Lincoln suddenly reached out to his wife, who was then in New York. On Monday, he sent her a brief note commenting on the cooler weather and healthier air. "Nothing very particular," he wrote, "but I would be glad [to] see you and Tad." What followed was then a typical miscommunication that somehow involved Mary Ann Cuthbert, the housekeeper. "Mrs. Cuthbert did not correctly understand me . . . ," Lincoln explained on Tuesday; "I did not say it is sickly &

that you should on no account come." He reiterated his earlier report. "So far as I see or know, it was never healthier, and I really wish to see you."[43]

By then, things in Tennessee looked somewhat better as reports had filtered back to Washington of the remarkable bravery exhibited by General George H. Thomas (later nicknamed the "Rock of Chickamauga") and his forces on the left side of the Union lines. Somehow, despite all of the madness and stampeding around them, Thomas and his men had held firm and delayed any potential Rebel advances on the critical city of Chattanooga. Yet Rosecrans was clearly shaken and his dispatches on the situation reflected fear that the Confederates were about to assault his position with the advantage of superior numbers. The general's nervous tone worried Secretary of War Stanton who finally decided late on Wednesday night, September 23, that something had to be done to reinforce Rosecrans. He called an emergency meeting of the Union high command.

John Hay, who had strolled over to the War Department just as Stanton was preparing to ride out to the Soldiers' Home, agreed to deliver the message to the president himself. "I went out to the Soldiers Home, through a splendid moonlight & found the Tycoon abed," Hay noted a few days later in his diary. "I delivered my message to him as he robed himself. Hay was surprised at how "considerably disturbed" the normally unflappable president had become. "I assured him as far as I could that it meant nothing serious," Hay reported, "but he thought otherwise, as it was the first time Stanton had ever sent for him."

The two men, and perhaps another messenger from the War Department, rode back to the hastily arranged meeting where they found Stanton had gathered General Halleck, Secretaries Seward and Chase, and a small handful of other leading Union generals. There was a heated discussion over the merits of sending two additional Army corps (20,000 men) via emergency rail transportation. The cipher-operators had delivered a new dispatch from Rosecrans that sounded more determined. From Hay's perspective, the "stampede seemed to be over." But Stanton was not satisfied and asked Major Eckert, who ran the War Department Telegraph Office but had worked for the railroads before the war, if it was even possible to arrange immediate transport over the existing rail lines. According to the recollection from cipher-operator David Bates, General Halleck had estimated that a transfer of that size over a distance of 1,200 miles would take weeks, even months. Instead, working until very late, Eckert and others in the office figured out how to move the troops in a matter of days. The president and his advisers finally agreed to execute the plan and several shared a late dinner at about one or two o'clock in the morning.[44]

The next day, shaking off his exhaustion, Lincoln wrote an important letter to his wife. He reported on the complicated military news from Chickamauga, but then turned to information with personal meaning for their family. He noted that Confederate Brigadier General Ben Hardin Helm, Mary Lincoln's brother-in-law, had been killed in the battle. It was difficult news to relate and the president did so in matter-of-fact fashion. Later that winter, the Lincolns would allow his widow, Emilie Todd Helm, to visit them at the White House. During her brief stay, which raised eyebrows in Washington, the president reportedly asked Mary Lincoln's older half-sister if she would consider returning in six months to live with them at the Soldiers' Home.[45]

The episode in Tennessee underscored the importance of Lincoln's evolving relationships. The effective teamwork that had developed between Lincoln and Stanton was on full display. Knowing each other as they did, they worked in quick concert to address a potentially serious problem with what historian James McPherson has labeled "the most impressive logistic achievement of the war."[46] In the immediate aftermath of Chickamauga, Rosecrans held his position but by October when there were no further encouraging results, the president again acted decisively, placing General Grant in full command over the region. Grant, never slow to action, immediately replaced Rosecrans with George Thomas. By the end of November, under Grant's direction, the Union forces had defeated the Rebels in a major battle near Chattanooga and had effectively gained control of Tennessee.

The interplay between husband and wife during the Tennessee crisis also highlighted the evolution of their marriage. The family was reunited by the end of September and passed a final month together at the cottage. Their long separation revealed a certain fundamental distance in their relationship, but also rekindled some of their affection for each other. "I really wish to see you," the president had written to his wife, and the words seemed utterly sincere.

Others also welcomed the return of mother and son to the cottage. Tad Lincoln brought with him yet another flag for the infantry guard at the Soldiers' Home, this one "10 ft long," according to a grateful Private Cutter.[47] The Bucktails and the Lincoln household remained in residence at the Home until Thursday, October 29, 1863, according to Cutter's letters. A professional mover—who hauled nineteen separate loads of furniture back to the White House—followed them the next Wednesday.[48]

The Lincolns returned to the White House amid much better spirits. Elections had gone well for the Republicans. Despite some setbacks, the campaign in Tennessee under Grant's direction was progressing again. The president and his wife subsequently decided to celebrate the good news and their return to the city with an evening out. On November 9, 1863, the first couple and several guests went to Ford's Theater to see actor John Wilkes Booth starring in

"The Marble Heart." The president reportedly enjoyed the play so much that he sent a note backstage offering an interview with the leading performer, who ducked the request because he was a Rebel sympathizer and perhaps, a Confederate agent. John Hay reported that he found the evening "rather tame."[49]

As Lincoln once again settled into his White House routine, it was clear that another summer at the Soldiers' Home had shaped him in ways deeper than might be expected. After spending a long summer walking past the fresh headstones at the nearby soldier's graveyard, the president now prepared to venture north to Gettysburg to assist in the dedication of a new military cemetery. As he crafted the ten elegant sentences of his brief address that would culminate months of work at explaining the war's purpose, Lincoln must have drawn on his solitary reflections at his wartime sanctuary. But he also shared his own set of vivid memories. When he urged his listeners to be resolved that "these dead shall not have died in vain," many images must have flickered through his mind—his son Willie, the crippled and dying soldiers he encountered each day, and perhaps Colonel Scott's poor wife drowned in the Potomac. The shining promise of a "new birth of freedom" was something he could have seen in the eyes of Frederick Douglass, or Mary Dines, or any number of unnamed ex-slaves whom he encountered on his daily commutes.

There is no proof for such speculation about Lincoln's mind-set, but there are fragments of memories that support some of these interpretations. The president was without doubt a sensitive and brooding man. Journalist Noah Brooks, for example, recalled that "one November day" while they were enjoying a ride out to the Soldiers' Home, the president "slowly and with excellent judgment" recited Oliver Wendell Holmes's melancholy poem, "The Last Leaf."[50] Francis Carpenter, the painter, recalled Lincoln telling him that "for pure pathos" there was "nothing finer" in the English language than the following six lines from "The Last Leaf."

> The mossy marbles rest
> On the lips that he has pressed
> In their bloom;
> And the names he loved to hear
> Have been carved for many a year
> On the tomb.

John Hay, too, heard these words from the presidential lips, but added that when Lincoln recited these particular lines, he invariably gave what the aide termed a "marked Southwestern pronunciation of the words 'hear' and 'year.'"[51]

These stories capture an elusive element of Lincoln's being—the same element that Walt Whitman had glimpsed during the shimmering heat of that quiet mid-August day. The president combined a hard, practical edge with an unusually deep and latent sadness. By 1863, he had become a man who embodied the ordinary accents of a common prairie attorney but whose innate qualities and evolving sense of history seemed to propel him steadily toward greatness. For those who despised him, like the Confederate sympathizer Booth, Lincoln was now clearly emerging as their primary target, the greatest object in the path of southern independence. To those who admired him, however, he truly seemed placed in his position by "the hand of God."

Part Three
1864

∞

7

"Present at Fort Stevens"

"ALL WELL," ABRAHAM LINCOLN WROTE TO HIS WIFE ON JUNE 29, 1864, "TOM IS moving things out." The president was referring to the relocation of his family's belongings for their third season at the Soldiers' Home. Mary Lincoln was once again in New York, waiting to rendezvous with Robert Lincoln, who was in the final days of his college experience at Harvard. "Tom" was probably Thomas Stackpole, a watchman familiar with the Soldiers' Home and a favorite of the Lincolns.[1] Everything seemed to be in order for another season at the private White House. The *New York Herald* reported that Robert Lincoln met his mother on July 2 and that the two then proceeded directly to Washington. Willard Cutter told his family that the presidential entourage formally occupied their cottage on Independence Day.

The Lincolns arrived to a residence that had recently undergone a few thousand dollars' worth of redecoration. In the spring, Mary Lincoln had hired John Alexander, a local upholsterer, to provide "repairs and refitting & furnishing" to the former Riggs country home. Alexander, who had previously worked on renovations at the White House, changed or added wallpaper to eight of the fourteen rooms. He washed the floors and windows and touched up the interior paint. He moved two large mirrors, hung pictures, and added a variety of new lace chamber curtains, linen sheets, and various types of parlor curtains. Across the hallway and in several rooms he placed a form of natural grass matting made from coconut husks that was designed to be cooler than regular carpeting, especially useful for nineteenth-century summer residences. Most of the chairs and sofas in the cottage received new covers. Alexander, whose business was located on Pennsylvania Avenue, also left the residence well stocked with a long list of household items, including three pairs of extra-fine blankets, four feather dusters, three brushes, two large hand towels, four large buckets, two pairs of andirons, and two silk bell pulls.[2]

The cumulative effect of these improvements was to restore a sense of fashion that had probably been fraying since 1851 when banker George Riggs sold the property to the government and vacated the residence. The banker represented a new class of wealthier Americans, made rich by the antebellum revolutions in transportation and communications. He and his partner, William W. Corcoran, had invested wisely in railroads and then later in other innovations, such as the telegraph, that helped shape the emerging national marketplace. When Riggs commissioned local architect William H. Degges to build his country home in 1842, it was a classic *arriviste* statement.

Degges chose to build the Riggs cottage in the Gothic Revival style that was just then becoming popular with the publication of Andrew Jackson Downing's *Cottage Residences* (1842).[3] Historian David Schuyler claims that Downing, a landscape designer and horticulturist, "more than any other individual, shaped middle-class taste in the United States" during the antebellum period. In his well-illustrated book on rural cottages, Downing had articulated a vision for integrating what were then modern conveniences (such as dumbwaiters, gaslights, and indoor water closets) into elegant homes that still demonstrated a respect for simplicity and for the beauty of their natural surroundings. He offered a sense of style and taste that was especially appealing to modern household patriarchs like Riggs or his partner Corcoran, who owned the neighboring estate, Harewood. The architect built a cottage residence for his demanding client that closely resembled a form in Downing's book labeled, Design II, English or Rural Gothic Style cottage.[4]

Riggs had certainly seemed to enjoy the simplicity of his country life, especially after falling out with Corcoran in the late 1840s over what he considered the latter's risky financial schemes. However, the death of a young daughter at the cottage in 1849, and perhaps the need for some belt-tightening, soured Riggs on the country and he returned with the surviving members of his family to live in the city during the 1850s.[5] The government took control of the residence and began altering the surrounding grounds. The interior of the cottage was then subject to heavy use, providing housing for the original inmates of what was called the Military Asylum until 1857. Following the transfer of the inmates, or residents as they preferred to be known, the cottage was occupied by a series of officers in temporary arrangements until the Lincoln family arrived.[6]

There is some confusion in the historical record as to exactly which season the Lincolns began occupying the Riggs cottage. The oral tradition at the Soldiers' Home places the first family there from 1862 onward. Subsequent histories of the institution and commemorations of the Lincoln era have always

An image of the former Riggs cottage as it appeared during the wartime era. The larger building on the right housed disabled veterans. EDWARD STEERS, JR.

assumed that the president lived in the same cottage during each of his three seasons in residence. Yet an 1864 letter from Benjamin French, commissioner of public buildings, suggests otherwise. Writing to the chairman of the House committee responsible for approving the funds provided to upholsterer John Alexander, the commissioner claimed that the money was necessary for fitting up a *new* cottage for the Lincolns. "The house heretofore occupied by President Lincoln," French wrote, "has, since last summer, been taken by some other person, & [the president] has been put to the expense of preparing another house for his own private residence there."[7]

What French told John H. Rice, the committee chairman, fits with some of the available evidence. President James Buchanan had stayed at Quarters 1, not the Riggs house, during his visits to the Soldiers' Home. This two-story cottage built in the 1850s, was nearby and was perhaps even better appointed than the older Riggs building. According to 1861 newspaper reports, the Lincolns had planned to stay in Quarters 1 before the Battle of Bull Run disrupted their original summer plans. A contemporary print by Charles Magnus clearly identifies that cottage as the "President's Villa" and labels the former Riggs residence as the "Military Governor's House." Lincoln scholars have assumed that the well-known publisher, perhaps confused by the Buchanan precedent, had simply mixed up the captions.[8] There was also a changeover in personnel at the Soldiers' Home in January 1864 that might have led to new housing arrangements in the summer. Colonel Justin Dimmick replaced acting governor Thomas L. Alexander as head of the institution, and longtime surgeon Benjamin King was relieved from his post. Vacancies and new faces could have prompted a presidential shuffle from Quarters 1 to the Riggs cottage.

On the other hand, none of the other contemporary accounts so far examined indicate that the Lincoln family moved from one cottage to another during the war. There is nothing documenting such a transition in any of the relevant letters, diaries, or newspaper reports. Mary Lincoln did not mention it. Neither did Willard Cutter, John Hay, Orville Browning, or anyone else who was in a position to observe the Lincolns throughout their three seasons at the Soldiers' Home. Most of the recollected accounts by one-time visitors are vague enough to make a clear-cut identification between homes with so many features in common almost impossible. The only description concrete enough to place the Lincolns definitively at the Riggs cottage comes from a California woman who visited in 1864 and thus does not answer the question for earlier years.[9] And unfortunately, records from the Board of Commissioners, always sparse to begin with, become practically nonexistent during the wartime period.

On further examination, there is also something suspect about French's letter to the House committee. He wrote that "the expense of preparing another house" had been "represented to me as a necessity" that was placing "a burden on the Chief Magistrate that he ought not to be subjected to." There is little doubt that it was Mary Lincoln who was making these representations to Commissioner French. She had repeatedly invoked the financial burdens of public office on the family. She was also the one who cared most deeply about the details of the family's accommodations. French, who was not a frequent visitor to the Soldiers' Home, might have simply misunderstood the rationale behind her request. He had made other minor errors in his report, and it would be a mistake to invest too much faith in the literal accuracy of his explanations. It is also conceivable that Mary Lincoln intentionally misled the commissioner, subtly enhancing the need for the appropriation, just as she exaggerated its financial burden on her family's healthy bank account. In the absence of additional proof, the most likely explanation of housing arrangements still appears to be that French was just wrong—for whatever reason—and that the Lincolns resided at the former Riggs cottage during each of their three seasons at the Soldiers' Home.

Regardless of these circumstances, the Lincolns were not able to enjoy the refurbished cottage for long. Shortly after their arrival, the Confederates threatened the city with an unexpected raid that came through Maryland. "Ever since we have been here," Private Cutter wrote on Monday, July 11, 1864, "the rebs have been near the city or advancing and [this] was rather a scary place for the President to stay."[10]

After enjoying nearly a six-month string of successes, President Lincoln had arrived at the Soldiers' Home in early July 1864 amid a number of dark omens. Following General Grant's 1863 victories in the Mississippi Valley and Tennessee, Lincoln had elevated him to the position of general in chief and had convinced the reluctant commander to come East to oversee General Meade and the Army of the Potomac in the all-important contest against Lee's army. The spring of 1864 had been a period of high hopes for the North as Union forces under Grant's implacable direction kept bearing down on Confederate positions around Richmond. But by early July, the advances had stopped. There were now reports filtering back to Washington that in six weeks of fighting against Lee in the "Wilderness" on the outskirts of the Rebel capital, Grant had incurred nearly 100,000 casualties—a figure almost twice the size of Lee's remaining army. Horrified, Mary Lincoln had called him a "butcher" and the man who had been a national hero was suddenly the object of intense scrutiny by the press and public.[11]

The news was not much better in the West. At the end of June, General William T. Sherman, who had become the principal western commander in Grant's absence, had ordered a tragically misguided assault at Kennesaw Mountain in central Georgia that resulted in his army's worst losses to date. The

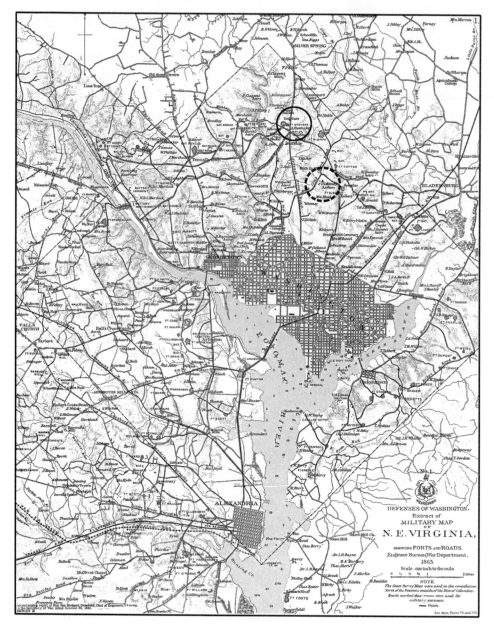

*A map of Washington's wartime defenses, with both Fort Stevens
and the Soldiers' Home (dotted) circled.*

OFFICIAL RECORDS OF THE UNION AND CONFEDERATE ARMIES; COURTESY BLAKE P. MAGNER.

Federal troops had been attempting to move down to Atlanta from the positions secured during the previous winter campaign in Tennessee. The advances of the previous year increasingly seemed to have been gained for nothing. Northern frustration was palpable as a renewed period of stalemate developed.

Politically, it was a difficult time as well. Secretary Chase had finally resigned. He had attempted to resign several times before, but Lincoln had always convinced him to remain inside the fold, certain that Chase's great talents were worth the price of his vanity and ambition. Yet after the president had received his formal renomination to serve as the presidential candidate of the Union coalition in early June, he no longer felt obligated to cater to his touchy subordinate. Chase's departure coincided with a renewed outbreak of discontent among congressional Republicans, primarily over the thorny problem of reconstruction policy or how to reintegrate conquered southern states back into the Union. The same day that Lincoln's military guard moved to the Soldiers' Home and the day after Congress had adjourned for its long summer recess, the president decided to pocket veto a congressional reconstruction plan called the Wade-Davis bill. This plan, backed by leading Radicals, was much tougher than the president's proposals for reconstruction and his refusal to endorse it created great animosity within his own party.

The summer storm grew worse for the president when Confederate General Jubal Early's tired and hungry troops crossed the Potomac and headed for Washington seeking mainly to steal food and supplies and to further rattle northern confidence. The Federal high command seemed unprepared for this maneuver, focused as they were on Grant's stalled progress outside of Richmond. In truth, from a military perspective, 15,000 poorly supplied Rebel soldiers were unlikely to inflict any serious damage on the heavily fortified capital. The defenses around Washington had been designed to withstand much greater offensive pressure. They were modeled after the Lines of Torres Vedras, a famous system of defensive redoubts or small forts that had been employed by the Duke of Wellington during one of his famous campaigns in Portugal at the beginning of the nineteenth century. Union engineers, led by John G. Barnard, had created what was considered a state-of-the-art network of nearly seventy forts that circled the District.[12]

Following the August 1862 debacle at Second Bull Run, Secretary of War Stanton had ordered a review of this defensive network to insure that no gaps existed. The study suggested a few improvements, most notably pointing out that the "weakest part of the system" lay along the northwestern boundary of the District, from the Potomac River to Fort Massachusetts (later renamed Fort Stevens) along the Seventh Street turnpike—and within a few miles from the Soldiers' Home.[13] In the spring of 1863, Union military leaders had tried to address these issues by reorganizing their forces. They created a separate Department of Washington, initially under the command of a political general, Samuel P. Heintzelman. By 1864, however, the forces were under the more competent direction of a professional military man, Christopher C. Augur. Nevertheless, the long stretches of inactivity had lowered the state of readiness and the recent spate of casualties during Grant's Wilderness campaign had depleted Washington's defenses of many able-bodied troops. The fort system around the city still looked formidable, but it was now a network built largely on the strength of novice or partially disabled soldiers. In addition, what military planners had failed to take into complete account was that even a temporary breakthrough by a force like Early's might have had disastrous political consequences.

Thus, when the Rebels swung south from Frederick, Maryland, on July 8, 1864, and headed toward the capital, they represented a real threat. The only significant body of Federal troops between Early's men and Washington was a rag-tag assortment of regular soldiers, short-term state militia volunteers and members of the Veteran's Reserves (partially disabled soldiers outfitted for combat). The Confederates quickly defeated these Union forces at the Battle of Monocacy on Saturday, July 9, 1864, but that single day's delay arguably helped save Washington because it provided the Union military leadership with extra time to call up a regular Army division to aid in the city's defense.[14]

These regulars were not yet available on Sunday, July 10, as Early's suspiciously well-informed forces headed directly toward the weakest link in the defensive shield—Fort Stevens on the Seventh Street turnpike. In his memoir, General Early did not disclose his intelligence sources for the 1864 campaign, but the Confederate spy network had been successfully infiltrating Washington since the outbreak of the hostilities. He probably knew about Stanton's 1862 report on the state of the defenses. Another possibility is that Early received key information from Colonel Bradley T. Johnson, a cavalry officer who later claimed that he had been authorized over the winter of 1863–1864 to develop a plan to capture President Lincoln once he began residing again at the Soldiers' Home. Johnson recalled that he had carefully prepared a "daring enterprise," approved by Confederate General Wade C. Hampton, that proposed to "make a dash" at kidnapping Lincoln once he relocated to his summer retreat. According to his postwar recollections, Johnson had abandoned this plan only reluctantly in June when he was ordered to support Early's initial movement into the Shenandoah Valley.[15]

The possibility that there was some scheme afoot to harm President Lincoln had occurred to Edwin Stanton. Following reports of the engagement at Monocacy, he had dispatched a War Department scout to monitor the president's movements to and from the Soldiers' Home. He soon received disturbing news, which he relayed immediately to Lincoln. "Your carriage was followed by a horseman," he reported, "not one of your escort and dressed in uniform unlike that used by our troops." The secretary was anxious, advising earnestly that the presidential guard "be on the alert tonight."[16]

Meanwhile, the next day, Sunday, Washington residents desperately tried to organize themselves. A soldier stationed in one of the city's other forts recalled the pathetic scene that he witnessed.

> That evening the motliest crowd of soldiers I ever saw came straggling out from Washington to man the rifle-pits which connected the forts. This force was composed of quarter-master's employees, clerks from the War, Navy, and State Departments, convalescents from the military hospitals, and the veteran reserves, the latter clad in the distinctive dress of the corps.

"They gabbled," he recalled, "and were evidently trying to keep up their courage by talking loudly and boastfully on their determination to hold the rifle-pits at all hazards." He added, "I smiled sorrowfully."[17] General Halleck, sharp-tongued as always, tartly rejected what he considered empty offers of help from officers stationed nearby. "We have five times as many generals here as we want," he stated, "but are greatly in need of privates. Any one volunteering in that capacity will be thankfully received."[18] Commenting on the chaos, William Doster, the District's provost marshal, noted in his diary that "Washington is at last waking up from the apathy which is become the fashion and which is an affectation of coolness very different from the genuine sentiment."[19]

While the citizens of Washington were waking up to their responsibilities, the commander in chief was still trying to rest peacefully at the Soldiers' Home, not too far from the scene of the impending skirmish. He and his family went to sleep as usual on Sunday night. Secretary of War Stanton, however, had finally had enough anxiety. At ten o'clock, he sent an urgent message to the president. "The enemy are reported advancing towards Tenallytown [on the northwest boundary of the District] and Seventh street road," he reported, "They are in large force and have driven back our Cavalry." Stanton made his point as clearly as he felt appropriate. "I think you had better come in to town tonight," he scribbled hastily.[20]

The messenger arrived to find the soldiers guarding the cottage full of anticipation and anxiously spreading rumors. Albert See, a private in the company, remembered seeing the president awakened. "I was on guard in front of the house and the president and his private secretary were in earnest conversation where I almost brushed against them as I walked my beat," he recalled. See claimed that when he heard the sounds of a horseman rapidly approaching, he panicked and ordered the president to step inside the cottage before yelling, "Co. K fall in! fall in!"[21] In the confusion that followed, some of the infantry troops thought Secretary Stanton himself had rushed out to the cottage. Willard Cutter later relayed to his mother how Stanton had arrived breathlessly around eleven o'clock to demand that the president and his family return to the city. "Well, Abe said he didn't think there was any danger," according to Cutter's version, "but he went along." The sleepy family did return quickly to the White House. "A little after midnight [Robert Lincoln] came into my room & got into bed," reported Hay, "saying Stanton had sent out for them all to come in."[22]

Describing the events two days later, journalist Noah Brooks explained to his readers that the "lonely situation of the President's Summer residence would have afforded a tempting chance for a daring squad of cavalry to run some risks for the chance of carrying off the President." Lincoln was the only political leader, Brooks pointed out, "we could ill afford to spare just now."[23] Years later Brooks expanded on his report, claiming that the president had been "irritated" by Stanton's fears and had returned "against his will." The journalist also suggested that during this emergency, Assistant Secretary of Navy Gustavus Fox had kept a ship ready on the Potomac for the president's possible escape, a fact that he claimed also "annoyed" the president when he discovered it.[24] Meanwhile, on the same night that the Lincoln family left their residence, General Augur ordered Lieutenant P. H. Niles of the Signal Corps to establish a post atop the main hall of the Soldiers' Home just across from the presidential cottage. From there the officer was able to communicate with other Signal Corps members stationed at the various forts and inside the city using a coded system of lights and flags, providing a communications service of "much importance" according to the official reports filed after the battle.[25]

The importance of good communications was demonstrated early the next day. At 6:20 A.M., Monday, July 11, 1864, General Augur received reports of "rapid firing" and a "large column of dust" near Rockville. He immediately went out to Fort Stevens to take a look for himself. General Horatio G. Wright, commanding the Sixth Corps from the Army of the Potomac, was due to arrive with his troops that morning. He had originally been ordered to occupy a position between the Chain Bridge and the main defenses near the Potomac— nowhere near the real action. Augur quickly convinced Halleck to countermand that directive and send the Sixth Corps toward the Seventh Street turnpike. "Please stop General Wright's movement up the Potomac," Halleck ordered at 1:40 P.M., "and send his command up Seventh Street to rendezvous near the Military Asylum."[26]

By midday it had become brutally hot and the streets were full of government employees heading out to the front and outlying residents fleeing into the safety of the city. "Great excitement in Washington," noted telegraph operator David Bates in his diary. "Department clerks are being armed and sent to the forts at the boundary."[27] Another member of the Telegraph Office, who had been ordered to take a mobile communications wagon out to the front, shared a vivid recollection of the day's confusion:

> It was one of the hottest days I ever experienced, and the dust rose in clouds blinding the vision. Beyond Georgetown we met a great number of people coming into Washington with their household effects, some driving cattle and leading horses. On each side of the road wherever a bush or tree cast any shade soldiers could be discerned prostrated by sunstroke. When half-way there my horses gave out and I started on foot, but the driver overtook me, the horses having a few minutes' rest. The office at General M.D. Hardin's headquarters was in a building left standing between the two forts [Reno and Stevens]. This building was demolished the next day because it was in line with the guns of the forts. On the roof in the blazing sun, signal-men were wigwagging their despatches. To the northeast we could see the dust of the enemy as they moved back and forth.[28]

For the president, the excitement and tension were too much. He simply could not remain in the White House while telegraph operators and quartermaster clerks raced out to join the fighting. "The President concluded to desert his tormentors today & travel around the defenses," noted White House aide Hay in his diary. "At three o'clock P.M. the President came in bringing the news that the enemy's advance was at Ft. Stevens on the 7th Street road. He was in the Fort when it was first attacked, standing upon the parapet. A soldier roughly ordered him to get down or he would have his head knocked off."[29] What the president saw, however, was not really a full-fledged attack. General Wright, whose troops were probably just arriving at the scene as the president was leaving, reported to General Augur at 4:10 P.M. that there had only been "a very light skirmish line" outside of Fort Stevens.

According to Jubal Early, it was the weather and the signal station at the Soldiers' Home that conspired to prevent him from reinforcing those advance skirmishers on Monday afternoon. "[T]he day was so exceedingly hot," the Confederate general recalled, "even at a very early hour in the morning, and the dust so dense, that many of the men fell by the wayside, and it became necessary to slacken our pace."[30] When they finally did arrive near the scene of the action, the Rebel troops found themselves under constant scrutiny and unable to choose the best location for their attack. "We could not move to the right or left without its being discovered from a signal station on the top of the Soldiers' Home," he later wrote.[31]

The result was only a scattered series of assaults and probes. Still, it was more than enough action for the local newsboys who sold their extra afternoon editions of the Washington *Star* by yelling, "'Hextry Staar. Second Edition. Great

Battle at Seventh Street."[32] It was also exciting for the president, who hurried over to the War Department after sharing his news with Hay and proceeded to sketch out a map of what he had seen that morning. "I have in my possession the diagram which Lincoln made in the telegraph office," recalled operator Albert Chandler. "This diagram showed the relative positions of the two bodies of troops and where the skirmish took place, all of which he explained to Major [Thomas] Eckert, [Charles] Tinker, [David] Bates and myself, who were, of course, extremely interested in his picturesque description."[33]

"The President is in very good feather this evening," Hay reported once Lincoln had returned to the White House. "He seems not the least concerned about the safety of Washington. With him the only concern seems to be whether we can bag or destroy this force in our front."[34] He even allowed his infantry guard from the Soldiers' Home to abandon their post and join the action. Willard Cutter and the Bucktail troops hurried to a position on the northwest side of the city.

Unlike the president, the professional military men did not see the same opportunity to "bag or destroy" the enemy. They had been convinced that Early's raid was intended merely as a distraction in order to undermine Grant's campaign in Virginia. Now they overestimated the size of the Confederate force and came to believe the full pursuit would be futile. Summarizing the day's events for General Grant, Assistant Secretary of War Charles Dana wrote:

> The force of the enemy is everywhere stated at from 20,000 to 30,000. The idea of cutting off their retreat would seem to be futile, for there are plenty of fords and ferries now in their control where they can cross the Potomac and get off, in spite of all our efforts to intercept them, long before our forces can be so concentrated as to be able to strike an effective blow.[35]

The Confederates were guilty of the same sort of miscalculation. "An attack in force is expected during the night," wrote William Doster nervously, "They would be fools if they waited." But the Rebels did wait. They debated attacking on Monday evening, but Jubal Early considered the fortifications too strong to assault and his battlefield intelligence too unreliable. "Under the circumstances," he wrote, "to have rushed my men blindly against the fortifications, without understanding the state of things, would have been worse than folly."[36] A captured Rebel soldier reportedly confessed "after necessary pressure" that the key factor behind the delay had been intelligence that General Early had received about the arrival of Wright's respected Sixth Corps.[37] In any event, whether through exhaustion, miscalculation, or fear, the Confederates failed to capitalize on their advantages and Monday night passed without any further confrontation at Fort Stevens.

The next day began less nervously for capital residents. "The city still survives and men feel relieved," Provost Marshal Doster wrote in his journal. The morning newspapers had announced that the fighting was continuing and that local grocer Peter Bacon was organizing the city's volunteer militia. Doster went to Bacon's store but found "no headquarters visible." He wrote dryly, "Asked Bacon's brother where headquarters were; [he] answered, 'Damned if I know.'"[38] Still, there were ominous reminders of the nearby danger. Orville Browning, who had finished his Senate term and was now a lobbyist in town, wrote in his journal that there was "some skirmishing going on all day—the sounds of guns occasionally heard." He noted that the telegraph wires had been cut and that there were reports of extensive damage to railroads and property.[39] The Rebels had burned Postmaster General Montgomery Blair's home in Maryland and were using his father's estate as their temporary headquarters. According to Doster, the city showed "no signs of alarm, except being subdued as children in a thunderstorm, listening and waiting for the issue." He wrote that it seemed "funny to hear the rumbling of street cars mixed with the rumbling of hostile cannon, the one of pleasure and business, the other of death and agony."[40]

Once again on Tuesday, July 12, the president refused to wait around in the city. Hay recorded the increasing physical danger to his boss in a matter-of-fact style. "The President again made the tour of the fortifications; was again under fire at Ft. Stevens," he wrote, adding, "a man was shot at his side."[41] What the aide failed to point out, however, was that on this occasion, the president apparently also took his wife with him. In fact, there were several leading figures from the administration and Congress present at Fort Stevens on the afternoon of July 12, including William Seward, Gideon Welles, and Senator Benjamin Wade. According to the recollection of a surgeon on duty at the Fort's infirmary, the president and first lady arrived at the scene "unattended, except by their coachman" because the "superbly mounted squadron of cavalry" lagged far behind. He recalled that the couple passed through the hospital ward first, consoling the wounded and encouraging the doctors, before heading up to the parapet or primary defensive wall. Not surprisingly, Robert McBride, a member of the cavalry detail, failed to mention this fact in his memoir, only reporting that his unit was "present" when Lincoln visited Fort Stevens.[42]

There had been various exchanges of fire since morning, but shortly after the president arrived, tensions escalated. According to David T. Bull, a soldier stationed in one of the rifle pits, he began to see "some warm work" at about 4 P.M. when the Rebels massed directly in front of the Fort, "thinking our force would not shell them thru fear of killing our own men."

> There was a large force of them gathered around a house in front of the Fort and there was a sharp shooter got up in the top of the house and thought he would kill some of our

men that was on the parapets. Old Abe and his wife was in the Fort at the time and Old
Abe and his doctor was standing up on the parapets and the sharp shooter that I speak of
shot the doctor through the left thigh, and Old Abe ordered our men to fall back.[43]

Bull was wrong about the wounded man being Lincoln's own doctor. The man
who was hit at the president's side was an assistant surgeon named Crawford
from the 102nd Pennsylvania Volunteers.

There is also some confusion over who gave which orders after the shooting
intensified. For many years, future Supreme Court justice Oliver Wendell
Holmes, Jr., who was then a captain in the Sixth Corps, claimed that without
thinking, he roughly told the president, "Get down, you fool!" after the sharp-
shooter began picking off targets along the parapet. However, most historians
discount the tale, pointing out, for example, that Captain Holmes spent part of
the next day with Robert Lincoln and John Hay yet failed to mention anything
about what surely would have been a terrific story.[44] General Horatio Wright,
who was present on the parapet and one of the ranking officers at the Fort, later
claimed that he was the one who insisted that the president stand down. "When
the surgeon was shot and after I had cleared the parapet of everyone else,"
Wright recalled, "[Lincoln] still maintained his ground till I told him I should
have to remove him forcibly. The absurdity of the idea of sending off the president under guard seemed to amuse him, but in consideration of my earnest-
ness in the matter, he agreed to compromise by sitting behind the parapet
instead of standing upon it."[45] Peter H. Kaiser, another soldier who was present,
remembered the situation in nearly identical terms, although in his version, the
president was more obedient.

> General Wright in command of the 6th Corps, stood near [Lincoln] with a field glass,
> viewing the contest, when a bullet wounded a surgeon nearby. The General turned at
> once with the order, "Mr. President, step down from the parapet, you are too conspicu-
> ous an object to remain in so exposed a position." Like a good soldier, he obeyed orders
> and stepped down.[46]

Secretary of Navy Welles and Senator Wade arrived just after this incident had
occurred. "We went together into the fort," Welles noted in his diary, "where
we found the President, who was sitting in the shade, his back against the
parapet towards the enemy." Welles added that a "man had been shot in the
fort a few minutes before we entered."[47]

After the parapet had been cleared, the officers in command ordered the
shelling of the nearby residence where the Rebel sharpshooters had been hid-
ing. Once the building was destroyed, the Sixth Corps conducted a final assault on the remaining Confederates. "When our men fell back far enough,"
David Bull related to his wife, "the cannon in the Fort opened on them and

At Fort Stevens, Lincoln twice came under enemy fire. LIBRARY OF CONGRESS.

fired the house, shelled them till they was in full retreat and then the Sixth Army Corps went after them and run them clean out of hearing."[48] Aldace Walker, a Vermont soldier stationed at Fort Stevens, explained to his father that while the cannons were "firing heavily," sometime after four o'clock, "[t]he Generals and President and Secretaries, &c. were looking on." Walker seemed to believe that Lincoln had been nearly hit himself. He noted in a letter, written the next day, that the president had "a hole in his coat sleeve."[49]

There is testimony from Lincoln himself on the events of that afternoon because months later one of the homeowners from the area petitioned Congress for redress of her damages. "I was present at Fort Stevens," Lincoln recalled, proudly, "(I think) on the afternoon of July 12th 1864." He noted that "some houses in front were shelled by our guns, and understanding that the Military officers in command thought the shelling of the houses proper and necessary, I certainly gave my approbation to its being done."[50] With the president's supportive testimony, Congress rejected the plea for restitution.

Lincoln's recollection is interesting for another reason as well. One of the homes that had been destroyed in order to build Fort Stevens in the first place belonged to a free black woman named Elizabeth Thomas, commonly known as "Aunt Betty." For years after the war, especially at occasions marking the anniversary of the attack on Fort Stevens, Thomas would share a story about how she tried to stop the demolition of her home. Her efforts finally exhausted, she recalled sitting under a tree, holding her infant child, sobbing as her "life savings" was being torn to pieces. She claimed that the officers in charge, distraught and guilty over her reaction, had called for the president to come and comfort her. According to her tale, he appeared as she cried under the tree and promised her that one day that she would "reap a great reward." It was on this basis that she asked Congress for six thousand dollars. As always, such anecdotes are hard to believe, especially since Lincoln's contemporary testimony suggests such a different attitude about eminent domain. Not surprisingly, Thomas also claimed that she was the one who yelled for Lincoln to "get down" during the attack.[51] Nonetheless, these stories still demonstrate that the invocation of Father Abraham as merciful and omnipresent, whether grounded in reality or not, were firmly part of the era's popular culture.

By the next morning, the Rebels were gone. "We had the 'Yanks' badly frightened," wrote Confederate soldier T. E. Morrow defiantly. "We got in sight of the Dome of the Capitol." Anxious to alleviate any impressions that they had been defeated, the soldier claimed to his father that the whole expedition had been a diversion. It had been "the intention of our Generals to draw the 'Yanks' from Grant's Army," he explained; "We had no idea of takeing [*sic*] the place."[52] Captured Confederates told a different tale, however. Aldace Walker reported that about fifty prisoners guarded by his unit "say they thought they were fighting militia" and "knew it was all up" when they realized the Sixth Corps had arrived.[53]

John Hay and Robert Lincoln rode around the area on Wednesday, July 13, looking for some adventures once the excitement had passed. They spoke with Captain Holmes, drank some beer with the tired troops, climbed the parapet at Fort Stevens where the day before Robert's father had been under fire, and encountered some prisoners being marched into the city. Hay described them as "ragged & dirty" and claimed that most "expressed themselves anxious to get out of the army."[54]

Rumors about the disheveled condition of Early's men soon spread around Washington. Montgomery Blair fumed over what he considered the incompetence of Union military commanders who had allowed his home to be destroyed by such troops. Gideon Welles quietly concurred. "The Rebels are making a show of a fight while they are stealing horses, cattle, etc. through Maryland," he wrote in his diary. "They might easily have captured Washington. Stanton, Halleck, and Grant are asleep or dumb."[55] The Union high command found itself beset by critics. Although Grant was shielded from most of this second-guessing by virtue of being with the Army near Richmond, Stanton and Halleck grew increasingly perturbed. Halleck authored a fiery letter demanding that any "slanderer" of the Army be "dismissed" from the cabinet—a stunning request that Stanton boldly passed along to the president.[56]

Even though the president was himself "disgusted" over the outcome of the raid, according to John Hay, he moved quickly to contain the recriminations. "I do not consider what may have been hastily said in a moment of vexation at so severe a loss, as sufficient ground for so grave a step," he calmly assured Stanton. He then added sternly, "I propose continuing to be myself the judge as to when a Member of the Cabinet shall be dismissed." To underscore his determination on this point, Lincoln followed his note to Stanton with a general memorandum for the cabinet, warning that it would "greatly pain me to discover any of you endeavoring to procure anothers removal, or, in any way to prejudice him before the public." For Lincoln, such complaints were best delivered in private. Thus, on his first ride back to the Soldiers' Home after the attack, a few hours following his warning to the cabinet about finger pointing, Lincoln vented his own feelings to John Hay. As they trotted along, the president complained sarcastically that General Wright was now hesitating in his pursuit of Early's forces "for fear he might come across the rebels & catch some of them."[57]

Meanwhile, as if to put a final exclamation point on the disheartening episode, the president arrived at his cottage on Thursday evening to find his military guard missing. The Bucktails had gone out to the front on Monday night to help in the defenses at Fort Reno (on the northwest side of the city, near present-day Wisconsin Avenue). However, according to Willard Cutter, they encountered an officer who ordered them to head instead for Fort DeRussy near Rock Creek. Somehow, in the chaos of battle, the military bureaucracy lost track of their whereabouts. "Where is Captain Getchell's company, One hundred and fiftieth Pennsylvania volunteers? I don't know where it is," admitted General Hardin, commanding at Fort Reno on Wednesday. "Is there any other name for that company?" It was not until 7 P.M. on Thursday night that Hardin could report to department headquarters that he had found Company K and sent them "on the road to the Soldiers' Home."[58]

Despite President Lincoln's efforts to limit the political fallout, there was a widespread sense of frustration in Washington following Early's raid. "My friend Abraham has got to do something to retrieve this awful blunder," Benjamin French confided in the pages of his journal, "or he is 'a goner.'"[59] Mary Lincoln, always sensitive to criticism of her husband, lashed out at Edwin Stanton. The secretary of war came to the cottage shortly after the episode and tried to engage the first lady by teasing that he intended to commission a portrait of her "standing on the ramparts at Fort Stevens overlooking the fight!" "That is very well," Mary Lincoln reportedly snapped back, "and I can assure you of one thing, Mr. Secretary, if I had had a few *ladies* with me the Rebels would not have been permitted to get away as they did!"[60]

To date, Lincoln's experience at Fort Stevens has been the only time in American history that a president has seen enemy fire during combat. Even though the raid was not a serious strategic assault and the skirmishing outside the fort was not intense by Civil War standards, the dangers were real and the president conducted himself with courage. A book discovered at the elder Blair's home after the raid contained an inscription left by a departing Virginia infantry soldier that suggested some of the Confederates may have been expecting a different reaction.

Near Washington, July 12, 1864.

Now Uncle Abe, you had better be quiet the balance of your Administration, as we only came near your town this time just to show you what we could do; but if you go on in your mad career, we will come again soon, and then you had better stand from under.

Yours respectfully, the worst rebel you ever saw.

58th Virginia Infantry.[61]

For some residents of Washington, such threats were particularly unnerving. President Lincoln received an anonymous letter shortly after Early's departure that pleaded with him to vacate the cottage. Signed simply, "Lizzie W. S.," the earnest note reported that when Lincoln rode out to his "Summer-retreat Soldiers Home," he often got "some distance invariably ahead" of his cavalry escort. The female correspondent noted that other travelers then occasionally followed the president, close enough to do him harm. "If you value your life!" she urged, "*discontinue* your visits, out of the City."[62]

If anything, however, the president's position hardened in July. Four days after returning to his residence at the Soldiers' Home, and one day after Commissioner French had worried that he was "a goner," Lincoln issued two public papers that revealed the extent of his determination. First, he called for 500,000 more men to enlist in the Union armies. After three long years of war, it was a stunning admission that the fighting was still far from over. Then, on the same day, he issued a general letter, addressed simply "To Whom It May Concern," stating that his conditions for beginning any negotiations on ending the war included "the abandonment of slavery."[63] There had been a flurry of proposals to negotiate a peace settlement in the summer of 1864, but by insisting on emancipation as a precondition, the president guaranteed that peace talks would never get off the ground. Seasoned by more than three years as commander in chief during the nation's bloodiest war—and now tested by fire himself—Lincoln appeared more determined than ever to see the conflict through to complete victory.

8

"Damned in Time & in Eternity"

By late July 1864, Jubal Early had become a more serious headache for President Lincoln. At first, the raid on Washington had been a fleeting embarrassment for the Union high command. Then it turned out that Early had other plans for making excursions into northern territory. On Tuesday, July 26, 1864, when Gideon and Mary Ann Welles paid a social call on the president and first lady at the Soldiers' Home, the men could talk about little else besides reports suggesting that the former Virginia state legislator turned Confederate general was now moving on southern Pennsylvania. "I told the President I trusted there would be some energy and decision in getting behind them, cutting them off, and not permitting them to go back," Welles noted in his diary, "instead of a scare and getting forces to drive them back with their plunder." The president said he agreed with those views "precisely" and told Secretary of Navy Welles that he had been urging General Halleck to guarantee that it would finally happen this time.[1]

Once again, however, the Rebel raiders escaped. Early's forces burned the town of Chambersburg, Pennsylvania, on Saturday, July 30, when the citizens failed to meet a demand for $500,000 in tribute. The same day, the Army of the Potomac launched a spectacularly failed assault on Petersburg, near the outskirts of Richmond. The encounter soon became known as the Battle of the Crater since Union engineers had attempted to blow up Confederate defenses with explosives that they had planted in a secret underground tunnel. Federal troops subsequently rushed into the crater that had been created by the explosion, turning themselves into easy targets once the stunned Rebel soldiers recovered their composure. It was yet another dismal day after several weeks of frustrating news.

The disappointing military developments coincided with another heat wave in Washington. "It is very warm & dusty here," Mary Lincoln informed son Robert who was then in New York. Writing on July 29, the first lady then suggested rather uncharacteristically that he might want to "remain a week or ten days longer" before coming to see them.[2] She might have been less focused on family at that moment because her husband had finally agreed to bring her along on an official trip. The president had made arrangements to hold a meeting with General Grant in the harbor outside Fort Monroe, on the Virginia peninsula. For some reason, he decided that on this occasion, Mary Lincoln and some of her friends could join him on the brief journey.

The decision thrilled the first lady who spent part of Friday at the Soldiers' Home penning several hasty invitations. "We propose returning on Monday morning," she wrote an acquaintance from Illinois who was visiting the city, "& in *this* excessively warm weather, we may perhaps be able to find an *occasional* cool breeze, on the river."[3] She informed another potential guest, whose recent visit to the cottage she had missed because of her headaches, that the "President has already several gentlemen friends to accompany him."[4]

There is no record of what Lincoln and Grant discussed at Fort Monroe. The taciturn general had written the president a rare letter on July 25 outlining his plans to consolidate the various departments around Washington in the aftermath of Early's raid. "Many reasons might be assigned for the change here suggested," Grant wrote in his terse fashion, "some of which I would not care to commit to paper but would not hesitate to give verbally."[5] Grant surely elaborated on those reasons at their meeting. They also certainly discussed who might head such a new command. Historian John Y. Simon points out that Lincoln made an interesting notation on the back of the general's July 25 letter. Between the abbreviations, "Md. & Penna.," indicating the scope of the proposed department, the president had scrawled, "McClellan." Simon believes that Lincoln was at least considering the possibility of reappointing the former commander to this field position. It was a move already being lobbied for by the Blair family. Defending the capital was indisputably the one task that McClellan had performed well in the past. In addition, the general was believed to be the front-runner for the Democratic party's nomination for president, a decision scheduled to be made in their national convention at the end of August. If McClellan was returned to active command, the Democrats would be thrown into disarray only about two months before the November presidential election.[6]

Another possibility is that President Lincoln was beginning to see in General Grant's recent behavior unhappy echoes of McClellan. There was a Confederate army loose in the Shenandoah Valley, dancing back and forth across the Potomac River, and nobody in the Union military appeared determined to seize the opportunity and destroy the enemy force. Lincoln might have used his five-hour conference at Fort Monroe to lecture Grant as he had done on previous occasions with McClellan. If so, that might explain why Grant omitted the painful episode from his *Memoirs*.[7] What is clear is that on Lincoln's departure, Grant raced into action. He informed General Halleck on August 1 that he wanted Philip H. Sheridan "put in command of all the troops in the field, with instructions to put himself south of the enemy and follow him to the death."[8] Lincoln had heard such talk before and was not impressed. He wrote Grant a short note calling his decision "exactly right" but warning that it was not being implemented and never would be "unless you watch it every day, and hour, and force it."[9]

It was good advice and would have been ignored by Lincoln's previous top generals—but not by Grant. This time the Union's senior military figure responded, came to Washington himself, and personally directed the consolidation of authority under Sheridan. The result was an autumn campaign of devastation in the Shenandoah Valley that utterly decimated the Rebel threat in northern Virginia and eventually made Sheridan a figure more reviled among ex-Confederates than anyone except perhaps General William T. Sherman. During the final year of the war, Lincoln almost never meddled with Grant's directives and found few occasions like the meeting at Fort Monroe that required a face-to-face consultation. But the fact that he ventured to confront Grant in early August and then kept the pressure on until he achieved a change in policy signaled an important message about his willingness to assert control when he felt it was necessary.

While his parents were visiting Fort Monroe, Robert Lincoln had been vacationing in Saratoga, New York, as a reward for his graduation from college. His mother had attended the July 20 ceremonies at Harvard, but his father had been too busy to break away.[10] By now, it had become painfully clear that father and son were simply not close. Robert later claimed in an autobiographical sketch that they had hardly ever talked or spent time together. His father had traveled frequently as a circuit lawyer when Robert was a young child. As he grew older, the family had sent him away to boarding school and then college in New England. The president's son later wrote that he could only recall receiving paternal advice about his future on just one occasion in his entire life—during the period when he returned to Washington in August 1864.

"I saw my father for a few minutes," Robert Lincoln recalled. "He said: 'Son, what are you going to do now?'" Robert remembered that he had answered, "As long as you object to my joining the army, I am going back to

Harvard to study law." "If you do," his father responded, "you should learn more than I ever did, but you will never have so good a time."[11] Robert Lincoln enrolled at Harvard Law School in September, and once again, spent no more than a few weeks with his father at the Soldiers' Home.

Robert was wrong on at least one fact. It was his mother, not father, apparently blocking his entry into the Union army. According to Mary Lincoln's half-sister, Emilie Todd Helm, who visited the White House briefly in the middle of the war and overhead the first couple heatedly discussing their son's desire to serve, the president was convinced it was their duty to let him go. "Many a poor mother, Mary, has had to make this sacrifice," he reportedly urged, "and has given up every son she had—and lost them all."[12] Ultimately, in the spring of 1865, President Lincoln convinced his wife to let Robert serve on General Grant's staff—not too far from the family, nor too close to the combat.

The dynamic that bound the Lincoln family together remained complicated and difficult to assess in the summer of 1864. Robert Lincoln was home from college but not apparently growing any closer to his father. Husband and wife also maintained some distance from each other. Despite her recent travels with the president, Mary Lincoln still planned to leave the Soldiers' Home for another extended vacation on her own in New York and New England. Sometime in early to mid-August, she left with Tad and escaped to the Equinox Hotel in Manchester, Vermont, not returning again until September 18. For about six or seven of the most critical weeks of his presidency, Lincoln was once again essentially alone and focused on his work.

As he had done in the past, the president sought whatever distractions he needed from his friends. Most important, he had the Stantons—not just the secretary of war but also his family, who lived for most of that summer at a nearby cottage on the Soldiers' Home grounds. Edwin Stanton, like Lincoln, had learned to find real comfort at the wartime sanctuary. For the secretary, whom journalist Noah Brooks described as a "bull-head," someone "opinionated, implacable, intent, and not easily turned from any purpose," this was a major accomplishment. David Bates, the cipher-operator who normally found the secretary "gloomy and peculiar," recalled a story in his memoir that illustrated how Stanton found peace at the Soldiers' Home.

> One evening, in the summer of 1864, I rode out to the Soldiers Home with important despatches for the President and Secretary of War, who were temporarily domiciled with their families in cottages on the grounds of the Home. I found Stanton reclining on the grass, playing with Lewis, one of his children (now living in New Orleans). He invited me to a seat on the greensward while he read the telegrams; and the business being finished, we began talking of early times in Steubenville, Ohio, his native town and mine. One of us mentioned the game of "mumble-the-peg," and he asked me if I could

*One Union general claimed that Secretary of War Edwin Stanton
had "a shaggy, belligerent sort of look."* LIBRARY OF CONGRESS.

play it. Of course I said yes, and he proposed that we should have a game then and there. Stanton entered into the spirit of the boyish sport with great zest, and for the moment all the perplexing questions of the terrible war were forgotten.[13]

The idea of Stanton playing a popular boy's game of knife-throwing skill would have struck almost all his contemporaries as nearly impossible to imagine. Gideon Welles found him occasionally "violent" and perpetually "alarmed." John Usher, secretary of interior, for one vowed never to speak to Stanton, calling him "rude and offensive."[14] One reason that Lincoln grew more attached to Stanton than others did might have been because he saw a relaxed side of the hard-driving secretary that most did not.

Stanton, who had lost his infant son in 1862, also indulged his younger children much the same way that Lincoln spoiled Tad. In fact, Stanton was equally indulgent with Lincoln's youngest son. "Tad was a great friend of Sec. Stanton," recalled Sergeant Charles Derickson of the military guard, "and almost any request he asked was granted." Derickson specifically remembered how going to the War Department with Tad Lincoln often meant barging past flabbergasted generals and contractors, who sometimes had to wait days to see the arrogant cabinet officer.[15]

The president, who spent so much time away from his children, also treated the Stanton boys as surrogate sons. Lewis Stanton, who was about Tad's age, once recalled how Lincoln helped them when the boys had tried to raise a small flock of peacocks at the Soldiers' Home. They grew frustrated when the birds kept flying away. The soldiers from Company K then tied small blocks of wood to the birds' feet that were light enough to allow them to roost in the nearby trees but heavy enough to prevent them from flying off. Yet one evening, according to Lewis Stanton, the birds and their wood contraptions got tangled up in the Soldiers' Home trees.

> Mr. Lincoln and my father arrived at the cottage. They at once noticed the peacocks who were roosting in a small cluster of cedar trees with the ropes and sticks caught in the many small branches and recognized the dangerous and uncomfortable position when on the morrow they would attempt to fly to earth. The two men immediately went to work, solemnly going to and fro unwinding the ropes and getting them in straight lines and carefully placing the small pieces of wood where without catching they would slide off when in the morning the birds flew down.[16]

In some small way, Lincoln's rescue of those poor peacocks symbolized the sanctuary he found at the Soldiers' Home. With or without his own family around him, he continued to seek out distractions in ordinary activities.

Entertaining old friends allowed Lincoln another way to achieve a sense of equilibrium. In the summer of 1864, two of his oldest and closest friends, Joshua Speed and Joseph Gillespie, spent a night at the cottage. They both later recalled that their experience that evening demonstrated to them that Lincoln had grown and matured significantly since their younger days together. Speed, who had lived with Lincoln in Springfield when the two men were bachelors, had probably been the closest friend of his life. He recalled that he was subsequently surprised to discover his old friend in his bedroom reading from the Bible. Alluding to their youthful late-night debates over faith, Speed gently teased his counterpart for abandoning his former skepticism. "You are wrong, Speed," Lincoln answered; "take all of this book upon reason that you can, and the balance on faith, and you will live and die a happier and better man."[17]

Gillespie remembered that earlier in the evening a group of visitors from New Jersey had arrived at the cottage seeking a presidential pardon for some young army deserters from their state who had been scheduled to be executed. Lincoln listened to their pleas, but refused to respond immediately to the request. He told the group to return the next morning to the White House to hear his verdict. Gillespie was unsure how his friend was leaning. "Before retiring," he recalled, "I told Mr. Lincoln that I could not sleep unless I had some inkling as to how he was going to decide in regard to these poor fellows." Lincoln responded by saying, "I can't tell you; but I will say this, that I have always found that mercy bears richer fruits than strict justice."[18]

The president also had some new friends interacting with him at the Soldiers' Home. Since the end of 1863, the Union Light Guard of Ohio had served as his cavalry escort, replacing Company A from the 11th New York Cavalry unit. From the beginning, this new cavalry detail had a special designation. Recruiters had sought only a handful of representatives from each of the state's eighty-eight counties in a whirlwind two-month tour during November and December 1863. They formed the 7th Independent Company of Ohio Voluntary Cavalry, better known as the Union Light Guard, under the command of Captain George A. Bennett and lieutenants Arthur W. White and James B. Jamieson. The Ohio men had arrived in the nation's capital at the very end of December.

For Willard Cutter and other members of the Bucktail infantry company already assigned to the president, the fact that a cavalry escort had been hand-picked for presidential duty struck them as confirmation of their own importance. "Guarding the president has got to be a big thing," Cutter had reported to his mother. From the infantry soldier's perspective, the new troops made his life easier. "They dont interfere with us any," he had written, noting that they guarded the White House gates. For the newly recruited cavalrymen, however, such mundane assignments represented an enormous letdown. Company member George C. Ashmun recalled that a small crisis in morale developed as the Union Light Guard spent most of the spring drilling and waiting for action. "To some of the men who had completed partial or full courses of collegiate education," he wrote after the war, "there was little glory or other satisfaction in two or three hours a day of rubbing the coats of those black horses!"[19]

"We enjoyed our summer work much more than we did the winter guard duty," recalled Private Smith Stimmel. "This part of the service gave us an opportunity to see a good deal of the everyday life of the President." Stimmel noted that Lincoln would often "take a stroll down along the edge of the grove where our tents were pitched," occasionally peeking inside the men's tents and "have a passing word with them." "We always felt that the President took a personal interest in us," Stimmel claimed; "He never spoke absent-mindedly, but talked to the men as if he were thinking of them."[20] Fellow company member Robert McBride shared an almost identical impression. "Occasionally Mr. Lincoln would go among the men and chat familiarly with them," he wrote. "Mr. Lincoln's manner on such occasions was that of one having a genuine, kindly interest in the members of the company and a wish to learn how matters looked from their point of view. There was nothing patronizing about it, nor anything savoring of condescension or superciliousness."[21]

On several occasions, the troops were impressed by Lincoln's down-to-earth qualities. Stimmel recalled that one afternoon in the summer of 1864 as the entourage was returning to the Soldiers' Home along the Seventh Street Road, they passed some cows grazing on the unoccupied land at the edge of the city. Suddenly, according to the young private, the president and Lieutenant White, who was accompanying him, veered off the road and began an impromptu inspection of the animals. "You see, just as I told you," Stimmel overheard the president saying to the lieutenant. Later he found out that the former frontiersman-turned-president had been explaining to his skeptical riding companion that the cow was "a lop-sided animal" with one side higher than the other, a biological fact he set out to prove by closer examination.[22]

Both McBride and Stimmel related a story that the president had shared with the men at the Soldiers' Home camp after hearing of their desire to see combat. Apparently by August, several members of the Union Light Guard were becoming anxious to enter the field. Jubal Early's raid on the capital in July had stoked their fighting instincts and there was some grumbling around the campfire that their talents were being wasted on this unnecessary duty. According to Stimmel, the members of the company later recalled this pointed anecdote, which they dubbed "The Pigtail Story." McBride recorded the president telling the story in this fashion:

> You boys remind me of a farmer friend of mine in Illinois, who said he could never understand why the Lord put the curl in a pig's tail. It never seemed to him to be either useful or ornamental, but he reckoned the Almighty knew what he was doing when he put it there.[23]

Stimmel claimed that Lincoln made the point with a "twinkle in his eye" but concluded his storytelling with a mild rebuke, reminding the soldiers that if they left for the front, some other unit would have to replace them and that ultimately it was a soldier's duty to obey orders.[24]

There were 108 members of the original Light Guard, including four free black cooks. One-third of the soldiers listed their occupation as farmers. There were several teachers like McBride and even some students. There were clerks, merchants, and hotelkeepers. A number of soldiers had experience as craftsmen or tradesmen, working before the war as carpenters, tinners, coopers, stonecutters, or bricklayers. Only a handful of the men had been professionals—a few dentists, one engineer, but not a single lawyer. And finally, a few more romantic combatants described themselves as painters or artists.[25]

From this unexceptional-sounding background, however, came a surprising degree of contentiousness. By mid-summer 1864, the company was literally at war with itself. Both its senior officers faced courts-martial and, by the end of the war, had been dismissed from service. Captain Bennett was charged with a variety of counts involving the misuse of government resources and men. He was accused by his own men of using government-issued forage to feed private horses, of keeping a cow for his own benefit at public expense, of using a corporal in the company to perform personal chores and of stealing rations and thereby starving his own men. Prosecutors added a final charge of making false returns.

In retrospect, it appears that Bennett was irascible, unpopular with his men, and perhaps because of his experience with the 11th New York Cavalry, treated as an outsider. He was guilty of charges that under different circumstances might have gone unreported by his soldiers. Robert McBride recalled one instance involving Tad Lincoln that illustrated the captain's discipline problems. During an inspection outside the White House, young Tad showed up to observe in his military-style uniform. "Captain Bennett took position in front of the company to deliver his usual scolding," reported McBride, "Tad stood by his side." The officer worked himself up toward a fiery conclusion, claiming that their quarters "look like . . ." but before he could let loose his string of curses, he was interrupted as "Tad's shrill voice rang out, completing the sentence in a manner more pungent than elegant and quite unprintable." According to McBride, even the Light Guard captain finally "relaxed in a broad smile" while the members of the company "burst into unrebuked laughter."[26]

As summer had approached, whatever laughter had existed was replaced by sullen determination. Malcontents in the unit had been gathering in Lieutenant Jamieson's tent during the slow months of guard duty. They had shared stories about Bennett's insults and infractions until their fury boiled over just before the company was reassigned to the Soldiers' Home.

Bennett protested fiercely during his court martial trial, which began in early July 1864 and continued for months. He claimed that disgruntled company members had plotted against him almost from the beginning of their tour of duty. With biting sarcasm, he implied that the men had been spoiled by their status as the presidential escort and bored by the absence of action.

Now on what does this specification [for the charge of starving the men] rest for support? Merely on the fact that the men of the company came here from Ohio to be the body guard of the President of the United States to live in Washington in the same style as his Excellency, to have servants and live in a palace. No soldiers' rations were to be fed to them. They were to have soft, fresh bread 3 times a day, Tenderloin Steak & Broiled Chickens—none of your hardtack or salt-meats for us. And while his Excellency occupied his winter quarters in town they had no occupation except that of seeking cause for grumbling. After a short time the occasion presented itself. Hardtack was issued and they were immediately starved. . . . As they could not command the accused, they . . . assembled in [Lieutenant] Jamieson's quarters night after night to lay plans for revenge as revenge they must have for being compelled to eat hardtack.[27]

Bennett was eventually found guilty and dismissed from service in June 1865. His second in command, Arthur White, also ran afoul of military rules and was accused in 1864 of misapplying forage, milking a government cow for his own benefit, "tormenting cows" on the White House grounds, filing false ration reports, and violating the terms of his arrest. According to the specifications of the charges, White ordered his men to "tie tin articles, namely cups, pans, and buckets, to the tails of said cows" near the Executive Mansion. On this count, and on the count of violating the terms of his arrest, White was found guilty and cashiered from the service.[28] With both Bennett and White dismissed from duty, Lieutenant James B. Jamieson finished the war with command of the contentious Union Light Guard detail.

Lincoln was surely aware of the problems within his cavalry escort though he made no recorded comments about them. That was probably because he was too busy facing down his own internal revolt. By August 1864, there was widespread disenchantment within the Republican party about his leadership of the Union coalition. Lincoln's job had always required a delicate balancing act of interests and principles. The unexpected military stalemate coupled with heated political disputes over legislative prerogatives and an endless variety of local patronage problems left the administration besieged and ultimately put the president's own renomination in jeopardy.

On the political front, Lincoln seemed to be suffering through the worst of all possible circumstances as factions on all sides found reason to be upset with him. Simmering resentment over the president's pocket veto of the Wade-Davis bill boiled over in early August with the publication of what was called a "manifesto" by Senator Benjamin Wade and Representative Henry Winter Davis. The document defended their reconstruction plan and charged Lincoln with encroaching on congressional authority and "holding the electoral votes of the Rebel states at the dictation of his personal ambition."[29] This was a statement of open political warfare from two leading congressional radicals and served to mobilize the various radical forces who had long been frustrated by the slow pace of Lincoln's decision making on questions such as emancipation and the conduct of the war. Several leading radicals began secretly discussing the feasibility of removing Lincoln from the Union ticket. A few considered endorsing a third-party candidate, such as General John C. Frémont, who had been the very first Republican presidential nominee in 1856 and now was attempting to run as an independent. Others jockeyed behind the scenes for a new nominee—Salmon Chase, Ulysses Grant, or some potentially unifying figure besides the unpopular president.

During this period, Lincoln attempted to sound out figures from all factions and to personally solicit help from those who might go out on the stump for him and the party in the fall. He reached out to Carl Schurz, a German-American politician from Wisconsin who was serving in the Union army and who was identified with the radical faction. On August 11, John Hay had summoned Schurz to Washington on behalf of the president.[30] This was not unexpected. Despite offering occasional criticism of the administration, Schurz had been willing over the previous months to provide intelligence about radical activities, particularly about those who supported John Frémont's third-party candidacy.[31]

Schurz spent an evening at the Soldiers' Home with Lincoln discussing the heated political situation. At the cottage, the guest recalled that the president asked him to sit "on a lounge in a sort of parlor which was rather scantily furnished." Then Lincoln "began to speak about the attacks made upon him by party friends, and their efforts to force his withdrawal from the candidacy." According to Schurz, the president went on at length about the injustice of the attacks, knowing his words would get repeated to key figures out in the country. "And now to have it said by men who have been my friends and who ought to know me better that I have been seduced by what they call the lust of power," complained the president, was an outrage. He was openly bitter. "Have they thought of that common cause when trying to break me down? I hope they have," he added grimly. Schurz, who was twenty years younger than the president, listened patiently until Lincoln exhausted his bile. Eventually, however, the president's mood brightened and before Schurz left for the evening, Lincoln "indulged himself in a few humorous remarks" and told his guest, "Well, things might look better, and they might look worse."[32]

Although many historians have emphasized the gloom hanging over the president during this period, his parting remarks to Schurz probably reflected both the core of his outlook and the focus of his determined strategy. He was concerned, maybe even tense, but definitely not panicked or even gloomy. Despite everything, he was methodically reaching out to stump speakers like the promising young German-American politician, assiduously preparing for the fall campaign. He had a message to deliver through Schurz, and he delivered it with authority. "Have they thought of that common cause when trying to break me down?" he had asked pointedly. Lincoln understood something that most of his radical critics did not. He was not going to be intimidated into resigning from office or pushed into stepping aside as a nominee for reelection. What the president had effectively told Schurz at the Soldiers' Home was that he was going to force a choice within the party: either rally behind his administration or allow the antiwar Democrats to win control of the White House and thereby lose the fight to end slavery. It was a stark choice, but Lincoln was in a stronger position than any of the malcontents appeared to understand.

Almost perversely, the president's political strength lay in the extent of the forces arrayed against him. His policies had frustrated not only radicals but also conservatives. In this case, what stoked the conservative fire was not his moderate approach to reconstruction—which they generally approved—but rather his stubborn insistence on upholding the emancipation doctrine. Their concern exploded with the release of the "To Whom It May Concern" letter in the aftermath of Early's raid on Washington. That document had been issued on July 18 with the intention of clarifying the Union position on conditions for holding peace negotiations with the Confederacy. At that time, newspaper editor Horace Greeley had been pressuring the administration to receive a self-appointed peace delegation from Richmond that was reportedly waiting at Niagara Falls, Canada. Skeptical of the situation, Lincoln had provided Greeley with a terse statement announcing that his administration would consider "any proposition" for ending the war which included the "integrity of the whole Union" and the "abandonment of slavery."[33] Since the Confederate states would never voluntarily abandon slavery, Lincoln's letter had the effect of scuttling the talks even before they could begin.

For conservatives, this intransigence on Lincoln's part was almost inconceivable. They believed that the continued military stalemate, the prospect of a Union party defeat at the November polls, and the rising body count of dead white men more than justified some horse-trading on the question of black freedom. On Tuesday, August 16, 1864, Alexander W. Randall, the former governor of Wisconsin and then an assistant postmaster general, handed the president a revealing letter from Charles D. Robinson, an editor of a Wisconsin Democratic newspaper that had been loyal to the administration. Robinson's letter, dated August 7, summarized the heated objections of many conservatives, both Republican and Democratic, who had been supporting the Union cause. Robinson claimed that by making "abandonment of slavery" a precondition for peace talks, the president had put "the whole war question on a new basis." He wrote that while he had supported the limited goals of the Emancipation Proclamation as "sound war policy," he had never intended to align himself with a sustained, national abolition effort. Ignoring the previous year's discussion about "a new birth of freedom," Robinson zeroed in on the politics of emancipation for the 1864 campaign. He blasted the president's July 18 letter, arguing that it "takes us War Democrats clear off our feet, leaving us no ground to stand upon" and threatened that he would be unable to support the reelection effort.[34] Lincoln took this threat seriously and immediately worked on drafting a response. Within a few days, he apparently informed William P. Dole, another administration official, that he was prepared to discuss his draft response with Randall on Friday evening at the Soldiers' Home.[35]

How Lincoln ultimately handled the Charles Robinson incident illustrated a great deal about his evolution as president. It is fair to say that this was one of the most pivotal moments of his administration—at least in political terms. The president was on the verge of being ousted as the Union Party nominee, his wartime coalition of Republicans and loyal Democrats having been ruptured almost beyond repair. Three years of controversial decisions finally seemed to have caught up with the beleaguered politician. There was no good news on the military front yet to save him or distract his rivals. And in this severe crisis, he was living alone at the Soldiers' Home. Even John Hay, his loyal young aide, was now out of town on vacation.

Under such intense pressure, Lincoln's first impulse was toward appeasement. He began his response to the conservative Wisconsin editor with uncharacteristically evasive political double-talk. "To me," he wrote in his pencil draft, "it seems plain that saying re-union and abandonment of slavery would be considered if offered is not saying that nothing else would be considered if offered." Looking over those words, the president must have quickly realized how offensive they would sound to other audiences. So he added in the next sentence, "But I will not stand upon the mere construction of language." Then he offered a powerful and incisive review of his statements on emancipation since the summer of 1862. Quoting from his letters to Horace Greeley—"What I do about slavery, and the colored race, I do because I believe it helps to save the Union"—and to James Conkling—"the promise being made, must be kept"—he vigorously defended emancipation as a military measure of continued importance. To negotiate without insisting upon the abandonment of slavery, he asserted, "would instantly ruin the Union cause itself" because African-American recruiting would "cease" and black soldiers would "throw down their arms."[36]

On Friday, August 19, Lincoln decided to test these arguments on Frederick Douglass, who, like Carl Schurz, had been called to Washington to discuss the upcoming electoral contest. If the president had imagined that his defense of emancipation would please the abolitionist orator, then he was sorely mistaken.

Douglass argued vehemently that the double-talk in the letter would be perceived as "a complete surrender of your anti-slavery policy, and do you serious damage."[37] Gazing across his White House desk at the former slave and contemplating his impossible position, Lincoln must have heard the words he had uttered to Schurz just a few days before echoing in his head—"*Have they thought of that common cause when trying to break me down?*"

Once again, the president decided to remind his guest about the high stakes of the election. Lincoln tersely suggested that "something should be done" to warn southern slaves that they must not expect emancipation if the Democrats won the 1864 elections. He urged Douglass to organize an effort that might prepare those slaves still in bondage after November to make their escape. The message was indisputable. Now was not the time for political in-fighting among loyal Unionists. The black abolitionist returned to New York, made some inquiries, and dutifully reported back to the president several days later on how such "desirable work" might be executed.[38] Historian David Blight has described the idea as offering "an unprecedented alliance between black leadership and federal power," almost a government-sponsored Underground Railroad.[39] But when Douglass reflected on the proposal to radical antislavery editor Theodore Tilton in October, he claimed it was what had "alarmed me most" about the meeting. By this point, however, he was also fully aware of the consequences of opposing Lincoln. The president's defeat meant the continuation of slavery. Swallowing his misgivings, he decided to support Lincoln's reelection.[40]

President Lincoln had told former governor Randall and Indian Affairs commissioner Dole to come to the Soldiers' Home that evening on August 19, to discuss his response to the Robinson letter. Randall decided to bring along Judge Joseph T. Mills, a prominent local Wisconsin politician who was in the capital on a visit. Mills recorded in his diary that Randall, apparently quite frugal, kept haggling with taxi drivers on Pennsylvania Avenue until he found one who would take them to the cottage for $1.50. "We got aboard his carriage, & drove out 4 or 5 miles to what is called the Soldiers Retreat," reported the out-of-towner. "We passed vast numbers of tents, entered into grounds intersected with gravil walks, running in all sorts of curves." The judge found the presidential cottage to be "not imposing in magnitude" and practically concealed by trees. After being admitted inside by a valet, the guests "entered a large, neat, plainly furnished room" dominated by a marble table in its center. "Soon appeared a tall slightly stooping gentleman, approaching with long, rapid strides," wrote Mills, noting that the president had "large feet with larger slippers."[41]

Governor Randall introduced Judge Mills to the president and the men exchanged pleasantries. Apparently noticing Lincoln's haggard demeanor, Randall asked why he did not "seek some place of retirement for a few weeks," assuring him that he "would be reinvigorated." Lincoln replied that three weeks "would do me no good." He told his guests that "my thoughts, my solicitude for this great country follow me where ever I go." Then the president turned abruptly to the issue at hand. "I don't think it is personal vanity, or ambition," he said, "but I cannot but feel that the weal or woe of this great nation will be decided in the approaching canvas."[42]

Lincoln was surprisingly firm about what he considered the mistaken assumptions of Democrats, like General McClellan, who claimed to support the war but not his wartime policies. "The war democrat depends upon conciliation," he stated, after asserting vigorously that "You cannot concilliate [*sic*] the South." At times, he grew openly sarcastic. "We have to hold territory," he noted, "Where are the war democrats to do it[?]" But his focus was on the sacrifices of black soldiers. Referring to recent encounters in which African Americans had demonstrated their heroism, the president grew passionate in his denunciation.

> There have been men who have proposed to me to return to slavery the black warriors of Port Hudson & Olustee to their masters to conciliate the South. I should be damned in time & in eternity for so doing.

Lincoln continued to assert that his grounds for supporting black freedom were both moral and practical. He claimed that "no human power can subdue this rebellion without using the Emancipation lever as I have done."[43]

Judge Mills was impressed. "The President appeared to be not the pleasant joker I had expected to see," he wrote, "but a man of deep convictions & an unutterable yearning for the success of the Union cause." William Dole showed up at the cottage in the middle of their conversation and extended their talk even longer. The president read them his response to the Robinson letter and they offered suggestions. Lincoln listened and then turned the topic of conversation to "reminiscences of the past" and began speaking about his famous 1858 debates against Stephen Douglas. With the question of race on his mind, the president related a funny story about a Democratic party orator during the campaign who had warned his audiences that if the Republicans won, then "darkies" would soon be allowed to vote. He recalled how the speaker then pointed out a white and a black man in the crowd, asking each which senatorial candidate he would vote for if he could. The white man answered Douglas, but the black man, "a Sambo," said, "I would vote for Massa Lincoln." "Now . . . what do you think of that," the Democrat had asked rhetorically. According to the president, an old farmer then cried out, "I think the darkey showd a damd sight of more sense than the white man."[44]

"The President was now in full flow of spirits," Mills reported, as Lincoln took a seat on the sofa by his side. "I was astonished at his elasticity of spirits," the visitor wrote in his journal. Eager to join in the conversation, Judge Mills then related to the president how he had run into Frederick Douglass earlier in the day at the White House. He claimed that in a darkened antechamber outside the presidential office, he had been "rivetted" by the great man's "remarkable physiognomy" and had been caught staring at him. In an earlier diary entry, Mills had described how he had cautiously approached the black man, asking if he was the famous orator, to which Douglass had stiffly replied, "That's what they call me." But during his conversation with the president, Mills now pretended that he had actually mistaken Douglass for Lincoln himself and had innocently asked the black orator, "Are you the president?" The men proceeded to joke about "miscegenation" or racial mixing before bringing their evening discussion to a close.[45]

By telling "Sambo" jokes and laughing at the wounded vanity of Frederick Douglass, President Lincoln used his "elasticity of spirits" to disarm men who might otherwise have questioned his political decisions. Randall, Dole, and Mills were loyal to the administration, but they were pragmatic politicians who expected him to offer a more generous response to War Democrats besides warnings of damnation if he rescinded emancipation. In a subsequent version of the letter to Robinson, Lincoln did attempt to mollify the disgruntled conservative element. He experimented with an opening line that would have been even more offensive to Frederick Douglass, now writing: "To me it seems plain that saying re-union and abandonment of slavery would be considered, if offered, is not saying that nothing *else* or *less* would be considered, if offered." He still kept many of the quotations from his earlier letters to Greeley and Conkling, but now defended his emancipation policy on almost exclusively practical grounds. "It is not a question of sentiment or taste," he wrote of the need for holding black troops in the army, "but one of physical force, which may be measured, and estimated as horsepower, and steam power, are measured and estimated." Then he ended his revised appeal with a stunning declaration. "If Jefferson Davis wishes, for himself, or for the benefit of his friends at the North, to know what I would do if he were to offer peace and re-union, saying nothing about slavery, let him try me."[46]

Sending this response to Robinson might have signaled the beginning of the end for black freedom as a Union war aim. Instead, the president never released his August 17 response—in any of its versions. He simply buried it in his papers. In retrospect, it appears that Lincoln had accomplished his goals in other ways. He had used the drafting of the letter and his discussion of the process to shape the attitudes of other political figures as much as to clarify his own think-ing. It was also no coincidence that he had accomplished this at the Soldiers' Home. The presidential sanctuary offered a more casual setting than the offi-cial residence—and a better forum to display his "elasticity of spirits." But most historians have missed this key bit of context because the passage from Judge Mills's diary that was included in Lincoln's *Collected Works* covered only the interview itself. To find out that this meeting with the judge, Governor Randall, and Commissioner Dole had taken place at the Soldiers' Home re-quires an examination of the original diary at the State Historical Society of Wisconsin.[47]

Lincoln's habit of floating and then withdrawing proposals was one that he employed with surprising frequency at the end of August 1864. He authorized Henry Raymond, editor of the *New York Times*, to undertake a secret peace mission to Richmond—only to change his mind and cancel his plans at the last minute. He drafted a memorandum for his cabinet that discussed the prospect of his own defeat in November, but then filed it away without even letting them read it. When a man named Isaac M. Schermerhorn asked for a letter to be read to a Union meeting in Buffalo, New York, the president initially wrote something that echoed his Robinson letter, but then declined to send it along.

One way to interpret these actions is to portray Lincoln as undecided and vacillating. But his deft handling of his various guests on August 19 suggests a more controlled frame of mind. The president had apparently decided by this stage in the war that he what needed to do was remind some of his so-called friends about the stakes of the contest. He needed them to see the complicated and contested nature of his decisions from his perspective. To accomplish this goal, he allowed several of them, in effect, to see him at work. In his unsent letter to Isaac Schermerhorn, Lincoln explained his decision making in terms that showed how thoroughly he had considered his difficult position and how confident he was in the rightness of his actions. "In taking the various steps which have led to my present position in relation to the war, the public interest and my private interest, have been perfectly paralel [*sic*]," he wrote, "because in no other way could I serve myself so well, as by truly serving the Union."

> The whole field has been open to me, where to choose. No place-hunting necessity has been upon me urging me to seek a position of antagonism to some other man, irrespec-tive of whether such position might be favorable or unfavorable to the Union. Of course I may err in judgment; but my present position in reference to the rebellion is the result of my best judgment, and according to that best judgment, it is the only position upon which any Executive can or could save the Union.[48]

9

"Whatever is, is right"

FEARS ABOUT POSSIBLE ATTEMPTS TO HARM OR KIDNAP ABRAHAM LINCOLN INCREASED throughout 1864. In March, the *New York Tribune* first reported on an alleged Rebel conspiracy to abduct the president. The same month, Willard Cutter noted that a man went "crazy" inside the White House, ranting about how "he would be the next President" before guards managed to arrest him.[1] By May, Senator James Lane of Kansas made a special trip to the White House to warn John Hay that the president "must now chiefly guard against assassination." The aide "poohpoohed" the concerns, in his words, arguing calmly that "every prominent man was more or less exposed to the attacks of maniacs."[2] A reported incident near the Soldiers' Home in mid-August 1864 added to the sense of rising anxiety.

About eleven o'clock one night, Private John W. Nichols of Company K was on guard duty at the large gate on the edge of the institution's grounds when he heard a rifle shot and then witnessed the "bareheaded" president riding quickly on horseback toward his cottage. Private Nichols asked the president about his missing hat and was told that "somebody had fired a gun off at the foot of the hill" which frightened Lincoln's horse and then led to a struggle to regain control that had "jerked his hat off." Concerned, Nichols recalled years later that he and another member of the company went down the twisting driveway toward the main road where they discovered the president's signature silk plug hat with a bullet hole through the crown. The next day Nichols claimed that he returned the item to the president, who assured him "rather unconcernedly" that the whole episode was the product of "some foolish gunner" and that he wanted the matter "kept quiet."[3]

Private John W. Nichols claimed after the war that he witnessed Lincoln escaping an assassin's bullet near the Soldiers' Home.
ILLINOIS STATE HISTORICAL LIBRARY, SPRINGFIELD, ILL.

The episode and Lincoln's response—if Nichols was remembering the story accurately—was characteristic of the president's determined posture during this generally tense period. He was continuing his daily commute, holding regular meetings at the White House, and even bringing more of his work back to the Soldiers' Home in the evenings. Fully aware of the precariousness of his position, the president appeared determined to make full use of his time in office.

On August 24, he spent part of an evening on the Soldiers' Home tower observing an exercise in nighttime Morse code signaling. Since the beginning of the conflict, Lincoln had demonstrated an interest in the technology of warfare. He had always provided an open door at the White House for inventors and innovators. On several occasions, he had even participated in tests of new weapons. This interest in the "tools of war" was not unexpected since Lincoln was the first (and so far only) president to have received a patent. In 1849, he had developed a method for improving the navigation of boats through shallow water.[4]

The test that Lincoln witnessed on August 24 involved hand-operated calcium lights that flashed Morse signals in the dark. Justin Dimmick, governor of the Soldiers' Home, and officers from the Naval Department and Signal Corps joined the president on the tower of the main hall. They observed cipher operators from the War Department Telegraph Office using the calcium lights to send Morse signals between the Smithsonian Institute and the Soldiers' Home, a distance of more than three miles. "Mr. Lincoln was greatly interested in this exhibition," recalled one of the operators, "and expressed the opinion that the signal system of both the army and navy could and would be improved so as to become of immense value to the Government."[5]

Four nights later, on Sunday, August 28, 1864, Lincoln was once again at work in the evening. In this case, a Baltimore attorney rousted him from his bed at midnight to discuss a presidential commutation for his clients, four men convicted of espionage and sentenced to death. Charles J. M. Gwinn was a War Democrat and son-in-law of U.S. Senator Reverdy Johnson (Unionist, Maryland). Gwinn was a combative figure, unafraid of violating protocol. Before the war, President James Buchanan had blackballed him for an appointment as U.S. attorney because he had dared to challenge the regular Democratic electoral slate.[6] Now he was fighting for the lives of four men and did not hesitate to rush down to Washington to confront the president himself. "For Gods sake," he had wired Postmaster General Montgomery Blair earlier in the day, "entreat the President to grant a respite to the four men condemned to die tomorrow."[7]

Nothing could have seemed more dramatic. Life and death literally appeared to hang in the balance as the sleepy president shuffled down the stairs in his oversized slippers to meet the agitated attorney, presumably pacing away in the parlor. But it was all a misunderstanding. Lincoln had received a telegram from Senator Johnson on Saturday and had already decided to commute the sentences for the four men to hard labor. John G. Nicolay, the senior White House aide, had transmitted this order to General Lewis Wallace on the afternoon of August 28, but Gwinn somehow had missed this news as he flew down to Washington. Naturally, he was apologetic, thanking the rumpled president for his "genuine kindness" and begging forgiveness for his unnecessary intrusion. "I shall always remember with grateful feelings," the attorney wrote the next day, "our mid-night interview at the Soldiers Rest."[8]

Shortly after the encounter with Gwinn, Lincoln invited Henry S. Huidekoper to the cottage to discuss a controversial plan for recruiting Union soldiers from among the Confederate prisoners of war. A native of Meadville, Pennsylvania, Colonel Huidekoper had been a primary organizer of the Bucktail regiment that had provided the infantry company currently serving as the president's military guard. In the spring of 1863, he had attempted to bring Company K into the field with the rest of the regiment but had been overruled by the president himself. If the men in Willard Cutter's unit had gone to the front with the Army of the Potomac, they would have ended up at the Battle of Gettysburg, where Huidekoper, a slim, young Harvard-educated officer, had lost his arm.

Unable to continue leading troops in the field, Huidekoper was interested in helping behind the lines. He and some other political figures from Meadville, including the president's friend David Derickson, conceived a plan to offer foreign-born Confederate prisoners of war the opportunity to avoid indefinite detention by taking a loyalty oath and agreeing to serve in the Union army. They had an interest in the proposal because they hoped to use these men to count against their local enrollment quotas. By this stage of the war, the customary exchanges of prisoners had ceased—owing, at least initially, to the refusal of Confederates to include black soldiers in the arrangements. The result was horrible overcrowding, especially in southern prisons, but also in the North. There was ample reason to believe that many Rebel prisoners held in northern camps would embrace almost any chance to escape the grueling conditions. Lincoln listened to Huidekoper on the night of August 31, 1864, and signed an order on the following day that authorized him to recruit volunteers for this program at the Rock Island, Illinois, prison camp.[9]

What is most interesting about this episode is not the results of the recruitment—Huidekoper later claimed about 2,400 ex-prisoners were sent to the West to fight Indians—but rather the temporary rupture it created between President Lincoln and Secretary of War Stanton and between the president and General Grant. Both Stanton and Grant vehemently opposed the idea. At first, Stanton even refused to execute Huidekoper's order. He did not object to employing foreign-born Rebels in the war effort, but he thought it an outrage to count them against local draft quotas. Provost Marshall General James B. Fry claimed that he witnessed an ugly scene between Lincoln and Stanton as a result of their disagreement over this proposal. "Mr. President I cannot do it," the Secretary reportedly said. "The order is an improper one, and I cannot execute it." Lincoln refused to back down, announcing heatedly, "Mr. Secretary, it will have to be done."[10] When Grant added his protests to the policy, Lincoln retreated, slightly. He refused to rescind the order but promised the general that "no other of the sort, will be authorized."[11]

Two factors probably explain Lincoln's stubborn insistence on this measure: politics and friendship. There had been draft riots in Meadville during the previous year. Pennsylvania was a critical state in the upcoming elections. Easing tension over the draft could only help stabilize an uneasy political situation. The president heard as much in a confidential report from David Derickson in mid-September. "Our people are much pleased with the arrangement," the officer wrote, "and fully appreciate the benefits it has secured to them." He added that "nothing could have been done that would have produced a better state of feeling in our midst."[12] This report from Derickson was not just a political analysis from an ordinary provost marshal. It was a friendly letter from a former companion. Huidekoper was not as close to Lincoln as Derickson had been when the latter was captain of Company K, but the young man still knew the president from his days of drilling troops around the Soldiers' Home. He had also attended Harvard at the same time as the president's son Robert, and his missing arm served as a solemn reminder of the terrible sacrifice he had already offered to the Union cause. Personal loyalty as well as political interest thus drew Lincoln into a rare confrontation with other members of the Union high command.

The same day that Lincoln signed Huidekoper's order, Confederate forces evacuated their positions around Atlanta, Georgia. Arguably no other military event in the war had a greater political impact than this one. Since March 1864, when General Grant had gone east to assume his new role as general in chief of the Union armies, William Sherman had been attempting to lead a successful Federal campaign from Tennessee into Georgia, the heartland of the Confederacy. For months, Sherman had been engaged in a frustrating campaign of maneuver with Confederate armies. His slow progress, coupled with Grant's bloody, stalemated campaign against Richmond, had demoralized many northerners and contributed significantly to Lincoln's summertime political problems. The fall of Atlanta appeared to change everything. Lincoln probably would have won the November contest even without the capture of this key Rebel stronghold (since the Democratic party was handicapped by the absence of southern electoral votes), but General Sherman's success lifted public morale and quieted the president's most severe critics.

The stunning Union victory also disrupted the political strategy of northern Democrats. The day before the evacuation of Atlanta, the Democrats had nominated General George B. McClellan as their presidential candidate. The move was not unexpected, but the dominance and vitriol of the antiwar forces at the national convention had been surprising to many. Party organizer August Belmont, a leading financier, told the assembled delegates in Chicago that four years of "misrule by a sectional, fanatical and corrupt party, have brought our country to the verge of ruin."[13] Antiwar delegates, or "Peace Democrats" as they were called, succeeded in winning approval for a plank in the platform that declared "after four years of failure," the time had come for a "cessation of hostilities."[14] These words made sense in August but sounded increasingly off-key after the fall of Atlanta. "Almost every Democratic candidate in the country," writes political historian David Long, "was hurt to some degree by the Chicago convention."[15]

The nomination of McClellan, one of the war's most notable generals, on such a vehement antiwar platform also appeared to be a strange balancing act that fooled nobody. The Democrats now appeared even more divided than the Unionists. In the upcoming days, McClellan tried awkwardly to distance himself from the language of his own party's platform. Union politicians gleefully capitalized on their opponents' problems by highlighting charges of domestic treason among the "Copperhead" Democrats. By some accounts, the damage to the Democratic party lasted for decades as their candidates repeatedly fought against an image of disloyalty that was seared into the public mind during the fall of 1864.

As the tide of the war and the campaign finally began to improve, Lincoln's thoughts returned to his family. "All reasonably well," he wired Mary Lincoln at the end of August. "Bob is not here yet. How is dear Tad?" The president's eldest son was due to arrive from New York carrying an important letter from John Nicolay. The White House aide was in the city trying to help sort out a contentious patronage issue that had been threatening the unity of the reelection effort. The problem was eventually settled, but Robert Lincoln, as usual, did not apparently feel pressed to rush back to Washington. A few days later, as the full impact of Atlanta's capture sank in, Lincoln sounded more certain about his status. "All well," he wrote on September 8, "including Tad's pony and the goats." The president reported to his wife that their son had already departed the capital, after only a brief visit, and had indicated that he was not necessarily planning to visit with his mother and brother in Vermont.[16]

In the same telegram, the president also noted for Mary Lincoln that the wife of the new Soldiers' Home governor, Colonel Justin Dimmick, had recently died. His decision to relay this sad news suggests that to some degree the Lincolns socialized with the senior officers at the Soldiers' Home while they were in residence. Dimmick was a retired colonel from Vermont who had been appointed in January 1864 to replace the long-serving acting head of the Home, Deputy Governor Colonel Thomas L. Alexander. The changeover had been contentious. Dissatisfied at being passed over, Alexander had resigned and had returned to Kentucky. Attending Surgeon Benjamin King, the other leading officer at the Home during the Civil War years, also fell out of favor and found himself forced out by December 1864 after eleven years of service.[17]

The story behind Alexander's resignation reveals a great deal about the challenges of managing a federal government institution in the Civil War era. From 1858 to 1864, there had been no formal governor of the Soldiers' Home. Alexander, the deputy governor, had served throughout this period as the acting chief. He had been a popular and respected figure, who seemed to excel at squeezing the most out of the Home's tight budget and limited resources. Prior to his tenure, residents were provided with practically no organized outlets for recreation—not even a library. Alexander recommended several changes aimed at improving morale among the residents, including the installation of a small bowling alley and a smoking lounge. The Soldiers' Home Board of Commissioners rejected those requests, but they did approve his plan to begin several newspaper subscriptions, and they authorized a handful of book purchases.

In retrospect, the strictness of the regime seems almost heartless. The disabled residents were expected, like regular Army soldiers, to clean their own rooms, cook their own rations, and attend to miscellaneous physical duties around the grounds. The institution employed only a few paid hands, such as a farmer, a gardener, and a hospital steward. In addition, early in the war the board cut back on extra pay for residents and even eliminated the tobacco allowance in what must have been perceived as a drastic cost-cutting measure.[18] Somehow, Alexander, a southerner, managed to juggle his competing pressures with aplomb. The official historian of the Soldiers' Home called his work "outstanding," and President Lincoln claimed that he found Alexander "very agreeable."[19] The praise from the commander in chief was especially noteworthy because at the beginning of the conflict Lincoln had received a small flurry of letters accusing the Kentucky-born Alexander of being a secessionist.[20] The continued rumors about Alexander's southern sympathies probably explain why he was passed over for promotion in January 1864.

During the period when the Lincoln family occupied their cottage at the Soldiers' Home, there was a total of about two hundred retired military personnel either admitted or already in residence at the institution. These men, some aging veterans from the War of 1812 and others much younger but hobbled by crippling injuries, often proved incapable of resting peacefully. Prior to the outbreak of the war, the attending surgeon had claimed that while a majority of the residents were "good and excellent men," there were others "so bad as to put to shame a penitentiary convict."[21]

Nearly half the 184 wartime residents whose presence was noted in the official reports deserted, went absent without leave (AWOL), or failed to return from furlough. Private John Carpenter, a forty-six-year-old Irish immigrant who had served in the infantry for twenty-two years, fled the Home on October 12, 1862, while the president was in residence. The official roster describes Carpenter as an "incorrigible drunkard" who came and went repeatedly before being dismissed in 1863. Alcohol was a common problem for the bored, often severely crippled men. Thomas Kirchner, a member of the Soldiers' Home band, was a "habitual drunkard" described as "a dirty & worthless character." A Swiss immigrant, Jules Hansjacob, had lost his leg in combat but could not seem to

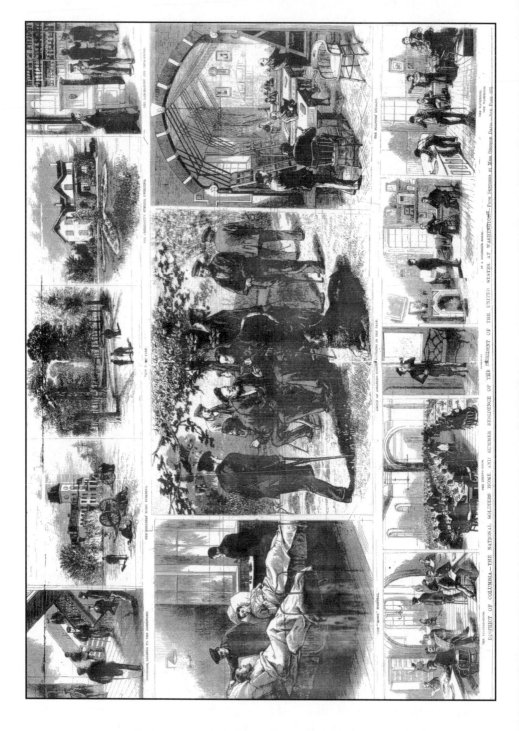

DISTRICT OF COLUMBIA.—THE NATIONAL SOLDIERS' HOME AND SUMMER RESIDENCE OF THE PRESIDENT OF THE UNITED STATES AT WASHINGTON.—From Sketches by Miss Georgie Davis.—[See Page 187.]

keep from running away, ultimately convincing the officials in charge that his "bad drinking" and "untrustworthy" conduct required his permanent expulsion.

Sometimes the institution invested special care in certain members only to be disappointed later. The Board of Commissioners agreed to pay for "artificial feet" for thirty-one-year-old resident John Connolly in 1862, but that did not prevent him from running away three years later.[22] Not all of the departures were the result of bad behavior. Several of the residents went in search of further military service. Dutch immigrant John DeGoy left in September 1863 to join the "Invalid Corps," a specially organized unit of disabled soldiers. Edmund Howard was admitted in 1864 after losing a leg in battle. Eventually, however, he managed to rejoin the regular Army, serving from 1867 to 1869 before finally retiring. Some left seeking employment. Private John Farrell entered the Soldiers' Home at the age of twenty-five in August 1864, but went AWOL for the first time in October. Somehow Farrell managed to remain a member of the Home until 1893, although he kept leaving without permission whenever he could obtain work.[23]

Newspaper reports from the period did not explore the turbulent underside of life at the Soldiers' Home. In 1861, the *Washington Sunday Chronicle* called the institution "a place where kings might dwell," praising the "good musicians" who formed a "very fine band" and the surgeon, Benjamin King, who guaranteed that the residents were "most attentively cared for." The article also featured a glowing profile of future deserter John Connolly, the one-legged resident who apparently served as the Home's volunteer librarian and hobbled around at that time on an old-fashioned wooden peg.[24]

The *San Francisco Bulletin* contained a report in 1865 from a California woman who had visited the previous year. She noted that a "jolly-faced, wooden-legged conductor" politely escorted her entourage around the grounds and the main building. "It is quite a study to wander through the abiding place of a hundred and fifty men who have spent years of their lives in active service," she wrote, "and know that until they change it for the shady graveyard on the hillside that stretches daily before their eyes, they shall have no other." She noted that the residents "necessarily live much in the past," and had covered the walls around their beds with "highly colored scenes" of past battles and portraits of favorite commanders. In the main hall that served as the principal sitting room during colder months, she described a "mammoth stove" in the center of a "cleanly arched space" that was only disturbed by a number of

---

(Facing page) Images of the Soldiers' Home residents from Frank Leslie's Illustrated Newspaper, *July 24, 1880, a popular nineteenth-century magazine.* LIBRARY OF CONGRESS.

"hickory arm-chairs" and an "indefinite quantity of spittoons." The visitors soon noticed the "agreeable smell of boiling coffee" and headed downstairs to the dining-room where they enjoyed "nice white bread, cold boiled ham and excellent coffee" served at a "spotless board." They left "charmed" by the "neatness and suitable comfort of everything."[25]

But if the public was generally unaware of problems at the Soldiers' Home, the Congress was fully engaged by them. According to Patrick Kelly, author of a study on the development of nineteenth-century U.S. veterans' benefits, the Military Asylum or Soldiers' Home was perceived during this period as "something of an institutional flop."[26] When Congress approved a name change in the late 1850s from the Military Asylum to Soldiers' Home—in a transparent attempt to improve poor public relations—Senator John P. Hale from New Hampshire gave voice to some surprisingly blunt complaints about the institution and what he considered its bothersome residents. "Since the attention of the Senate has been called to this subject," he said,

> I can say with perfect truth that not a day has gone over my head, not even Sunday, that some old cripple on his crutches, or some lame or infirm old soldier, has not been to me, as I had moved in this matter, with complaints of the manner in which they are treated in this institution.[27]

In 1864, Hale introduced a resolution calling for a Senate investigation to consider closing the Home. There were other scattered congressional calls for greater accountability, but the institution survived and then grew dramatically after the conflict as it received an influx of Civil War veterans.[28] The postwar period also witnessed the establishment of a national network of Soldiers' Homes; authorized in legislation signed by President Lincoln only weeks before his death.

There is no evidence however that Lincoln got involved in the debate over the future of the Soldiers' Home in Washington. He was certainly busy with other priorities. It is also not clear how much direct contact he had with the residents. Willard Cutter noted their presence occasionally in his letters, but nothing appears in Lincoln's own writings or in those of his wife. There is also surprisingly little direct testimony that has been discovered from the crippled veterans of the Civil War era. One resident recalled that Lincoln "used to walk about in these paths" and that "he was very kind and familiar with us all."[29] But that fleeting memory recalled anonymously over twenty years later offers little ground for anything but tentative conclusions.

One such interpretation involves a consideration of how Lincoln reacted to being surrounded by immigrants. Over 65 percent of the wartime residents at the Soldiers' Home had been born outside the United States. That is a remarkable figure considering that only about 24 percent of the Union army during this period was foreign-born. The explanation for this discrepancy surely lies in the disruption to kin networks wrought by the great trans-Atlantic migrations of the 1840s and 1850s. Many of the immigrant soldiers found themselves separated from their families as they faced the catastrophe of physical disability. They were thus compelled to seek institutional support. Fully one-third of the Soldiers' Home residents during the Civil War era were Irish immigrants. About one out of six members were of German descent. The rest came from a variety of European nations—Great Britain, France, Holland, Spain, and Switzerland. In addition, many of these men were relatively young. The average age at the time of admittance was only forty-one years. At least 10 percent of the residents living in the Soldiers' Home during the Civil War era were still under thirty. Although visitors tended to characterize the residents as "respectable looking, cleanly old men," they were not the homogeneous crew of elderly pipe-smokers that they appeared to some observers.[30]

The question of integrating foreigners into the American republic was one that Lincoln had wrestled with frequently during the latter years of his political career. In the 1850s, he had privately objected to the Know-Nothing or nativist political movement that briefly threatened to curtail the rights of immigrants and was often characterized by blatant anti-Catholic bigotry. However, he also received considerable Know-Nothing support in his campaigns and there is evidence that he avoided publicly condemning the movement prior to the war for calculated political reasons. There were Irish and German immigrants living in Springfield, Illinois, but nothing like the percentages at the Soldiers' Home. Perhaps the proximity to these men, who had proven their loyalty in service to a country that still often condoned public discrimination against them, moved the sensitive president. In his final message to Congress, delivered in December 1864, he struck the most enthusiastic endorsement for immigration of his entire career—though still couched carefully in strategic terms. "I regard our emigrants," he wrote, "as one of the principal replenishing streams which are appointed by Providence to repair the ravages of internal war, and its wastes of national strength and health."[31]

One conclusion about Lincoln's state of mind in the autumn of 1864 is certain: he was seeking any allies he could find. Despite the divided Democratic convention and the fall of Atlanta, the president was taking nothing for granted in regard to the impending election. The campaign was a rough affair. Union politicians accused Democrats of "domestic treason." In return, Republicans were labeled supporters of "miscegenation" or interracial coupling. Both sides raised and spent money without any rules to guide them. There was, as with most nineteenth-century campaigns, a high level of scurrilous personal charges. Democrats claimed that the president had acted disrespectfully by laughing and singing with his entourage while touring the bloody Antietam battlefield in October 1862. Lincoln took this slander seriously enough to spend the better part of an afternoon drafting a statement for his friend and travel companion Ward Lamon denying the charge.[32] Meanwhile, the Republican *New York Times* made an anti-Semitic charge against Democratic National Committee chairman August Belmont, pointing out that he worked for the Rothschild family. "Yes, the great Democratic party has fallen so low that it has to seek a leader in the agent of foreign Jew bankers," snarled the newspaper.[33]

By outward appearances, the president remained above this messy electoral fray. During this era it was considered inappropriate for presidential candidates to campaign for themselves. Both Lincoln and McClellan stayed in the background while their supporters slugged it out on their behalf. Occasionally, the president gave brief responses to public serenades from his supporters, but otherwise he offered no stirring campaign speeches and there were definitely no Lincoln-McClellan debates. Yet a careful examination of the president's activities between the Democratic convention at the end of August and Election Day on Tuesday, November 8, suggests that he became quite involved behind the scenes.

One striking example of Lincoln's covert political activities that has been overlooked in previous studies of the election contest occurred at the Soldiers' Home on Sunday, September 11, 1864, at eight o'clock in the morning. On that day, the president had invited Congressman Fernando Wood for a private discussion at the cottage. Wood was a principal leader of the antiwar Democrats.[34] The fact that Lincoln was talking with a political enemy probably explains why the conversation did not take place at the White House. According to journalist Noah Brooks, the president was wary about Wood's reputation and kept notes on their occasional meetings. In the past, Wood had urged Lincoln to rescind the banishment of leading Peace Democrat Clement Vallandigham—or at least to ignore the former congressman's violations of that 1863 order. Years later Brooks recalled that the September 11 conversation, which he believed had occurred in August, involved reaching an accommodation over how far the administration should allow other Peace Democrats to push their campaign attacks. "We don't expect to elect our candidate for President this fall," Wood reportedly said; "the people of the North are not yet ready for peace."

> But peace must come sooner or later; and when it does, the Democratic party will be the party which will act and assimilate with the dominant party in the South, and so we shall again have our rightful ascendancy.

In case Lincoln was missing his message, Wood, a smooth political operator, spelled it out for him. "Now, Mr. President, you cannot find any fault with that," he said; "it is not going to hurt you any."[35] This message had two meanings. Wood was asking the president to give Democrats an opportunity to make the show of making their case, assuring him that it would have no effect on the immediate outcome of the presidential contest.[36]

It is impossible to determine for certain whether Brooks's recollection of Lincoln's notes on this meeting accurately reflects what happened, but it would have been in character for Wood to address the president in such a cynical manner. He was a former mayor of New York City, the first elected by the notorious Tammany Hall political machine, and has been ranked by urban historians as one of the ten most corrupt big-city mayors in American history.[37] William "Boss" Tweed once said jealously of his predecessor, "I never yet went to get a corner lot that I didn't find Wood had got in ahead of me."[38]

There is also contemporary evidence from within the White House that suggests Lincoln wanted something from the dapper New York politician and might have been open to horse-trading. Almost two weeks after the Soldiers' Home meeting, John Hay recorded a remarkable story in his diary about the president's being engaged in a top-secret opposition research project that involved Wood and had the potential to destroy McClellan. Lincoln told him that Fernando Wood had visited McClellan twice in 1862 for the purpose of persuading the general to write a secret letter pledging to conduct the war in an "inefficient conciliatory style" in exchange for the 1864 Democratic presidential nomination. "Now that letter must be in the possession of Fernando Wood," Lincoln said, "and it will not be impossible to get it." Clearly, at least, this was something he had discussed with Wood at the Soldiers' Home. The president then explained to his surprised aide that he had heard the story originally from John G. Smith, the governor of Vermont, who had heard about it from his brother, General William "Baldy" Smith, a former subordinate of McClellan. Hay expressed his skepticism, leading the president to confess that when the general had failed to pursue Lee's army after the battle of Antietam, his excuses had been so transparent that Lincoln suspected "he was playing false."

If the story about McClellan's letter were true it meant that proof existed documenting that the general had betrayed the Union for his own political benefit. But, as with so many other rumors, this one was grounded in a rather simple mistake. Historian Michael Burlingame has located a note from Governor Smith written to the president after the election admitting that he had misinterpreted his brother's story and that McClellan's letter, as far as Baldy Smith had known, only concerned disapproval of emancipation and mentioned nothing about the presidential nomination. Presumably this was a reference to the famous Harrison's Landing letter that the commander had presented to

Lincoln in July 1862. But the president did not know this in September when he met with Wood or explained the bizarre story to Hay.[39]

In the afternoon following his meeting with Fernando Wood, the president turned to personal matters. He had not received a response to the telegram he had sent his wife a few days earlier, updating her on Robert's travels, Tad's goats, and the demise of Mrs. Dimmick. Assuming that she had finally left Manchester, Vermont, he now directed his note to New York. "All well," he again reported. "What day will you be home?"[40] The first lady then appeared about a week later and Tad was finally reunited with his pets. "Mrs. Lincoln come home night before last," Willard Cutter wrote on September 17, 1864, "she had been over the white mountains. She and Tad, they were gone 6 or seven weeks and of course had a good time for all I know."[41]

Upon her return, Mary Lincoln tried to engage in her own round of politicking on behalf of her husband's reelection. She sent New York politician and friend Abram Wakeman a long letter from the Soldiers' Home on September 23 that focused almost exclusively on election news. "You doubtless rejoiced with us over Sheridan's last victory," she wrote, referring to General Philip Sheridan's campaign to drive Jubal Early's forces out of the Shenandoah Valley; "these successes, will be beneficial in the rapidly approaching Election." Commenting on "villainous aspersions" that she had read about her husband in the "miserable" *New York World*, a leading Democratic newspaper, Mary Lincoln responded by denying all the allegations of corruption. "Poor Mr. L," she wrote, "is almost a monomaniac on the subject of honesty." She stated flatly, "we have not enriched ourselves," claiming that she had been "economical . . . more so than I have ever been before in my life."[42] As the attacks persisted and the signs of reelection continued to look hopeful, her defiance grew. By October, she announced to Wakeman that she was "much amused" by the "falsehoods" of the Democratic press. "When will their vile fabrications cease?" she wrote. "Not until they find Mr. L reelected!"[43]

The heat of the campaign and their long separation from each other appeared to stoke the affections of the first couple. A member of the Union Light Guard recalled that when the weather turned chillier, he often observed the president tenderly arranging a shawl over his wife's shoulders before they started off together on their daily carriage rides.[44]

By October 1864, state elections and local reporting from across the North suggested that the Unionists had built up a considerable advantage in the bitter campaign. More good news from the military front only further boosted morale. Attorney General Edward Bates noted dourly in his diary that at a cabinet meeting in late October there was "nothing talked of but election matters." "I wish the election was over," he complained, predicting that afterward Lincoln would be "a freer and bolder man."[45]

In the final weeks of the contest, the president continued to stay focused on the race, but in the evenings he seemed to relax. His reaction to a group of unexpected visitors from abroad illustrated this new attitude. English traveler George Borrett recalled that around this period, Assistant Secretary of Treasury George Harrington had asked his daughter, who claimed she knew the Lincolns "well," to escort his small delegation to the retreat. "It was dark when we reached the President's residence," Borrett remembered, "so that we could see little of what it was like, beyond the fact that it stood in a sort of park, and was guarded by a regiment of troops, encamped picturesquely about the grounds."

> We drove up to the door, and being challenged by the sentry, replied with becoming modesty that we wanted to see Mr. and Mrs. Lincoln. He let us pass, and we rang. I rather expected the door to have been opened by the disreputable coachman; but we were waited upon by a buttonless 'buttons,' apparently the sole domestic on the premises, to whom we told our wish. He suggested that it was rather late for an interview with Mr. and Mrs. Lincoln, and as it was then considerably past eight, I thought the hint very reasonable. Not so the Secretary's daughter. With ready wit and admirable aplomb, she bade the officious page to go in and tell his master that there were three gentlemen there, who had come three thousand miles for the express purpose of seeing him and his lady, and did not intend to go away until they had done so.

Borrett then recalled how a sleepy Lincoln appeared in his slippers and graciously agreed to sit with them in the parlor. He described his childhood. "It was a treat," according to the English guest, "to hear him talk of his early life, with a certain quiet pride in his rise from the bottom of the ladder." The president kept up the conversation "briskly," commenting at length on the constitutional and legal differences between the British and American systems of government and law. Still, this part of the discussion bored the Englishman until Lincoln finally turned the talk to the poetry of Alexander Pope, whom he said he admired greatly. The president quoted from memory the closing lines from the first epistle of Pope's famous "Essay on Man."

> All nature is but art, unknown to thee;
> All chance, direction, which thou canst not see;
> All discord, harmony not understood;
> All partial evil, universal good:
> And, spite of pride, in erring reason's spite,
> One truth is clear, whatever is, is right.

Although he claimed to admire the poet, Lincoln noted the potential for abuse in the philosophy of the last line. "You see," he pointed out to his visitors, "a man may turn it, and say, 'Well, if whatever *is* is right, why, then, whatever *isn't* must be wrong.'" The skeptical English gentleman left charmed, calling his encounter with Lincoln "a much more pleasant one than I ever had with any other potentate."[46]

The closer electoral victory appeared, the more convivial Lincoln became. Noah Brooks recalled an evening during this period when Lincoln, "standing with his back to the fire and his legs spread apart," read to a small group from humorist Petroleum V. Nasby's papers. During this evening at the cottage, he also recited one of Orpheus C. Kerr's stories poking fun at Secretary of Navy Gideon Welles. The Nasby piece, which Brooks claimed that Lincoln carried around in his pocket, pretended to attack the president for allowing contrabands, or runaway slaves, to populate the North. The climax of the essay, in full regional dialect, was intended as a mock rallying cry for the nation's racists.

> Arowse to wunst! Rally agin Conway! Rally agin Sweet! Rally agin Hegler! Rallyer agin Hegler's family! Rally agin the porter at the Reed House! Rally agin the cook at the Crook House! Rally agin the nigger widder in Vance's addishun! Rally agin Missis Umstid! Rally agin Missis Umstid's childern by her first husband! Rally agin all the rest uv Missis Umstid's chdern! Rally agin the nigger that kum yisterday! Rally agin the saddle-kulurd gal that yoost 2 be hear! Ameriky fer white men!

According to Brooks, whenever the topic of racial integration came up, Lincoln was prone to recall these lines with a rueful chuckle. On that same night, he also shared with his visitors Kerr's story about how the ancient-looking Welles once put off an urgent request for his presence by claiming that he was "very busy examining a model of Noah's ark, with a view to its introduction into the United States Navy."[47]

There was an interesting footnote to the evening that Brooks described. The journalist claimed that at the end of the night he felt insulted by the president who had announced to him loudly that he must not repeat any of the stories to Secretary of Navy Welles "for he would be dreadfully mortified if he knew it." Brooks, a relatively old friend, considered such warnings unnecessary, but he discovered after the other guests had gone that Lincoln was intending the message for one of them, whom he confessed had worried him as a potentially "leaky vessel."[48]

On another brisk autumn evening before the election, Hugh McCulloch, a senior administration official, recalled watching Lincoln swap tales with Alexander Randall, the former governor of Wisconsin. "For two hours there was a constant run of story-telling," McCulloch reported, "Lincoln leading and Randall following, a contest between them as to which should tell the best story and provoke the heartiest laughter."[49]

As always with politicians such as Randall, however, Lincoln had more on his mind than simply anecdotes. When Chief Justice Roger B. Taney died in mid-October, McCulloch wrote a letter to Lincoln alluding to an earlier conversation they had shared at the Soldiers' Home about replacing the ailing Supreme Court leader. Referring delicately to "the Gentleman whose name was mentioned in connection" with the pending nomination, he appeared to be placing the discussion at the time of the evening of the story swapping with Randall. After the election, President Lincoln named former Treasury Secretary Salmon Chase to the post.[50]

The only significant shadow hanging over the president as November approached concerned his safety. Following the gunshot incident in August, there was a noticeable increase in security around the president. Prior to this period, Lincoln had been allowed to determine for himself whether he needed an escort and often rode back and forth between the Soldiers' Home and the War Department late at night, alone or in the company of only a messenger or aide.[51] He frequently rode to the theater from the White House and walked to nearby government offices without any military guard.

Those policies changed in the fall of 1864. The guards were now on full alert; Ward Lamon began sleeping at the White House, and by November, the War Department initiated the practice of assigning a former city police detective to accompany the president at all times as a personal bodyguard. Writing to a friend in October, Rebecca Pomroy, the Lincoln family nurse, related information she had heard from cook Mary Dines—apparently back in her old post at the cottage—about the extent of the new security measures.

> Aunt Mary, from Mrs. Lincoln, called to have me go out to the Soldiers' Home and spend a few days with the family. She says that the President has had several threatening letters, his house is guarded all round the outside, and a private guard inside the house.[52]

One of these threats had come apparently from a southern spy named Thomas Nelson Conrad who had arrived in Washington in late September, hoping to abduct the president on his daily commute to and from the Soldiers' Home. In some ways, the plan was reminiscent of the scheme devised over the winter of 1863–1864 by Bradley T. Johnson and aborted by Early's raid on Washington. In this case, Conrad claimed in his memoir that he had received direct approval for his covert operation from James A. Seddon, the Confederate secretary of war.[53] According to his account, Conrad slipped into Washington in late September and began conducting surveillance of the president's movements from among the trees in Lafayette Park near the White House. He soon learned that Lincoln typically left for the Soldiers' Home "in the cool of evening" and rode out on Fourteenth Street.

Assisted by two others, a man identified only as Norton and a former classmate of Conrad from Dickinson College named Daniel Cloud, the spy prepared to follow Lincoln's carriage out on a Saturday evening in October, attempting the bold abduction along the winding paths not far from the cottage.

> It was all planned out to the last detail and the minute the driver of Mr. Lincoln's equi-page passed into the forest, he should be made to stop by means of a pistol at his head, and Mr. Lincoln, served in similar manner, would be compelled to cross from his car-riage to the close vehicle.[54]

The day before the plan was supposed to be executed, Conrad claimed that a cavalry detail suddenly appeared at the White House and began the practice of escorting the president. He attributed the increased security to a newspaper report that had documented similar abduction plans by another group of Con-federate irregulars. After observing Lincoln's new routine for a period of time, Conrad finally left the city, conceding the "unsuccessful termination" of his operation.[55]

The biggest problem with Conrad's recollection is his failure to acknowl-edge that Lincoln's cavalry escort had already been in place, in one form or another, for three years by the fall of 1864. His account makes it appear as if the president had been unguarded prior to the undocumented newspaper leak, which Conrad claims ruined his plans. There are other minor problems with the story—including misspelled names and many self-aggrandizing details—but the fundamental mistake in the account makes it difficult to accept.

In recent years, however, there has been a resurgence of interest in the pos-sible connections between John Wilkes Booth's plot and the Confederate government's interest in abducting President Lincoln. Some scholars believe that Booth's conspiracy, which apparently began as a kidnapping plot, had au-thorization from Richmond. William A. Tidwell, an expert on the Lincoln assassination, and two co-authors noted in a controversial 1988 study of the murder that there were several circumstantial ties that they believe strongly suggest that Booth was acting as an operative of the Confederate government. Part of their thesis rests on the similarities in the recollected accounts of the various kidnapping plots. "The Bradley Johnson scheme, the plan described by Thomas Nelson Conrad, and the plan actually used by John Wilkes Booth," writes Tidwell, "all involved capturing Lincoln on the outskirts of Washington at or near his summer residence at the Soldiers' Home."[56]

Resolving such contested issues is ultimately quite difficult, if not impos-sible, but assessing the state of anxiety around the president in the autumn of 1864 is far easier. Too much evidence exists to document that people around Lincoln were growing increasingly worried about him. One of the officers from the Union Light Guard recalled an incident during this period that reveals the high level of anxiety. He was on guard duty near the cemetery when he encountered a man who turned out to be the president. Lincoln, who was a "light and capricious" sleeper according to John Hay, was accustomed to taking late night walks around the grounds of the Soldiers' Home. "I saw a man walking alone and leisurely across the path I was taking," related Lieutenant George C. Ashmun, "and as I came near him I saw it was Mr. Lincoln."

> At an earlier hour I would have kept from speaking, but, prompted by anxiety, I said, "Mr. President, isn't it rather risky to be out here at this hour?" He answered, "Oh, I guess not—I couldn't rest and thought I'd take a walk." He was quite a distance outside the line of infantry guards about the house where the family was staying. He turned back after I spoke to him, and I passed on to where the escort was camped."[57]

Whether frightened or simply growing colder, by Election Day, November 8, 1864, the Lincolns had returned to residence in the city. On that day, the president's military guard voted in the field, at an impromptu polling place established at their camp near the White House. Absentee voting was a new custom in American politics, developed during the war to help the soldiers participate in the political process. According to Willard Cutter, the vote was nearly unanimous for the president. "Com. K went all right this time," wrote the Bucktail private, "67 Union to one Copperhead and that one not by us boys." In general, the military vote went overwhelmingly for President Lincoln and the Union ticket. According to most estimates, Lincoln won nearly 80 percent of the ballots cast by soldiers (compared to his 55 percent share of the popular vote overall).[58] By midday, Cutter was already ecstatic. "As far as heard from this morning Old Abe is ahead by a big majority," he wrote. "The Copperheads will find out in a few days where their little Mc is for he hasn't a gunboat to get in to save his bacon as he used to have while in command."[59]

Even though the election campaign had been dismally negative and petty in some respects, it was nonetheless an awesome accomplishment for a nation to hold a presidential election in the middle of a Civil War. Soldiers and their male relatives at home voted on whether they would remain in the field, continuing to risk their lives in support of an effort that had become a crusade for freedom. The president, who had suspended civil liberties on several occasions during the course of the conflict, refused to disrupt the national electoral process. "We can not have free government without elections," he said afterward, "and if the rebellion could force us to forego, or postpone a national election it might fairly claim to have already conquered or ruined us."[60]

Lincoln's victory marked the end of any Confederate hopes for survival. Their strategic position had looked dismal since the summer of 1863 when Vicksburg had fallen and Lee had lost at Gettysburg. But there had always been some hope that the North might become too weary and accept a negotiated peace settlement that recognized the division of the Union, or at the very least, the existence of slavery. By holding firm on the promise of emancipation and by winning an election on those grounds, Lincoln thereby guaranteed the war would end with the restoration of a Union freed from slavery. On election night, Ward Lamon, his close friend and self-appointed bodyguard, seemed to realize the danger of Lincoln's indispensability. John Hay's diary records a poignant scene:

> [Lamon] took a glass of whiskey and then refusing my offer of a bed went out & rolling himself up in his cloak lay down at the President's door; passing the night in that attitude of touching and dumb fidelity with a small arsenal of pistols & bowie knives around him. In the morning he went away leaving my blankets at my door, before I or the President were awake.[61]

By the winter of 1864, it was clear that even loyal border states would have to abandon the peculiar institution. Over the winter, as desertions wreaked havoc on the collapsing Rebel armies, the Lincoln administration lobbied for an amendment to the Constitution that would enshrine the Emancipation Proclamation and make its effects national and permanent. Although Lincoln would not live to see the ratification of the 13th Amendment, he was the president responsible for making it possible.

Looking backward, it is easy to attribute everything to a spirit of destiny— to explain each tragedy as a necessary stepping-stone to the ultimate triumph. The narrative is so compelling that it is difficult not to embrace the circular logic of Alexander Pope—*Whatever is, is right*—and to find in each apparently minor detail, like the seasons spent at the Soldiers' Home, some mystical representation of the story's final verdict. And yet, it is clear that the president's time at the Soldiers' Home did have meaning in the story of his evolving presidency. The place was not just a backdrop to great events but also a participant in them. No period better embodies this insight than the late summer and early autumn of 1864. Here Lincoln used his wartime retreat not only as a sanctuary but also as a private workplace. He cultivated political support, using the informal setting of the Soldiers' Home as a factor in his outreach. And here was the place where Lincoln became a target for embittered conspirators. Even if some of the tales have been inflated by time and by the pollution of memory, it was clear throughout the summer of 1864 that by choosing to live outside the White House, the president helped make himself a target. In some way, that is the most fitting end point for a study of the presidential sanctuary. Lincoln went to the Soldiers' Home seeking privacy and aspiring to be ordinary and discovered that above all being ordinary means being vulnerable.

Conclusion
"There is something else there"

How dearly I loved the "Soldiers' Home" & how little I supposed, one year since, that I should be so *far removed* from it, broken hearted, and praying for death, to remove me, from a life, so full of agony.

—Mary Lincoln, August 25, 1865

THE LINCOLNS NEVER AGAIN RETURNED TO TAKE UP RESIDENCE AT THE SOLDIERS' Home. The Confederacy began collapsing in the winter following the 1864 election. Richmond fell on April 2, 1865. Lee surrendered the Army of Northern Virginia a week later at Appomattox Court House. Confederate President Jefferson Davis and remnants of the Rebel army remained at large, but there was a spirit of celebration in Washington. Lincoln was sometimes too exhausted to fully share in this exultation, but he was obviously satisfied with the Union war effort and was beginning to look ahead to the national reconstruction and to his own retirement from politics. He discussed with Mary Lincoln how they might spend their time together after the second term of his administration concluded in 1869.

Those plans fell apart on Friday night, April 14, when well-known actor John Wilkes Booth entered Lincoln's box at Ford's theater and assassinated the president who had once admired his stage talent. Originally, Booth, an avid secessionist, had organized a conspiracy to abduct the president, a plan that resembled the botched job undertaken by spy Thomas Conrad the year before. But the actor was not so easily discouraged. He realized that it might be easier to assassinate the president while he attended a public event, such as an evening at the theater, where Booth had easy access and the bodyguards tended to relax. The conspiracy was ambitious. At the same time that Booth murdered Lincoln, another member of his gang attacked and severely injured Secretary of State Seward. A planned assault on Vice President Andrew Johnson failed to materialize. Booth also proved himself to be resourceful and difficult to capture. Despite a broken leg, he managed to escape from the city and remained at large for weeks before Federal troops finally cornered and killed him in northern Virginia.

The Lincoln family was devastated. Gideon Welles reported that after spending most of the night of the assassination at the Peterson House, across from the theater, watching the president's final hours with several other key military and political figures, he went home briefly and then returned to the White House later in the morning. "There was a cheerless cold rain and everything seemed gloomy," he noted in his diary. By that time, there were "several hundred" African Americans outside the Executive Mansion, "weeping and wailing their loss." They remained all day. Mary Jane Welles was already inside with the first lady, where everything seemed "silent and sad." The Navy secretary tried to console Mary Lincoln in the second floor library but she was beyond any help. As he was leaving, Tad Lincoln burst out, "Oh, Mr. Welles, who killed my father?" The sharp-tongued Connecticut politician confided in his diary that at those words he finally lost control of his emotions and began to cry.[1]

Mary Lincoln remained in the White House for weeks after the funeral. She finally left to return to Illinois with Tad and Robert. They lived in hotels and rented rooms in Chicago for a time—Mary Lincoln refused to return to Springfield—but ultimately the expense of that lifestyle proved too great. She lobbied unsuccessfully for a pension but only received the remainder of the president's 1865 salary. With that money she purchased a home in the city but was unable to maintain it as her residence and ended up renting it out to make her mortgage payments.[2] Embarrassed and annoyed by her financial difficulties, Mary Lincoln auctioned off clothes and furniture until the proceeds of her husband's estate finally allowed her to live independently. She took Tad on an extended trip to Europe and continued to fight for a pension, which Congress finally authorized in 1870. The next year, mother and son returned to the United States, but along the way Tad, who had always been sickly, contracted pleurisy, a severe lung disease that initially appeared to be nothing more than a bad cold. Yet somehow the illness turned fatal, and Tad died at the age of eighteen.

The continued tragedy and isolation affected Mary Lincoln. She found practically no solace from Robert Lincoln, who had married the daughter of a U.S. senator and had begun his own career as an attorney. He considered his mother unstable and an embarrassment to his father's memory. Her continued obsession with spiritualism and her spending habits concerned him so much that in 1875 he had her committed to an insane asylum. There the former first lady remained for three months until she finally secured permission, over her son's objections, to return to live with her sister and brother-in-law in Springfield. Seven years later, she died in the house where she had lived as a young woman during the period when Abraham Lincoln had first courted her.[3]

Robert Lincoln, the only son who survived, ultimately became a prominent and respected figure, although always cold and distant in his demeanor. In 1881, President James Garfield appointed the son of the former president, then only thirty-eight years old, to be secretary of war. Later Robert also served as U.S. ambassador to Great Britain before leaving government service to become president of the Pullman Company, one of the nation's largest railroad interests. Beyond his professional career, Robert acted as the principal guardian of his father's legacy. When he came to believe that too many biographers and would-be intimates were invading the family's privacy and tarnishing the great president's image with offensive stories and recollections, he made a decision to shut off access to Lincoln's personal and public papers. Scholars would not be able to examine many of the letters received and sent by President Lincoln until 1947 when the restrictions imposed by his son finally expired. Yet as if to offer a final piece of evidence on Robert Lincoln's ambivalent relationship with his mother and father, when he died in 1926, his wife had him buried at Arlington National Cemetery, far away from the family crypt in Springfield.

Former aides John Nicolay and John Hay wrote a ten-volume authorized biography of Lincoln that stood for years as the definitive source on his public career. Hay later became secretary of state under Presidents William McKinley and Theodore Roosevelt. Noah Brooks, the journalist who was supposed to replace John Nicolay in the spring of 1865 as Lincoln's top aide, continued to work as an editor and writer, producing several volumes of reminiscences about the Civil War era.

The young men from Meadville who had served as the president's favorite military guard returned to their lives after the conflict. Willard Cutter, for instance, lived in Meadville until the age of eighty-three, carefully passing along the 150 letters he had sent home from camp at the White House and Soldiers' Home to his granddaughter, Irene Sprout. She was equally tenacious in preserving these vivid glimpses of life around Lincoln, holding them in private possession until the 1970s. For years, only the family, a few local residents, and a group of very dedicated Civil War reenactors even knew of their existence. David Derickson died in 1891 but not before he wrote for the local newspaper an extensive recollection of his service. According to a pension application filed by his second wife Sarah, he suffered from rheumatism of the feet and cardiac asthma before he passed away. His son Charles became a lumber merchant and Republican party functionary in the 1890s.

Edwin Stanton continued to serve as secretary of war under Lincoln's successor Andrew Johnson, but the two had a falling out over Reconstruction policy. Ultimately, Johnson's desire to remove Stanton triggered the impeachment crisis of 1868. The former cabinet officer died the following year.

Gideon Welles, the secretary of the navy, fell out of favor with President Johnson himself but proved to be one of only two men (along with William Seward) who served the complete terms of both the Lincoln and Johnson administrations. Lincoln's frequent Soldiers' Home guest, Orville Browning, also served in the Johnson cabinet, as the secretary of the interior. He finally left Washington in the late 1860s, returning to practice law in Illinois until his death in 1881. Copperhead Democrat Fernando Wood died the same year as Browning. He had been defeated for reelection to Congress in the election that followed his secret 1864 meeting with Lincoln but returned to Capitol Hill after the war. Always a survivor, Wood eventually became chairman of the House Ways and Means committee. George McClellan, the Democratic presidential nominee in 1864, found some of his own redemption in politics, serving as governor of New Jersey from 1878 to 1881.

President Johnson never used the Soldiers' Home as a retreat, but some others who followed him in office did. Rutherford B. Hayes and Chester A. Arthur both took advantage of the standing offer to live in the former Riggs cottage in summertime. Arthur also stayed at the cottage in the winter of 1882 while repairs were being made on the White House. Meanwhile, the Soldiers' Home grew dramatically as an institution in the years after the Civil War. In the aftermath of the extensive conflict, veterans became one of the nation's most powerful political interests and established a series of precedents for public benefits and support. On the other hand, the regular Army demobilized quickly after the conflict, reducing in size from over one million troops in uniform to about 25,000 during the postwar period.

Although officers and residents at the Soldiers' Home often discussed President Lincoln's connection to their institution with pride, there were few formal attempts to preserve his legacy at the cottage. The building itself continued to serve a variety of functional purposes. When not hosting special guests, the Riggs house was used as a hospital and dormitory. The larger meaning of Lincoln's affiliation with the Soldiers' Home also remained largely unexamined. Over one hundred years passed after the announcement of the president's Emancipation Proclamation before the officers at the Soldiers' Home moved to end racial segregation at the institution.[4] Not until the summer of 2000 was the place where Lincoln had lived for more than a quarter of his presidency declared a national monument. Credit for this belated accomplishment belongs primarily to the National Trust for Historic Preservation and then First Lady Hillary Rodham Clinton, who spearheaded the final successful efforts at protecting the Lincoln Cottage at the Soldiers' Home.

The efforts to preserve a physical site associated with the Lincoln presidency are important because observers can no longer "see the President" as Walt Whitman did so memorably in 1863. Historians might build engaging narratives out of their evidence in order to help readers imagine the past, but for many the inspiration of a place stands unmatched. Visitors cannot see the president any longer, but they certainly can see where he walked and lived. They can pass the gravestones that he passed in the summer before his journey to Gettysburg, or they can trot up and down the stairs where his oversized slippers once shuffled.

For historians, this very human attachment to place offers a powerful reminder about the practice of biography. Especially with a monumental figure such as Lincoln, it is easy to overlook the importance of daily life in shaping larger political experiences. Details that matter—like the location of a meeting, the absence of a wife, or the day of the week—tend to get squeezed out for more obviously significant fare. All biographers try their best to explore the boundaries between the public and private lives of their subjects, but rare is the narrative that can command both the mundane and the sublime in the same story.

This book makes an attempt to do so, at least for one family sharing three long seasons together at a summer cottage in the middle of that all-consuming Civil War. The story of the Lincolns at the Soldiers' Home is a story of sanctuary but not in the ordinary sense of that word. For Abraham Lincoln, the sanctuary he found by leaving the White House was in discovering a new state of mind and in finding a greater sense of equilibrium. For him as well, the physical place was but a gateway to a more enriching inner world.

To understand how important this achievement was in shaping Lincoln's presidency, consider just two of the more dramatic stories from the Soldiers' Home experience. In the tense summer of 1862, Colonel Scott showed up at the cottage unannounced seeking special dispensation to recover the body of his dead wife. Exhausted and out of patience, the president initially lashed out at the poor officer. "Am I to have no rest?" he exploded. By the summer of 1864, so much had changed. Despite all of the hardships and remaining dangers, when George Borrett and his party of unexpected visitors arrived at the cottage, the tired president rallied to charm them with wide-ranging conversation and a deft commentary on Pope's claim that "Whatever is, is right."

These stories, recollected and fleeting as they are, still suggest an important new perspective on Lincoln's growth as a presidential leader. Almost everyone acknowledges that he evolved in office and became increasingly more capable of uniting the nation and managing the war, but demonstrating such change can prove challenging. By examining the narrative through a more intimate lens, the story should become more vivid and hence more understandable. That is the underlying hope of this effort. But Whitman once again offers a sober reminder of our limitations. The great poet complained in the pages of his wartime journal that nobody could seem to capture the full spirit of Lincoln's expression. "There is something else there," he wrote on August 12, 1863, perplexed and frustrated. Despite all the years, it is the one observation that still seems as powerful as ever.

Afterword

Occupying a breeze-swept wooded hilltop a few miles north of the tourist magnets on the Mall, the modest building known as the Lincoln Cottage is one of Washington's greatest hidden treasures. I believe—and many others agree—that this place, as tranquil and beautiful today as it was in Lincoln's time, is the most important site associated with the man who was arguably our most important president. It is certainly the most important "unknown" presidential site in the nation.

For several months each year from 1862 to 1864, a period totaling almost one quarter of his presidency, Lincoln used the cottage to meet with cabinet members and military leaders, conceive and refine his doctrine of emancipation, relax with his family, and restore his own inner peace. Yet despite its enormous significance, remarkably little has been known about this nineteenth-century equivalent of Camp David. Happily, the appearance of Matthew Pinsker's rich and insightful history means that the cottage's days as an unknown landmark will soon be over.

Efforts to bring the Lincoln Cottage into the public spotlight and help ensure its preservation have been under way for several years. The Armed Forces Retirement Home, which owns the site, has provided decades of sensitive stewardship but has lacked the funds to carry out needed restoration. To call attention to its plight, the National Trust included the cottage on its annual list of America's 11 Most Endangered Historic Places in 2000. A short time later, President Clinton officially designated the site the President Lincoln and Soldiers' Home National Monument, thereby ensuring its protection under federal law. Since then, the National Trust and the Armed Forces Retirement Home have worked in close and productive partnership. With invaluable assistance from the National Park

Service and a dedicated group of scholars, local officials, historians, and preservationists with a wide range of organizational affiliations, we've developed a vision for the future of this important piece of the nation's history.

The cottage will be restored and interpreted as the premier center for learning about Lincoln the man, his ideas, his presidency, the development of the Emancipation Proclamation, and his family life at the Soldiers' Home. The learning center we envision will produce publications, sponsor conferences, and establish strong working partnerships with leading universities. It will help teachers enhance their understanding of American history by bringing educators and scholars together and by developing curriculum materials and traveling exhibitions.

Preservation will focus on authenticity in the spaces, architectural details, and landscaping still in place from Lincoln's time, and on the acquisition or long-term loan of selected Lincoln artifacts and documents. We don't intend to create a traditional house museum filled with period antiques. Instead, we will use a limited number of furnishings and artifacts, combined with innovative interpretive techniques, to engage visitors in a full range of learning experiences.

Because of its somewhat out-of-the-way location, we don't expect the restored cottage to attract huge numbers of tourists, but we do want it to be open to visitors—especially schoolchildren and teachers, Civil War enthusiasts, and students and scholars of Lincoln, the Civil War, and American history. And we're eager to collaborate with other Lincoln sites to provide a fuller understanding of the man and his impact on the world—in both his own day and the decades since his death.

We knew we couldn't convert our vision into reality without knowing much more about the Lincolns' life at the cottage. With the help of funds from the Gilder Lehrman Institute of American History, we were very fortunate to be able to engage the services of historian Matthew Pinsker. He has produced a work that will be enormously rewarding to Lincoln scholars and laymen alike. In addition to revealing much that was previously unknown, the book offers a wealth of humanizing detail—such as the president's daily commute to and from the White House and his habit of bringing work home from the office—that links the world of the 1860s to that of today. The information and insight resulting from Pinsker's research will be indispensable to our task of illuminating and interpreting the Lincoln experience at the Soldiers' Home.

Work on the cottage is already under way. Finishing the job will be a huge challenge, but I'm confident that the public will share our conviction that this is an extraordinarily important undertaking, eminently worthy of our best efforts.

In his first annual message to Congress, with the Union teetering on the brink of catastrophe, Lincoln declared that "the struggle of today is not altogether for today—it is for a vast future also." We are part of the "vast future" Lincoln spoke of. As the beneficiaries of his work, we must—and we will—do everything in our power to ensure that the Soldiers' Home cottage is preserved for all time to help us understand and honor the great man who saved the Union, elevated freedom as a human principle, and helped shape contemporary America.

March 2003   Richard Moe
                                                    President, National Trust
                                                    for Historic Preservation

Chronology
Lincoln at the Soldiers' Home

1861

March 6   Mary Lincoln visits the Soldiers' Home just two days after Lincoln's inauguration. She is probably acting on the advice of outgoing president James Buchanan, who believed that he slept better at the Military Asylum or Soldiers' Home than he did at the White House.

March 7   President Lincoln visits the Soldiers' Home for the first time. Both his excursion and his wife's the day before are covered by the *New York Times*.

May 10–24   Mary Lincoln leaves Washington for a shopping excursion to New York and Boston.

July 11   Calling the Soldiers' Home "a very beautiful place," Mary Lincoln predicts in a letter to a friend that her family will be moving there for the summer within three weeks.

July 21   Union troops suffer a surprising defeat at the First Battle of Bull Run.

August   Mary Lincoln, along with Robert Lincoln, John Hay, and niece Elizabeth Todd Grimsley, begins an extended vacation in Long Branch, New Jersey.

1862

February 20   Willie Lincoln dies, probably from typhoid fever contracted through the contaminated White House water supply.

May 21   Board of Commissioners for Soldiers' Home report to Secretary of War Stanton that the institution "is in fine order" with 132 "inmates" as of May 1862.

May 29   Upset over the distractions of the White House during her period of mourning, Mary Lincoln writes a friend predicting that her family will be residing at the more secluded Soldiers' Home by July 1.

June 8–13   About this time, the Lincoln family moves out to the Soldiers' Home for their first summer in residence.

June 18   Lincoln shares breakfast at his new summer cottage with Senator Orville Browning (R, Ill.), government contractor Alexander T. Stewart, and New York Judge Henry Hilton. The group argues over General George McClellan's strategy to attack the Rebels via the Virginia peninsula.

June 18   Vice President Hannibal Hamlin discusses emancipation policy with President Lincoln in the evening at the Soldiers' Home.

June 25   The president entertains Senator Browning and his guests, Mr. and Mrs. Ihrie, and Browning's daughter Emma. They probably discuss emancipation policy since earlier that day Browning gave a major speech against the proposed "confiscation" bill, a congressional measure to end Rebel slavery.

June 29   Lincoln shares breakfast with Assistant Secretary of War Peter H. Watson at the Soldiers' Home cottage of Secretary of War Edwin Stanton, because Stanton had been forced to rush into the city earlier in the morning when his child became gravely ill.

June 30   Secretary of War Stanton telegraphs Secretary of State William Seward, who was then meeting with Union governors in New York City over problems with the pace of army enlistment. He notes that President Lincoln had "gone to the country very tired" and would not be able to answer the governors' concerns about military recruitment until the next morning.

June 30   Senator Browning visits the Soldiers' Home in the evening,
                 bringing along Mr. and Mrs. William Dorman from Florida.
                 Lincoln discusses the military situation on the Virginia pen-
                 insula with Browning, relying on a pocket map of Virginia
                 that he carried with him. According to Browning's diary, they
                 sat together "on the stone steps of the portico." The president
                 also read from a copy of satirical verse by the poet Fitz-Greene
                 Halleck.

July   Later in the war, Lincoln recalls to aide John Hay that sometime
                 at the beginning of this month General Montgomery Meigs, the
                 Union Army's chief quartermaster, rode out to the Soldiers'
                 Home in panic, urging the president to evacuate McClellan's
                 army from the peninsula.

July 4   President Lincoln meets wounded soldiers from the Virginia
                 peninsula campaign while returning in the evening to the Sol-
                 diers' Home.

July 5   Senator Browning and an associate named Daniel G. Whitney
                 ride out to the Soldiers' Home in the evening. William T.
                 Carroll, the chief clerk of the Supreme Court, also visits the
                 first family that evening. Lincoln shows Browning dispatches
                 from General George McClellan suggesting that the penin-
                 sula campaign is going better "than was previously supposed."

July 9–17   Mary Lincoln leaves the Soldiers' Home, with both sons Rob-
                 ert and Tad, and travels to New York for a brief excursion.

July 13   During a carriage ride to the funeral for Secretary of War
                 Stanton's child, President Lincoln reveals to Secretary of State
                 Seward and his son and Secretary of Navy Gideon Welles that
                 he plans to issue an emancipation proclamation.

July 25   Before leaving Washington for the season, Senator Browning
                 and his wife, along with naval officer J. C. P. DeKrafft and the
                 wife of New Mexico territorial delegate John S. Watts, visit
                 with the Lincoln family at the Soldiers' Home. The president
                 informs Browning that he has given General Henry Halleck
                 full authority to replace McClellan. In addition, he shares with
                 the senator a confidential request from Great Britain to allow
                 $50 million worth of cotton to pass through the Union naval
                 blockade.

July 26	Mary Lincoln writes to a local social acquaintance that her family is "delighted" with life at the Soldiers' Home, especially with the "drives & walks" around the grounds.
July	Elbert S. Porter, a minister and editor of the *Christian Intelligencer*, discusses emancipation with President Lincoln at the cottage.
July	Probably in July 1862, some of Lincoln's oldest friends from Illinois—Leonard Swett, William Hanna, and Ward Hill Lamon—visit him at the Soldiers' Home and try desperately to convince him to increase his personal security. He says he cannot be "shut up" in a cage.
August 8	Margaret Heintzelman, wife of General Samuel P. Heintzelman, reviews the failed peninsula campaign with the president while visiting the Lincoln family at their retreat. She is joined by a friend named Miss Hurd.
August 13	Union steamers *George Peabody* and *West Point* collide on the Potomac, creating a terrible tragedy that results in over seventy deaths.
August 23	Colonel Charles Scott, whose wife died in the Potomac steamer tragedy, appeals to the president for permission to enter a closed military zone to recover her body. He is escorted to the Soldiers' Home by fellow New Hampshire native and Treasury Department official, John R. French.
August 29	Union troops suffer another devastating defeat at the Second Battle of Bull Run.
August 30	Lincoln bemoans General McClellan's "dreadful cowardice" while riding in from the Soldiers' Home with White House aide John Hay.
August	Sometime in August or September, General James Wadsworth, commander of the defenses of Washington, orders members of the 11th New York Cavalry to accompany President Lincoln on his daily commute between the Soldiers' Home and the White House.
August–September	During this period, painter Francis Carpenter claims that President Lincoln told him he "finished" the "second draft" of the Emancipation Proclamation at the Soldiers' Home.

September   Lincoln family nurse Rebecca Pomroy recalls that during this month, as she rode with the president from the Soldiers' Home one morning, he informed her that he seemed "cheerful" because during the previous night he had finally finished drafting the emancipation proclamation.

September 2   McClellan meets with Lincoln at the Soldiers' Home while trying to reorganize the defenses of Washington in the aftermath of the Union defeat.

September 3   Newspapers report that Secretary of State Seward conferred with President Lincoln at the Soldiers' Home until midnight. There is widespread panic in Washington as General Lee launches an invasion of Maryland.

September 5   General McClellan orders a military guard placed around the Soldiers' Home.

September 6   After a mix-up in the assignment caused by confusion with the "Soldiers' Rest" (a transit camp for Union troops near the B&O Railroad station located in the city), two companies from the 150th Pennsylvania Volunteers—Company K and Company D—arrive to guard the president.

September 7   President Lincoln meets Captain David V. Derickson, Company K, and rides with him into the city. The two men soon form a close friendship.

September 13   Lincoln sprains his wrist while attempting to control his runaway horse on the morning ride into the city.

September 17   Union forces stop the Confederate advance at the Battle of Antietam.

September 20   The *Chicago Daily Tribune* reports that Mary Lincoln insists on a cavalry escort for her husband during his commutes from the Soldiers' Home.

September 21   White House aide John Hay notes that in the morning the president was "carefully" finishing his preliminary emancipation proclamation at the White House.

September 22   President Lincoln announces his decision to endorse an emancipation policy to his cabinet and formally issues the Preliminary Emancipation Proclamation.

September 25   Lincoln informs White House aide John Hay while they are riding to the Soldiers' Home in the evening that General McClellan "was doing nothing to make himself either respected or feared."

September 28   Secretary of Navy Welles informs his wife in a letter that the Lincoln family continues in residence at the Soldiers' Home.

October 4   Mary Lincoln writes a letter to newspaper editor James Gordon Bennett from the Soldiers' Home, openly discussing her husband's problems with his cabinet.

October 13   Vice President Hamlin recalls that he and Lincoln "talk all night" at the cottage about the fate of General McClellan.

October 20   Mary Lincoln, along with son Tad, travels to New York and then to Boston. She is gone for five weeks before returning on November 27.

November 1   President Lincoln writes a letter of endorsement for Captain Derickson and the men of Company K, who guard the Soldiers' Home, claiming that they were "very agreeable."

November 4   Postmaster General Montgomery Blair convinces his father, noted political adviser Francis P. Blair, Sr., to visit Lincoln at the Soldiers' Home and try to convince him to keep General McClellan in command. Lincoln refuses, claiming that McClellan has "the slows."

November 9   Reporting that it had grown cold, Lincoln wires his wife, then on a trip to Boston, asking permission to return the household and servants to the White House. The move probably occurs that week.

1863

January 1   President Lincoln signs the Emancipation Proclamation at the White House.

January 1   Mary Lincoln and Orville Browning ride out to the Soldiers' Home in the afternoon and discuss the first lady's recent experiences with spiritualists.

April | Captain David Derickson leaves his command as head of Lincoln's military guard and returns to Pennsylvania to serve as his district's provost marshal, the Union official responsible for organizing recruitment, and if necessary, the draft. He is replaced by Captain Thomas Getchell.

May 2–4 | Union troops suffer a demoralizing defeat at the Battle of Chancellorsville.

June 8–17 | Mary Lincoln and Tad enjoy an excursion to Philadelphia.

June 22 | The Lincoln family begins another season in residence at the Soldiers' Home.

June 24 | Confederate troops cross the Potomac River as General Robert E. Lee launches his second invasion of the North, this time toward Pennsylvania.

June 26 | Silas W. Burt and two other New York politicians journey to the Soldiers' Home to discuss the Union's troubled political and military situation. An obviously exhausted President Lincoln falls asleep near the end of their interview.

July 1–3 | The Battle of Gettysburg results in a pivotal victory for the Union.

July 3 | Mary Lincoln suffers serious head injuries when she falls from a carriage while riding from the Soldiers' Home to a nearby hospital. Her wounds later become infected and she nearly dies.

July 4 | Confederate troops in Vicksburg surrender. Within a week, Union forces will control the entire Mississippi River.

July 6 | Lincoln sends a sharp message to General Henry Halleck from the Soldiers' Home complaining that he was "a good deal dissatisfied" with the failure of Union generals to follow up their victory at Gettysburg.

July 10 | President Lincoln interviews ordnance expert John Absterdam and two of his associates about a new type of shell that Absterdam has invented.

July 14 | On or about this day, Robert Lincoln comes to get his father at his White House office so they can head off to the Soldiers' Home and discovers the president in an uncharacteristically bad mood. Lincoln complains to his eldest son bitterly about the failures of Union generals to capture Lee's army after the Battle of Gettysburg.

July 19   President Lincoln meets with the British minister at his cottage.

July 25   White House aide John Hay spends the evening with President Lincoln discussing philology. He reports riding home in the dark amid "a party of drunken gamblers & harlots."

July 28   At about this time, Mary Lincoln begins an eight-week vacation from Washington with Tad by heading for New York City. Later they will travel to Vermont. They will not return until September 28.

August 12   Walt Whitman records in his journal that he observes the president and his cavalry escort traveling into Washington each morning.

August 22   Lincoln and young aide John Hay view the stars from the Naval Observatory and spend the night at the Soldiers' Home. Hay falls asleep while the president recites passages from Shakespeare.

August 23   Lincoln and Hay share an early breakfast and ride into the city together. Later that day, the president will draft a public letter to James C. Conkling defending the course of his administration and its policies on the draft and emancipation.

September 1   Late in the afternoon, Union army officer and former journalist Donn Piatt discusses the court-martial of General Robert H. Milroy with an aggravated President Lincoln, who is trying to leave the White House for the Soldiers' Home.

September 16   General Joseph Hooker visits President Lincoln at his wartime retreat.

September 20   General Samuel P. Heintzelman notes in his diary that Lincoln spent the night at the White House. The president was clearly waiting for news from the Battle of Chickamauga, an important engagement outside Chattanooga, Tennessee, that resulted in yet another Union defeat.

September 23   Secretary of War Stanton sends John Hay to retrieve Lincoln from the Soldiers' Home for an emergency meeting to deal with the aftermath of the Chickamauga defeat. Union military officials conceive an inspired plan to reinforce Federal troops in Tennessee by using commercial rail lines.

September 27　　General Hooker takes aide John Hay with him to the Soldiers' Home to meet with the president before Hooker transfers to the western theater of the war.

September 28　　Mary Lincoln and Tad return from their summer vacation travels.

October 8　　General Dan Sickles, a former congressman who lost his leg at the Battle of Gettysburg, spends an evening with Lincoln at the cottage.

October 29　　Company K, the president's military guard, moves from the Soldiers' Home to the White House.

November 4　　Movers haul nineteen loads of furniture from the summer cottage to the White House.

December　　The Union Light Guard, a specially recruited cavalry unit from Ohio, begins guarding the president as he moves about town; the Light Guard replaces the 11th New York Cavalry. A portion of the Light Guard will be stationed at the Soldiers' Home with Company K of the 150th Pennsylvania in the summer of 1864.

December　　President Lincoln asks his wife's half-sister, Emilie Todd Helm, if she would come and live with the family in six months once they return to their Soldiers' Home cottage. Helm declines.

1864

January　　The Board of Commissioners of the Soldiers' Home appoints retired Colonel Justin Dimmick as the new governor of the institution. He replaces Colonel Thomas Alexander, who had been serving as acting governor since 1858. Many Union officials suspected Alexander, a Kentucky native, of having Rebel sympathies.

February 11　　Confederate President Jefferson Davis vetoes legislation proposing to create a Soldiers' Home in the Confederacy.

May 3　　Mary Lincoln enjoys an afternoon ride to the Soldiers' Home with the wife and daughter of a New York congressman.

May 21	Local upholsterer John Alexander submits invoices totaling $3,000 to the Commissioner of Public Buildings for work on refurbishing the Lincoln cottage at the Soldiers' Home.
June 29	President Lincoln wires his wife, "All is well. Tom is moving things out," presumably referring to the impending seasonal move out to the Soldiers' Home.
July 4	The Lincoln family begins its third season in residence at the Soldiers' Home.
July 9	Confederate troops under the direction of General Jubal Early defeat Union forces at Monocacy in Maryland and head toward the District of Columbia.
July 10	After an urgent request from Secretary of War Stanton, the Lincoln family hurriedly leaves the Soldiers' Home and arrives at the White House about midnight.
July 11	Confederate General Early's forces begin a light assault on the outskirts of Washington.
July 11	In the afternoon, President Lincoln leaves the White House and observes the Rebel troops from an outpost at Fort Stevens near the Maryland line. He is present when the fort comes under enemy fire.
July 12	President and Mrs. Lincoln visit Fort Stevens together and both are present when the fort again comes under light enemy fire. A surgeon standing near the president is wounded in the leg.
July 14	President Lincoln returns to the Soldiers' Home, complaining along the way to aide John Hay that his generals are once again slow in trying to capture the fleeing Rebels.
July 18	Lincoln drafts a letter for possible negotiations with the Confederates, addressed "To Whom It May Concern," that lists "abandonment of slavery" as a precondition for talks.
July 19	Suffering from a headache, Mary Lincoln is unable to entertain guests George Ramsey, chief of Ordnance, and his niece.
July 26	Secretary of Navy Welles and his wife Mary Ann visit the Lincoln family at their cottage. Welles and Lincoln complain about the failures of Union military leaders.

July 28	Court-martial of Captain George Bennett of Union Light Guard begins.
July 29	Mary Lincoln warns her eldest son Robert in a letter that Washington is exceptionally "warm & dusty" that summer.
July 30–August 1	The president and first lady travel to Fortress Monroe in Virginia for a meeting with General Ulysses Grant.
August	Union general Carl Schurz, a German-American Republican leader, visits Lincoln at the Soldiers' Home to discuss the upcoming 1864 election. Lincoln complains bitterly about the Radical critics within their own party.
August–September	Mary Lincoln and Tad again spend a large portion of the summer in Vermont.
August	Joshua Speed, probably Lincoln's closest friend, visits the family at their cottage and recalls that when he saw the president reading the Bible, they had a discussion about faith in which Lincoln revealed that he had abandoned the skeptical views of his youth.
August 19	Postmaster General (and former Wisconsin governor) Alexander Randall brings Wisconsin judge Joseph T. Mills to the Soldiers' Home. Indian Commissioner William P. Dole joins them. The four men discuss Lincoln's "To Whom It May Concern" letter of July 18, the fate of emancipation, and famous black abolitionist Frederick Douglass.
August 24	Lincoln observes a demonstration of Morse code from the tower at the Soldiers' Home.
August 28	An attorney for four men sentenced to death for treason arrives at the Soldiers' Home at midnight to plead with the president for mercy. Lincoln treats him kindly, revealing that he had already commuted their sentence.
August	Private John Nichols of Company K recalls that sometime during this month, he heard a gunshot and witnessed President Lincoln racing on his horse hatless into the Soldiers' Home. The president denied that he had been shot at, but Nichols reported that the next day he discovered Lincoln's hat with a hole in the brim.

September 8   The wife of Soldiers' Home governor Justin Dimmick dies.

September 11   Democratic congressman and notorious "Copperhead" Fernando Wood meets secretly with President Lincoln at the Soldiers' Home. They discuss the 1864 election.

September 16   Mary Lincoln and Tad return from their summer vacation in Vermont. They bring gifts for the soldiers of Company K who protect their cottage.

September   Sometime in the autumn of 1864, English visitor George Borrett spends an evening with President Lincoln at the Soldiers' Home cottage. Lincoln recites verses from Alexander Pope's "Essay on Man" from memory.

October   Lincoln family nurse Rebecca Pomroy reports in a letter that she has been urged to come to the Soldiers' Home, told by first family cook "Aunt" Mary Dines that the president has received several threatening letters.

October   Confederate spy Thomas N. Conrad observes President Lincoln's daily routine, trying to determine if he is vulnerable to kidnapping along the route between the Soldiers' Home and the White House.

October 3   Former senator Orville Browning tries to meet with President Lincoln at the White House but discovers that he is still in residence at the Soldiers' Home.

October 15   Secretary of War Stanton removes his household from the Soldiers' Home, returning to his residence in the city.

November 8   Lincoln reelected as U.S. president.

1865

April 13   According to a recollection by Treasury Department official Maunsell Field, President Lincoln rode out to the Soldiers' Home in the afternoon, just one day before he was fatally shot by John Wilkes Booth.

August 25   Mary Lincoln writes to friend Elizabeth Blair Lee (daughter of Francis P. Blair), a touching letter recalling her grief and including the phrase, "How dearly I loved the Soldiers' Home . . ."

Notes

Introduction

1. *Specimen Days*, "Abraham Lincoln," No. 45 [August 12, 1863], Walt Whitman, *Prose Works* (Philadelphia: David McKay, 1892); Bartleby.com, 2000. www.bartleby.com/229/ [October 29, 2002].
2. The others were James Buchanan, Rutherford B. Hayes, and Chester Arthur. See Paul R. Goode, *The United States Soldiers' Home: A History of Its First Hundred Years* (Richmond, Va.: William Byrd Press, 1957).
3. *Washington Sunday Chronicle*, April 14, 1861. I owe special thanks to Michael Burlingame for sharing this newspaper clipping.
4. Buchanan, quoted in Goode, p. 62, *New York Times*, March 8, 1861; *Washington Sunday Chronicle*, April 14, 1861.
5. Mary Lincoln to Hannah Shearer, Washington, July 11, 1861, reprinted in Justin G. Turner and Linda Levitt Turner, eds., *Mary Todd Lincoln: Her Life and Letters* (New York: Alfred A. Knopf, 1972), 94.
6. Mary Lincoln to George D. Ramsay [Soldiers' Home], July 20 [1864], in Turner and Turner, *Mary Todd Lincoln*, 177.
7. For details on the Lincolns' cottage and the questions surrounding their choice of residence, see chapter 7.
8. Mary Lincoln to Elizabeth Blair Lee, Chicago, August 25, 1865, in Turner and Turner, *Mary Todd Lincoln*, 267.
9. John Hay to William H. Herndon, Paris, September 5, 1866, in Douglas L. Wilson and Rodney O. Davis, eds., *Herndon's Informants: Letters, Interviews, and Statements about Abraham Lincoln* (Urbana: University of Illinois Press, 1998), 331.
10. David V. Derickson, "The President's Guard," typescript recollection courtesy of Jane Westenfeld, Ida M. Tarbell Papers, Allegheny College, Meadville, Pa.
11. Edward Dicey, *Spectator of America*, ed. Hebert Mitgang (orig. pub. as *Six Months in the Federal States* by Macmillan, 1863; Chicago: Quadrangle Books, 1971), 61.
12. Notes on interview with Charles M. Derickson, undated, courtesy of Jane Westenfeld, Ida M. Tarbell Papers, Allegheny College, Meadville, Pa.
13. Aldace F. Walker to Father, Fort Massachusetts, October 8, 1862, transcripts available from Fort Ward Museum Library, Alexandria, Va.

14. George Borrett, "An Englishman in Washington in 1864," *The Magazine of History with Notes and Queries* 38 (Extra no. 149; 1929), 6–7.

15. Quoted in Allen Clark, "Abraham Lincoln in the National Capital," *Records of the Columbia Historical Society* 27 (1925), 89.

16. John Hay, "Life in the White House in the Time of Lincoln," *Century* 41 (November 1890), 34. John Hay to William H. Herndon, Paris, September 5, 1866, in Wilson and Davis, *Herndon's Informants*, 331.

17. Isaac N. Arnold, *Life of Abraham Lincoln*, quoted in Allen Clark, "Abraham Lincoln in the National Capital," *Records of the Columbia Historical Society* 27 (1925), 90.

18. Dispatch of December 4, 1862, appearing in *Sacramento Daily Union*, December 30, 1862, in Michael Burlingame, ed., *Lincoln Observed: Civil War Dispatches of Noah Brooks* (Baltimore, Md.: Johns Hopkins University Press, 1998), 13–14.

19. F[rancis] B. Carpenter, "Personal Impressions of Mr. Lincoln," (New York) *The Independent*, April 27, 1865, 1: 2.

20. John Hay, "Life in the White House in the Time of Lincoln," *Century* 41 (November 1890), 35–36. Passage from *Richard II* 3.ii.155–160.

21. Abraham Lincoln to James H. Hackett, Executive Mansion, August 17, 1863, Roy P. Basler, ed., *The Collected Works of Abraham Lincoln*, (11 vols., New Brunswick, N.J.: Rutgers University Press, 1953), 6: 392–393.

22. Invoices from John Alexander, upholsterer, Washington, May 21, 1864, Record Group 217, Records of the U.S. General Accounting Office (GAO), Records of the First Auditor, Audit 151.223, October 24, 1864, National Archives. For details on the cottage interior, see chapter 7.

23. George Borrett, "An Englishman in Washington in 1864," *The Magazine of History with Notes and Queries* 38 (Extra no. 149; 1929), 2–15.

24. Leonard Swett, "The Conspiracies of the Rebellion," *North American Review* 144 (February 1887), 187–188.

25. Diary entry, Saturday, July 25, 1863, in Michael Burlingame and John R. Turner Ettlinger, eds., *Inside Lincoln's White House: The Complete Civil War Diary of John Hay* (Carbondale: Southern Illinois University Press, 1997), 67–68.

26. Mary Lincoln to Mrs. Charles [Fanny] Eames, Soldiers' Home, July 26 [1862], in Turner and Turner, *Mary Todd Lincoln*, 130–131.

27. *Specimen Days*, "Abraham Lincoln," No. 45 [August 12, 1863], Walt Whitman, *Prose Works* (Philadelphia: David McKay, 1892); Bartleby.com, 2000. www.bartleby.com/229/ [October 29, 2002].

28. Maunsell B. Field, *Memories of Many Men and of Some Women* (New York: Harper & Brothers, 1874), 321.

29. *Charleston Mercury*, February 26, 1861, Herbert Mitgang, ed., *Abraham Lincoln: A Press Portrait* (orig. pub. 1956; New York: Fordham University Press, 2000), 234.

30. Willard A. Cutter to Elizabeth Cutter, Washington, D.C., March 31, 1864, Willard A. Cutter Papers, Allegheny College, Meadville, Pa.

Chapter 1. "Gone to the country"

1. Mary Lincoln to John Hay [Washington] [May 23, 1862], in Thomas F. Schwartz and Kim M. Bauer, eds., "Unpublished Mary Todd Lincoln," *Journal of the Abraham Lincoln Association* 17 (Summer 1996), 4.

2. John Hay to J. G. Nicolay, April 9, 1862, in Tyler Dennett, ed., *Lincoln and the Civil War in the Diaries and Letters of John Hay* (orig. ed. 1939; New York: Da Capo Press, 1988), 41.

3. Mary Lincoln to John Hay [Washington] [May 25, 1862], in Schwartz and Bauer, "Unpublished Mary Todd Lincoln," 4–5.

4. Jean H. Baker, *Mary Todd Lincoln: A Biography* (New York: W.W. Norton, 1987), 211.

5. Mary Lincoln to Julia Ann Sprigg, Executive Mansion, May 29 [1862], in Turner and Turner, *Mary Todd Lincoln*, 128.

6. John G. Nicolay to Therena Bates, Washington, June 15, 1862, John G. Nicolay Papers, Library of Congress. The exact date of the Soldiers' Home departure is unclear. Local newspapers did not report on the move. A friend found that the family had left by Friday, June 13. See Diary entry, June 13, 1862, in Theodore C. Pease and James G. Randall, eds., *The Diary of Orville Hickman Browning* (2 vols., Springfield: Illinois State Historical Society, 1925–33), 1: 551.

7. Diary entry, June 16, 1862, in Benjamin Brown French, *Witness to the Young Republic: A Yankee's Journal, 1828–1870* (Hanover, N.H.: University Press of New England, 1989), 399–400.

8. Diary entry, Wednesday, June 18, 1862, in Pease and Randall, *The Diary of Orville Hickman Browning*, 1: 552.

9. For a good discussion of the March 8, 1862, council of war, see Stephen W. Sears, *George B. McClellan: The Young Napoleon* (New York: Ticknor & Fields, 1988), 158–160. The other Union generals who joined Heintzelman in questioning the peninsula campaign were John G. Barnard, Irvin McDowell, and Edwin Sumner.

10. Abraham Lincoln to George B. McClellan, June 18, 19, 1862, *Collected Works* 5: 276–277.

11. Charles E. Hamlin, *The Life and Times of Hannibal Hamlin* (2 vols., orig. pub. 1899; Port Washington, N.Y.: Kennikat Press, 1971), 2: 428–429.

12. "Message to Congress," March 6, 1862, *Collected Works* 5: 145.

13. Diary entry, Monday, April 14, 1862, in Pease and Randall, *The Diary of Orville Hickman Browning*, 1: 541.

14. David Herbert Donald, *Lincoln* (New York: Simon & Schuster, 1995), 654n.

15. Remarks to a Delegation of Progressive Friends, June 20, 1862, *Collected Works*, 5: 278.

16. For a balanced appraisal of the Lincoln-Browning relationship, see Maurice G. Baxter, *Orville H. Browning: Lincoln's Friend and Critic* (Bloomington: Indiana University Press, 1957), 172–179.

17. Diary entry, Sunday, June 22, 1862, in Pease and Randall, *The Diary of Orville Hickman Browning*, 1: 553.

18. "Remarks to Baltimore Presbyterian Synod," October 24, 1863, *Collected Works* 6: 535–536. The editors of the *Collected Works* have also included an alternate version of this statement on faith: "I have often wished that I was a more devout man than I am. Nevertheless, amid the greatest difficulties of my Administration, when I could not see any other resort, I would place my whole reliance in God, knowing that all would go well, and that He would decide for the right." For a lively analysis of this topic, with a skeptical eye toward attempts to "Christianize" Lincoln, see Allen C. Guelzo, *Abraham Lincoln: Redeemer President* (Grand Rapids, Mich.: William B. Eerdmans, 1999).

19. Mary Lincoln to Mrs. Charles [Fanny] Eames, Soldiers' Home, July 26 [1862], in Turner and Turner, *Mary Todd Lincoln*, 131.

20. Laura Redden (later Laura Redden Searing) was not only a female correspondent for a St. Louis–based newspaper (using the pseudonym "Howard Glyndon"), but also she was deaf and communicated only by writing notes. Thus, at least part of this recollection, which describes a conversation with Mary Lincoln, engages in a degree of poetic license. Howard Glyndon, "The Truth about Mrs. Lincoln," *The Independent*, August 10, 1882. See also Ruth Painter Randall, *Mary Lincoln: Biography of a Marriage* (Boston: Little, Brown, 1953), 296.

21. Baker, *Mary Todd Lincoln*, 216, 218.

22. Noah Brooks, "Glimpses of Lincoln in War Time," *Century* 49 (January, 1895), 462.

23. Thomas Coulson, *Joseph Henry: His Life and Work* (Princeton, N.J.: Princeton University Press, 1950), 308; Randall, *Mary Lincoln*, 292–293; Brooks, "Glimpses of Lincoln in War Time," *Century* 49 (January, 1895), 463.

24. Baker, *Mary Todd Lincoln*, 221; Donald, *Lincoln*, 427.

25. The 1860 Census listed 31,183,582 people and 5,155,608 families. Combatant and civilian deaths are estimates taken from James M. McPherson, *Ordeal by Fire: The Civil War and Reconstruction* (2d ed., New York: McGraw-Hill, 1992). Other calculations by the author.

26. The note suggests that by "house" Stanton meant his Soldiers' Home cottage, by "home" he meant his family's residence in the northwest section of the city, and by "town" he meant his office at the War Department. Edwin M. Stanton to Abraham Lincoln [June 29, 1862], Abraham Lincoln Papers, Library of Congress. Transcribed and annotated by the Lincoln Studies Center, Knox College, Galesburg, Ill. Available online at http://memory.loc.gov/ammem/alhtml/alhome.html.

27. David Homer Bates, *Lincoln in the Telegraph Office: Recollections of the United States Military Telegraph Corps during the Civil War* (orig. pub. 1907; Lincoln: University of Nebraska Press, 1995 ed.), 392; Peter Cozzens and Robert I. Girardi, eds., *The Military Memoirs of General John Pope* (Chapel Hill: University of North Carolina Press, 1998), 115.

28. Abraham Lincoln to William Seward, June 28, 1862, *Collected Works*, 5: 292.

29. Abraham Lincoln to William Seward, June 28, 1862, *Collected Works*, 5: 292.

30. Call for Troops, New York, June 30, 1862, *Collected Works*, 5: 294n.

31. The editors of Browning's diary do not identify "Mr & Mrs Dorman of Florida," but the editors of John Hay's diary are surely correct in believing that it was Orloff and Margarette Dorman, formerly of Chicago. See Pease and Randall, *The Diary of Orville Hickman Browning*, 1: 555, and Burlingame and Ettlinger, *Inside Lincoln's White House*, 300.

32. Diary entry, Monday, June 30, 1862, in Pease and Randall, *The Diary of Orville Hickman Browning*, 1: 555.

33. Ibid.; Abraham Lincoln to James G. Wilson, Springfield, May 2, 1860, *Collected Works*, 4: 48; "Fanny" (1819) appears in Fitz Greene Halleck, *The poetical works of Fitz-Greene Halleck. Now first collected. Illustrated with steel engravings, from drawings by American artists* (2d ed., New York: D. Appleton & Co., 1848), 111–211, available online at "Making of America: University of Michigan," http://moa.umdl.umich.edu/; "American Poets," *North American Review* 33 (October 1831), 309, available online at "Making of America: Cornell University Library," http://cdl.library.cornell.edu/moa/. For a recent biography of Halleck, see John W. M. Hallock, *The American Byron: Homosexuality and the Fall of Fitz-Greene Halleck* (Madison: University of Wisconsin Press, 2000).

34. Diary entry, Tuesday, July 1, 1862, in Pease and Randall, *The Diary of Orville Hickman Browning*, 1: 555.

35. Call for 300,000 Volunteers, July 1, 1862, *Collected Works* 5: 296–297. Abraham Lincoln to Edwin D. Morgan, July 2, 1862, *Collected Works* 5: 302.

Chapter 2. "Am I to have no rest?"

1. *New York Tribune*, July 8, 1862.

2. Remarks to Delegation of Veterans of 1812, July 4, 1862, *Collected Works*, 5: 306.

3. Diary entry, Thursday, April 28, 1864, in Burlingame and Ettlinger, *Inside Lincoln's White House: The Complete Civil War Diary of John Hay*, 191. Lincoln did not identify a date for this curious episode, but John Nicolay includes extracts from Meigs's diary attesting to a

late night visit on July 4, 1862, with Governor Sibley. See entry in Earl S. Miers, ed., *Lincoln Day by Day: A Chronology 1809–1865* (Dayton, Ohio: Morningside, 1990), 125.

4. Diary entry, Saturday, July 5, 1862, in Pease and Randall, *The Diary of Orville Hickman Browning*, 1: 557; Abraham Lincoln to George B. McClellan, July 5, 1862, *Collected Works* 5: 307.

5. George B. McClellan to Abraham Lincoln, July 7, 1862, Abraham Lincoln Papers, Library of Congress. See also Sears, *George B. McClellan*, 227–228.

6. July 5, 1862, entry from John A. Dahlgren diary quoted in Miers, *Lincoln Day By Day*, 126.

7. F[rancis] B. Carpenter, *The Inner Life of Abraham Lincoln: Six Months at the White House* (orig. pub. 1866; Lincoln: University of Nebraska Press, 1995), 86–87.

8. Gideon Welles, "History of Emancipation," *Galaxy* 14 (December 1872), 842.

9. Thomas T. Eckert quoted in Bates, *Lincoln in the Telegraph Office*, 138–141.

10. Mark E. Neely, Jr., *The Last Best Hope of Earth: Abraham Lincoln and the Promise of America* (Cambridge, Mass.: Harvard University Press, 1993), 108–109.

11. David Donald, for one, generally accepts Eckert's story. See Donald, *Lincoln*, 363–364.

12. Appeal to Border State Representatives, July 12, 1862, *Collected Works*, 5: 317–318. See Gideon Welles, "History of Emancipation," *Galaxy* 14 (December 1872), 843.

13. Welles recorded several versions of this conversation. For the original diary entry, see Howard K. Beale, ed., *Diary of Gideon Welles: Secretary of Navy under Lincoln and Johnson* (3 vols., New York: W. W. Norton, 1960), 1: 70–71. Note, however, that the entry for July 13, 1862, is undated and appears to have been entered at some time after the day itself. Welles also referred to the episode in his diary entry for September 22, 1862; see ibid., 1: 144. A decade later, the former secretary recalled the chain of events and related matters in a series of magazine articles that were eventually turned into a book. See Gideon Welles, "History of Emancipation," *Galaxy* 14 (December 1872), 843.

14. There are many good, scholarly accounts of congressional action on emancipation. One of the most succinct and insightful comes from Herman Belz, "Protection of Personal Liberty in Republican Emancipation Legislation," in his collection of essays, *Abraham Lincoln, Constitutionalism, and Equal Rights* (New York: Fordham University Press, 1998), 101–118.

15. Diary entry, Tuesday, July 15, 1862, in Pease and Randall, *The Diary of Orville Hickman Browning*, 1: 559–560.

16. George W. Julian, "Lincoln and the Proclamation of Emancipation," in Allen Thorndike Rice, ed., *Reminiscences of Abraham Lincoln by Distinguished Men of His Time* (orig. pub. 1885; New York: Harper & Brothers, 1909 rev. ed.), 237–238.

17. Emancipation Proclamation—First Draft [July 22, 1862], *Collected Works*, 5: 336–337. Several cabinet officers described the historic moment in their diaries and in later recollections.

18. Quoted in Carpenter, *The Inner Life of Abraham Lincoln*, 20–24.

19. Diary entry, Monday, July 21, 1862, in Pease and Randall, *The Diary of Orville Hickman Browning*, 1: 562.

20. Diary entry, Saturday, February 6, 1864, in Pease and Randall, *The Diary of Orville Hickman Browning*, 1: 659.

21. Diary entry, Friday, July 25, 1862, in Pease and Randall, *The Diary of Orville Hickman Browning*, 1: 563.

22. A good discussion of these complicated developments appears in Mark E. Neely, *The Fate of Liberty: Abraham Lincoln and Civil Liberties* (New York: Oxford University Press, 1991), 52–65. See also Philip Shaw Paludan, *The Presidency of Abraham Lincoln* (Lawrence: University Press of Kansas, 1995), 192–193, who correctly points out that although the Militia Act *authorized* a draft, the President never formally exercised this power in 1862. That

is why the Enrollment Act of March 1863 is often described as the first full-fledged conscription law in U.S. history.

23. Diary entry, Thursday, July 24, 1862, in Pease and Randall, *The Diary of Orville Hickman Browning*, 1: 562.

24. Diary entry, Friday, July 25, 1862, in Pease and Randall, *The Diary of Orville Hickman Browning*, 1: 563.

25. Mary Lincoln to Mrs. Charles [Fanny] Eames, Soldiers' Home, July 26 [1862], in Turner and Turner, *Mary Todd Lincoln*, 130–131.

26. Mary Lincoln to Julia Ann Sprigg, Executive Mansion, May 29 [1862], in Turner and Turner, *Mary Todd Lincoln*, 128.

27. *New York Herald*, August 18, 1861.

28. Abraham Lincoln to Joshua F. Speed, Springfield, October 22, 1846, *Collected Works* 1: 391.

29. Rebecca Pomroy to unidentified person, Washington, August 1862, quoted in Anna L. Boyden, ed., *War Reminiscences: A Record of Mrs. Rebecca R. Pomroy's Experience in Wartimes* (Boston, Mass.: D. Lothrop, 1884), 105.

30. William Seward to John Bigelow, Washington, July 15, 1862, reprinted in U.S. Department of State, *Assassination of President Lincoln* (Washington, D.C.: Government Printing Office, 1867), 134.

31. Leonard Swett, "The Conspiracies of the Rebellion," *North American Review* 144 (February 1887), 187–188. Swett, Hanna, and Lamon were all residents of Bloomington, Illinois. Swett tentatively dates their conversation with Lincoln as occurring in the summer of 1863 but guards were already in place by then and records indicate that Swett was in Washington on August 2, 1862. See *Collected Works* 5: 353. The image of not being shut up in an "iron cage" is one Lincoln repeated frequently. See J. G. Nicolay and John Hay, "A History of Abraham Lincoln," *Century* 39 (January 1890), 432. Other less credible sources who claimed credit for convincing the president to increase his security were Ward H. Lamon and Union general Benjamin F. Butler. See Benjamin F. Butler, "Some of Lincoln's Problems," in Rice, *Reminiscences of Abraham Lincoln*, 252–253, and Ward Hill Lamon, *Recollections of Abraham Lincoln, 1847–1865* (Chicago: A. C. McClurg, 1895), 261–263.

32. Abraham Lincoln to Reverdy Johnson, July 26, 1862, *Collected Works* 5: 343. Note that this letter is in John Hay's handwriting and even though it was included in Lincoln's *Collected Works*, it probably represents only an approximation of Lincoln's own thoughts and phrases.

33. Address to Union Meeting in Washington, August 6, 1862, *Collected Works*, 5: 359.

34. Address on Colonization to a Deputation of Negroes, August 14, 1862, *Collected Works* 5: 371–372.

35. Abraham Lincoln to Horace Greeley, August 22, 1862, *Collected Works* 5: 388–389. See Allen C. Guelzo, *Abraham Lincoln: Redeemer President* (Grand Rapids, Mich.: William B. Eerdmans, 1999), 340–341.

36. Memorandum: Appointment of Gabriel R. Paul, August 23, 1862, *Collected Works* 5: 390–391. The officer received his promotion in September.

37. John R. French, "Reminiscences of Famous Americans," *North American Review* 141 (September 1885), 237–239.

38. E. B. Long with Barbara Long, eds., *The Civil War Day by Day: An Almanac 1861–1865* (Garden City, N.Y.: Doubleday, 1971), 250. A preliminary list of victims printed in the *Baltimore Sun*, August 16, 1862, includes Scott's wife and comments from Scott himself. French's recollection omits Colonel Scott's first name, his wife's name, the names of the ships involved in the accident, and even the date of the visit to the cottage—all details that tend to vanish in the mists of memory. I owe special thanks to Eddie Daniels for tracking down many of these corroborating details.

Chapter 3. "Forever free"

1. George B. McClellan to Ellan Marcy McClellan, August 29, 1862, and George B. McClellan to Abraham Lincoln, August 29, 1862, quoted in Sears, *George B. McClellan*, 254.

2. Diary entry, Monday, September 1, 1862, in Burlingame and Ettlinger, *Inside Lincoln's White House*, 37.

3. Gideon Welles diary entry, September 2, 1862, quoted in Benjamin Franklin Cooling, *Symbol, Sword, and Shield: Defending Washington during the Civil War* (Shippensberg, Pa.: White Mane Publishing, 1991), 128.

4. George B. McClellan to Abraham Lincoln, September 2, 1862, Abraham Lincoln Papers, Library of Congress. Transcribed and annotated by the Lincoln Studies Center, Knox College, Galesburg, Ill.

5. Diary entry, Friday, September 5, 1862, in Burlingame and Ettlinger, *Inside Lincoln's White House*, 38–39. It is worth noting, however, that Lincoln apparently took steps to distance himself publicly from the decision to elevate McClellan. See Sears, *George B. McClellan*, 259–261.

6. Quoted in Sears, *George B. McClellan*, 263–264.

7. George B. McClellan to Abraham Lincoln, Washington, September 5 [1862], in Ibid., 435.

8. Reprinted in Thomas Chamberlin, *History of the One Hundred and Fiftieth Regiment Pennsylvania Volunteers, Second Regiment, Bucktail Brigade* (Philadelphia, Pa.: F. McManus, 1905), 27.

9. Willard A. Cutter to Elizabeth Cutter, Camp Soldiers Home, September 10, 1862, transcript courtesy of Mike Dallas, Meadville, Pa. Chamberlin, *One Hundred and Fiftieth Regiment*, 36–37.

10. Willard A. Cutter to Elizabeth Cutter, Camp Soldiers Home, September 10, 1862, transcript courtesy of Mike Dallas, Meadville, Pa.

11. Charles M. Derickson recollection, December 15, 1897, Ida M. Tarbell Papers, Allegheny College, Meadville, Pa.

12. No record of this appointment has been found. Lincoln might have been familiar with Derickson's name because the Meadville Republican wrote him in January 1861 urging the appointment of Pennsylvania senator Simon Cameron as secretary of Treasury in the new administration. See David Derrickson [*sic*] to Abraham Lincoln, January 24, 1861, Abraham Lincoln Papers, Library of Congress. Transcribed and annotated by the Lincoln Studies Center, Knox College. Galesburg, Ill.

13. [R. C. Browne], *History of Crawford County: Part II* (Chicago: Warner, Beers, & Co., 1885), 2: 344–345.

14. Samuel P. Heintzelman diary, quoted in Miers, *Lincoln Day By Day*, 138.

15. Quoted in Chamberlin, *One Hundred and Fiftieth Regiment*, 41.

16. Willard A. Cutter to Elizabeth Cutter, Camp Soldiers Home, September 10, 1862, transcript courtesy of Mike Dallas, Meadville, Pa.

17. *Cincinnati Gazette*, "The President's Cavalry Escort, and How It Happened," September 18, 1862, reprinted in *Chicago Daily Tribune*, September 20, 1862.

18. Thomas West Smith, *The Story of a Cavalry Regiment: Scott's 900 Eleventh New York Cavalry* (n.p.: Veteran's Assocation, 1897), 14. Bostwick's 5 cent note is currently being traded as a Civil War memento over the Internet. See http://www.rrcoins.net/images/Scotts.jpg.

19. Smith, *The Story of a Cavalry Regiment*, 25.

20. Harry M. Kieffer, *The Recollections of a Drummer-Boy* (Boston: Houghton Mifflin, 7th ed., 1890), 48.

21. Colonel Halpine quoted in Carpenter, *The Inner Life of Abraham Lincoln*, 67.

22. Smith, *The Story of a Cavalry Regiment*, 25–26.

23. Abraham Lincoln to George B. McClellan, July 5, 1862, *Collected Works* 5: 307.

24. (Washington, D.C.) *The Evening Star*, September 13, 1862 (2d ed.), 3: 5.

25. Reply to Emancipation Memorial [Washington], September 13, 1862, *Collected Works*, 5: 420. Although included in his official writings, it is worth noting that Lincoln did not put these remarks on paper. Rather, participants at the meeting attributed them to Lincoln shortly afterward.

26. Willard Cutter to George Cutter, Camp Soldiers Home, September 16, 1862, Willard A. Cutter Papers, Allegheny College, Meadville, Pa.

27. McPherson, *Ordeal by Fire*, 286.

28. *Union County (Pa.) Star and Lewisburg Chronicle*, September 19, 1862, 1:5. Available on-line at http://bertrand.bucknell.edu/sheary/newspapers/uc&lc09_19_62.htm

29. Diary entry, Tuesday, July 14, 1863, in Burlingame and Ettlinger, *Inside Lincoln's White House*, 62.

30. Diary entry, September 22, 1862, in Beale, *Diary of Gideon Welles*, 1: 143–145.

31. Diary entry, September 22, 1862, in David Donald, ed., *Inside Lincoln's Cabinet: The Civil War Diaries of Salmon P. Chase* (New York: Longmans, Green, 1954), 150.

32. George S. Boutwell to Josiah G. Holland, June 10, 1865, J. G. Holland Papers, New York Public Library. George S. Boutwell, *The Lawyers, the Statesman, and the Soldier* (New York: D. Appleton, 1887), 116–117. I owe special thanks to Allen Guelzo for pointing out this discrepancy.

33. Carpenter, *The Inner Life of Abraham Lincoln*, 20–24.

34. Boyden, *War Reminiscences*, 121–122.

35. F[rancis] B. Carpenter to William H. Herndon, New York, December 4, 1866, in Wilson and Davis, *Herndon's Informants*, 495.

36. For the full passage, see Carpenter, *The Inner Life of Abraham Lincoln*, 20–24. The mistakes are subtle but not likely from a president blessed with an exceptional memory. In the painter's version of the conversation, for example, Lincoln cannot remember the exact date of the critical July 22 cabinet meeting and confuses some of the chronology around the battle of Antietam. *New York Times* columnist William Safire does a good job of exposing these and others inconsistencies in the "Underbook" to his novel, *Freedom*; see William Safire, *Freedom: A Novel of Abraham Lincoln and the Civil War* (New York: Avon Books, 1987), 1376–1377. Carpenter's Lincoln also uses distinctive phrases, such as "Things had gone on from bad to worse" and "we had reached the end of our rope," that don't otherwise appear in the canon of his writings. Even more revealing, some of the phrases attributed to Lincoln, such as "touching it up here and there," sound suspiciously like the metaphors of a painter, not a politician.

37. Quoted in Donald, *Lincoln*, 15.

38. Philip W. Ogilvie, "Elizabeth Thomas (1821–1917)," unpublished paper, 2000. Allan John Johnston, "Surviving Freedom: The Black Community of Washington, D.C., 1860–1880" (Ph.D. dissertation, Duke University, 1980), 177.

39. *Washington Post*, "Former Woman Slave, 92, Pays Tribute to Father Abraham" [December 27, 1936], Soldiers' Home Files.

40. Notes on interview with Charles M. Derickson, undated, typescript courtesy of Jane Westenfeld, Ida M. Tarbell Papers, Allegheny College, Meadville, Pa.

41. Mary Dines, quoted in John E. Washington, *They Knew Lincoln* (New York: E. P. Dutton, 1942), 84–87.

42. Washington, *They Knew Lincoln*, 87. It is worth pointing out that in her recollection, Dines attributes various statements to President Lincoln, but Don and Virginia Fehrenbacher, editors of an edition of Lincoln's "recollected words," consider there to be "more than average doubt" regarding the accuracy of these quotations. See Don E. Fehrenbacher and Virginia

Fehrenbacher, eds., *Recollected Words of Abraham Lincoln* (Stanford, Calif.: Stanford University Press, 1996), 142.

43. Diary entry, September 21, 1862, in Donald, *Inside Lincoln's Cabinet*, 149.

44. Diary entry, Wednesday, September 24, 1862, in Burlingame and Ettlinger, *Inside Lincoln's White House*, 40.

45. Preliminary Emancipation Proclamation, September 22, 1862, photocopy provided courtesy of Kathi Stanley, New York State Library, Albany, N.Y.

46. David V. Derickson, "The President's Guard," typescript recollection courtesy of Jane Westenfeld, Ida M. Tarbell Papers, Allegheny College, Meadville, Pa.

47. Nibbie Slade, quoted in Washington, *They Knew Lincoln*, 111.

48. Preliminary Emancipation Proclamation [Washington], September 22, 1862, *Collected Works*, 5: 433–436.

49. Response to Serenade, September 24, 1862, *Collected Works*, 5: 438.

50. Dateline, September 25, 1862, appearing in *Missouri Republican*, September 29, 1862, in Michael Burlingame, ed., *Lincoln's Journalist: John Hay's Anonymous Writings for the Press, 1860–1864* (Carbondale: Southern Illinois University Press, 1998), 312–313.

51. Diary entry, Wednesday, September 24, 1862, in Burlingame and Ettlinger, *Inside Lincoln's White House*, 41.

Chapter 4. "Capt. D and his company"

1. Diary entry, Friday, September 26, 1862, in Burlingame and Ettlinger, *Inside Lincoln's White House*, 41.

2. Diary entry, Saturday, November 29, 1862, in Pease and Randall, *The Diary of Orville Hickman Browning*, 1:589–590.

3. Lincoln's famous remark about novice soldiers, "You are green, it is true, but they are green also; you are all green alike," was a comment attributed to him in the days before the Battle of First Bull Run. Quoted in James M. McPherson, *Battle Cry of Freedom* (New York: Oxford University Press, 1988), 336.

4. Willard Cutter to William S. Cutter, Camp Soldiers' Home, September 28, 1862, Willard A. Cutter Papers, Allegheny College, Meadville, Pa.

5. Record of Dismissal of John J. Key," September 26–27, 1862, *Collected Works* 5: 442–443.

6. Abraham Lincoln to Hannibal Hamlin, September 28, 1862, *Collected Works* 5: 444. Considering Hamlin's later claim that he first heard Lincoln's emancipation plans in June 1862, it is worth noting that his letter of September 25 made no mention of this fact. If anything, the vice president sounded slightly alienated from the president. He began his correspondence with the admission that "I do not know as . . . this note will ever meet your eye." See Hannibal Hamlin to Abraham Lincoln, September 25, 1862, Abraham Lincoln Papers, Library of Congress. Transcribed and annotated by the Lincoln Studies Center, Knox College, Galesburg, Ill.

7. Montgomery Blair to George B. McClellan, September 27, 1862; Francis P. Blair to George B. McClellan, September 30, 1862, quoted in Sears, *George B. McClellan*, 326–327. See also Donald, *Lincoln*, 386–387.

8. Abraham Lincoln to George McClellan, October 13, 1862, Abraham Lincoln Papers, Library of Congress. Transcribed and annotated by the Lincoln Studies Center, Knox College, Galesburg, Ill. Quoted in Sears, *George B. McClellan*, 330.

9. Henry W. Halleck to George B. McClellan, October 6, 1862, quoted in Basler, ed., *Collected Works* 5: 452n.

10. George B. McClellan to Abraham Lincoln, October 7, 1862, Abraham Lincoln Papers, Library of Congress. Transcribed and annotated by the Lincoln Studies Center, Knox College, Galesburg, Ill.

11. Diary entry, Friday, September 23, 1864, in Burlingame and Ettlinger, *Inside Lincoln's White House*, 230.

12. Mrs. [Mary] Lincoln to James Gordon Bennett, Soldiers' Home, October 4, 1862, in Turner and Turner, *Mary Todd Lincoln*, 138.

13. For an especially thoughtful treatment of this period, see Douglas L. Wilson, *Honor's Voice: The Transformation of Abraham Lincoln* (New York: Alfred A. Knopf, 1998).

14. There are widely differing views on the dynamics of the Lincoln marriage. For a sophisticated portrait generally sympathetic to Mary Lincoln, see Baker, *Mary Todd Lincoln*. For a well-researched interpretation that claims the marriage was mostly "a fountain of misery," see Michael Burlingame, *The Inner World of Abraham Lincoln* (Urbana: University of Illinois Press, 1994).

15. Benjamin B. French, diary entry, December 16, 1861, quoted in Fehrenbacher and Fehrenbacher, *Recollected Words of Abraham Lincoln*, 382.

16. Notes on interview with Charles M. Derickson, undated, courtesy of Jane Westenfeld, Ida M. Tarbell Papers, Allegheny College, Meadville, Pa.

17. Willard A. Cutter to Elizabeth Cutter, Soldiers Home, October 8, 1862, Willard A. Cutter Papers, Allegheny College, Meadville, Pa.

18. Albert N. See, *Autobiography of Albert Nelson See* with an introduction by Joseph S. Northrop (orig. pub. by author 1921; Huntington, Ind.: Joseph S. Northrop, 1983) [24], Henry Horner Lincoln Collection, Illinois State Historical Library, Springfield, Ill.

19. Charles M. Derickson recollection, December 15, 1897, courtesy of Jane Westenfeld and Michael Burlingame, Ida M. Tarbell Papers, Allegheny College, Meadville, Pa. Notes on interview with Charles M. Derickson, undated, courtesy of Jane Westenfeld, Ida M. Tarbell Papers, Allegheny College, Meadville, Pa.

20. Baker, *Mary Todd Lincoln*, 255. See also, Donald, *Lincoln*, 428, and Ruth Painter Randall, *Lincoln's Sons* (Boston, Mass.: Little Brown, 1955), 137–138.

21. See, *Autobiography of Albert Nelson See*.

22. Wayne C. Temple, "Mary Todd Lincoln's Travels," *Journal of the Illinois State Historical Society* 52 (Spring 1959), 186–188.

23. Abraham Lincoln to George B. McClellan, October 25, 1862, *Collected Works* 5: 474.

24. C[harles]. M. Derickson to Ida M. Tarbell, March 26, 1898, courtesy of Jane Westenfeld, Ida M. Tarbell Papers, Allegheny College, Meadville, Pa.

25. C[harles]. M. Derickson to Ida M. Tarbell, March 26, 1898, courtesy of Jane Westenfeld, Ida M. Tarbell Papers, Allegheny College, Meadville, Pa. An edited version of this story appears in Ida M. Tarbell, *The Life of Abraham Lincoln* (4 vols., New York: S. S. McClure, 1895), 3: 156–157.

26. Smith, *The Story of a Cavalry Regiment*, 26–27.

27. Judge Advocate General's Office Records, Record Group 153, File No. MM773, NN748, George W. Flemming, August 1, 1863, National Archives, Washington, D.C. I owe special thanks to Tom and Beverly Lowry and the Index Project Inc. for helping to identify this case. Flemming was convicted of desertion in February 1864, and sentenced to death. The harsh verdict was eventually commuted, however, and Flemming returned home with the rest of his company in June 1865.

28. William C. Davis, *Lincoln's Men: How President Lincoln Became Father to an Army and a Nation* (New York: Free Press, 1999).

29. James Sloan Gibbons, "We Are Coming Father Abraham," *New York Evening Post*, August 16, 1862.

30. David V. Derickson, "The President's Guard," typescript recollection courtesy of Jane Westenfeld, Ida M. Tarbell Papers, Allegheny College, Meadville, Pa. Mix quoted in Carpenter, *The Inner Life of Abraham Lincoln*, 261–262.

31. Chamberlin, *One Hundred and Fiftieth Regiment*, 40–41.

32. H. S. Huidekoper, "On Guard at White House," *National Magazine* 9 (February 1909), 510. I owe special thanks to Mary Beth Corrigan for turning up this recollection.

33. David V. Derickson, "The President's Guard," Ida M. Tarbell Papers, Allegheny College, Meadville, Pa.

34. *New York Herald*, October 5, 1862.

35. Abraham Lincoln to Whom It May Concern, Executive Mansion, November 1, 1862, *Collected Works*, 5: 484–485.

36. Willard A. Cutter to George Cutter, November 1, 1862, Willard A. Cutter Papers, Allegheny College, Meadville, Pa.

37. Willard A. Cutter to Elizabeth Cutter, November 1, 1862, Willard A. Cutter Papers, Allegheny College, Meadville, Pa.

38. Diary entry, November 16, 1862, Virginia Woodbury Fox in Levi Woodbury Papers, container 1, reel 1 (1862), Library of Congress. Dr. C. A. Tripp and journalist Philip Nobile deserve credit for helping to bring this entry to my attention.

39. Mary Todd Lincoln to Abraham Lincoln, New York, November 2, 1862, Abraham Lincoln Papers, Lincoln of Congress. Transcribed and annotated by the Lincoln Studies Center, Knox College, Galesburg, Ill.

40. Mary Todd Lincoln to Abraham Lincoln, New York, November 2, 1862, Abraham Lincoln Papers, Lincoln of Congress. Transcribed and annotated by the Lincoln Studies Center, Knox College, Galesburg, Ill.

41. This story comes from an unpublished recollection written by Cooke in 1890. His memory was faulty on at least one minor detail. He claims that the interview, which he places in the week before McClellan's dismissal, occurred while the president playfully bounced his youngest son Tad on his knee. In early November, however, Tad Lincoln was in New York and Boston with his mother. See Jay Cooke, "Interview with Lincoln," *American History Illustrated* 7 (November 1972), 11.

42. Montgomery Blair's recollection comes from a letter to one of George McClellan's early biographers. See Montgomery Blair to George Ticknor Curtis, Washington, January 21, 1880, quoted in George Ticknor Curtis, "McClellan's Last Service to the Republic, Part III," *North American Review* 130 (June 1880), 567–568. Francis Blair, Sr.'s, description of the meeting comes from his November 7, 1862, letter to his son Montgomery Blair, excerpted in William E. Smith, *The Francis P. Blair Family in Politics* (2 vols., New York: Macmillan, 1933), 2: 144.

43. Quoted in Smith, *The Francis P. Blair Family in Politics*, 2: 144.

44. Quoted in George Ticknor Curtis, "McClellan's Last Service to the Republic, Part III," *North American Review* 130 (June 1880), 567–568.

45. Abraham Lincoln to Mary Lincoln, Washington, November 9, 1862, *Collected Works* 5: 492.

46. Willard A. Cutter to George Cutter, Camp Soldiers' Home, November 9, 1862, Willard A. Cutter Papers, Allegheny College, Meadville, Pa.

Chapter 5. "Mother very slightly hurt"

1. Benjamin B. French, "Address Delivered at the Dedication of the Statue of Abraham Lincoln, Washington, April 15, 1868, Benjamin B. French Papers, Library of Congress. During his 1868 speech, French did not specify exactly when the episode with Tad's cat had

taken place, but the context of his recollection suggests that June 1863 would have been the most likely moment for it to have occurred.

2. Diary entry, Monday, June 22, 1863, in Donald B. Cole and John J. McDonough, eds. *Benjamin Brown French, Witness to the Young Republic: A Yankee's Journal, 1828–1870* (Hanover, N.H.: University Press of New England, 1989), 424.

3. Willard A. Cutter to George Cutter, Soldiers' Home, June 24, 1863, Willard A. Cutter Papers, Allegheny College, Meadville, Pa.; Washington *Star*, June 22, 1863.

4. Quartermaster's Annual Report, FY 1863–64, *Official Records*, Series 3, Vol. 4, p. 903.

5. Willard A. Cutter to George Cutter, Camp at Soldiers' Home, July 18, 1863, Willard A. Cutter Papers, Allegheny College, Meadville, Pa. Cutter sometimes refers to "Aunt" Mary as Mary Williams (not Dines) in his letters about the Lincoln family's cook, but this was probably the same woman.

6. Unidentified clipping, "Former Woman Slave, 92, Pays Tribute to Father Abraham," [December 27, 1936] Soldiers' Home Vertical Files, U.S. Soldiers' and Airmen's Home, Washington, D.C.

7. Emancipation Proclamation, January 1, 1863, *Collected Works* 6: 28–31.

8. Gabor S. Boritt, "The Voyage to the Colony of Linconia: The Sixteenth President, Black Colonization, and the Defense Mechanism of Avoidance," *Historian* 37 (August 1975), 619–632. See a revised version of this essay in Gabor S. Boritt, ed., *The Lincoln Enigma: The Changing Faces of an American Icon* (New York: Oxford University Press, 2001), 1–19.

9. Diary entry, Friday, July 1, 1864, in Burlingame and Ettlinger, *Inside Lincoln's White House*, 217. According to some wartime diary entries and postwar recollections, Lincoln did occasionally bring up compensated emancipation and colonization in political discussions after January 1, 1863, but the absence of these issues from his public papers was nevertheless significant.

10. James M. McPherson, *For Cause & Comrades: Why Men Fought in the Civil War* (New York: Oxford University Press, 1997), 123–124.

11. Aldace F. Walker to Father, Fort Massachusetts, October 26, 1862, transcripts available from Fort Ward Museum Library, Alexandria, Va.

12. Quoted in Donald, *Lincoln*, 402.

13. Diary entry, Wednesday, December 31, 1862, in Pease and Randall, *The Diary of Orville Hickman Browning*, 1: 606–607.

14. Diary entry, Monday, January 19, 1863, in Pease and Randall, *The Diary of Orville Hickman Browning*, 1: 616.

15. Diary entry, Monday, January 1, 1863, in Pease and Randall, *The Diary of Orville Hickman Browning*, 1: 608–609. Browning spells the name of the medium as "Laury." Cranston and Margaret Laurie, and their daughter Belle, all acted as spiritualists from their home in Georgetown. See http://www.spirithistory.com/lincoln.html for a well-documented history of this prominent cluster of mid-nineteenth-century Washington spiritualists.

16. Andrew B. Hart to Margaret Hart, Washington, January 1, 1863, Civil War/Written Accounts, Crawford County Historical Society, Meadville, Pa. Hart died the next year from smallpox.

17. Willard A. Cutter to Elizabeth Cutter, Washington, D.C., January 1, 1863, and Willard A. Cutter to Grandmother, Washington, D.C., January [1], 1863, Willard A. Cutter Papers, Allegheny College, Meadville, Pa.

18. McPherson, *For Cause & Comrades*, 123–124.

19. David V. Derickson, "The President's Guard," typescript recollection, Ida M. Tarbell Papers, Allegheny College, Meadville, Pa.

20. Willard A. Cutter to Elizabeth Cutter, Washington, D.C., February 16, 1863, Willard A. Cutter Papers, Allegheny College, Meadville, Pa.

21. Willard A. Cutter to George Cutter, Washington, D.C., May 6, 1863, Willard A. Cutter Papers, Allegheny College, Meadville, Pa.

22. Judge Advocate General's Office Records, Record Group 153, File No. NN252, Augustus Halfast, August 1, 1863, National Archives, Washington, D.C. I owe special thanks to Tom and Beverly Lowry and the Index Project Inc. for helping to identify this case.

23. Quoted in McPherson, *Ordeal by Fire*, 317.

24. McPherson, *Ordeal by Fire*, 248.

25. Willard A. Cutter to George Cutter, Soldiers' Home, June 24, 1863, Willard A. Cutter Papers, Allegheny College, Meadville, Pa. Cutter was referring to a cavalry engagement near Gainesville, Maryland, that took place on Sunday, June 21, 1863.

26. Silas W. Burt, "Lincoln on His Own Story-Telling," *The Century Magazine* 73 (February 1907), 500.

27. Abraham Lincoln to Erastus Corning and Others, June 12, 1863, *Collected Works* 6: 266.

28. Silas W. Burt, "Lincoln on His Own Story-Telling," *The Century Magazine* 73 (February 1907), 499–502.

29. Bates, *Lincoln in the Telegraph Office*, 155.

30. Washington *Evening Star*, July 2, 1863, 2:1. Abraham Lincoln to Robert T. Lincoln, Washington, July 3, 1863, *Collected Works*, 6: 314.

31. Memorandum [Washington], July 17, 1863, *Collected Works Supplement*, 194.

32. Diary entry, Tuesday, July 14, 1863, in Burlingame and Ettlinger, *Inside Lincoln's White House*, 62.

33. Abraham Lincoln to Henry W. Halleck, Soldiers' Home, July 6, 1863—7pm, *Collected Works*, 6: 318.

34. Abraham Lincoln to Henry W. Halleck [July 7, 1863], *Collected Works* 6: 319.

35. Response to a Serenade, July 7, 1863, *Collected Works* 6: 319–320. For a good brief description of this episode see James R. Heintze, "Abraham Lincoln's Independence Day Address of July 7, 1863," 2002, http://gurukul.american.edu/heintze/Lincoln.htm.

36. Abraham Lincoln to Robert Lincoln, July 11, 1863, *Collected Works* 6: 323.

37. Boyden, *War Reminiscences*, 143–144.

38. Abraham Lincoln to Robert T. Lincoln, Washington, July 14, 1863, *Collected Works*, 6: 327.

39. Robert Todd Lincoln reminiscence, January 5, 1885, quoted in Michael Burlingame, ed., *An Oral History of Abraham Lincoln: John G. Nicolay's Interviews and Essays* (Carbondale: Southern Illinois University Press, 1996), 88.

40. Diary entries, Saturday, July 11; Sunday, July 12; Monday, July 13; Tuesday, July 14; and Wednesday, July 15, 1863, in Burlingame and Ettlinger, *Inside Lincoln's White House*, 61–63.

41. Gabor S. Boritt, "'Unfinished Work': Lincoln, Meade, and Gettysburg," in Gabor S. Boritt, ed., *Lincoln's Generals* (New York: Oxford University Press, 1994), 100. Boritt concludes that if Hamlin was the secret envoy, he was an ineffectual one. He quotes Meade's son, who was present, as questioning both the mission and messenger. "Vice President Hamlin has been here and went away this morning," he wrote, "what they sent him for, God only knows, he does not look as if he had an idea in his old beastly head" (100).

42. John S. Goff, *Robert Todd Lincoln: A Man in His Own Right* (Norman: University of Oklahoma Press, 1969), 52. Donald, *Lincoln*, 448.

43. Baker, *Mary Todd Lincoln*, 227–228. Notes on interview with Charles M. Derickson, undated, courtesy of Jane Westenfeld, Ida M. Tarbell Papers, Allegheny College, Meadville, Pa.

44. Charles M. Derickson recollection, December 15, 1897, courtesy of Jane Westenfeld and Michael Burlingame, Ida M. Tarbell Papers, Allegheny College, Meadville, Pa.

Chapter 6. "In fine whack"

1. Dispatch of July 4, 1863, appearing in *Sacramento Daily Union*, July 28, 1863, Burlingame, *Lincoln Observed*, 57. Burlingame points out that "prog" was a slang reference for food. Willard's was the famous hotel located near the White House.

2. Diary entry, Saturday, July 25, 1863, in Burlingame and Ettlinger, *Inside Lincoln's White House*, 67–68.

3. Constance McLaughlin Green, *Washington: Village and Capital, 1800–1878* (Princeton, N.J.: Princeton University Press, 1962), 251.

4. *Washington Daily Morning Chronicle*, July 7, 1863, p. 2:7.

5. William Doster and *Washington Star* quoted in Margaret Leech, *Reveille in Washington: 1860–1865* (New York: Harper & Brothers, 1941), 261.

6. Abraham Lincoln to Mary Lincoln, September 21, 1863, *Collected Works* 6: 471.

7. Willard A. Cutter to Elizabeth Cutter, Washington, D.C., July 22, 1863, Willard A. Cutter Papers, Allegheny College, Meadville, Pa.; Wayne C. Temple, "Mary Todd Lincoln's Travels," *Journal of the Illinois State Historical Society* 52 (Spring 1959), 189.

8. John Hay to John G. Nicolay, Executive Mansion, August 7, 1863, quoted in Dennett, *Lincoln and the Civil War*, 75–76. Hay, like many others, thought the Lincoln family was vacationing in the White Mountains of New Hampshire.

9. Abraham Lincoln to Mary Lincoln, July 28, 1863, *Collected Works* 6: 353. Robert Lincoln returned to Washington briefly near the end of August. See entry for August 18, 1863, Miers, *Lincoln Day by Day*, 203.

10. John Hay to John G. Nicolay, Executive Mansion, August 7, 1863, in Dennett, *Lincoln and the Civil War*, 76.

11. John Hay to John G. Nicolay, Executive Mansion, August 7, 1863, in Dennett, *Lincoln and the Civil War*, 76.

12. Burlingame and Ettlinger, *Inside Lincoln's White House*, xi–xvi.

13. Dispatch of November 7, 1863, appearing in *Sacramento Daily Union*, December 4, 1863, in Burlingame, *Lincoln Observed*, 83–84.

14. John Hay to William H. Herndon, Paris, September 5, 1866, in Wilson and Davis, *Herndon's Informants*, 331.

15. Hay's comment on Stoddard in Diary entry, Friday, October 30, 1863, and Philbrick's comment on Hay in Charles H. Philbrick to Ozias M. Hatch, December 30, 1864, both quoted in Burlingame and Ettlinger, *Inside Lincoln's White House*, 105, xv. Other White House aides included Nathaniel S. Howe, Gustave Matile, and Edward D. Neill.

16. Abraham Lincoln to Joseph Gilmore, Executive Mansion, August 7, 1863, *Collected Works* 6: 368.

17. Abraham Lincoln to Horatio Seymour, Executive Mansion, August 7, 1863, *Collected Works* 6: 369–370.

18. Abraham Lincoln to Mary Lincoln, August 8, 1863, *Collected Works* 6: 371–372. Interestingly, this letter never reached the first lady. Somehow it fell into the hands of a soldier in the Army of the Potomac. Eventually, one of the president's friends heard about the letter and had it returned it to its author in 1864.

19. *Collected Works* 6: 372. Diary entry, August 10, 1863, Samuel P. Heintzelman Papers, Library of Congress, Washington, D.C. Willard A. Cutter to Brother, Washington, D.C., August 11, 1863, transcript courtesy of Mike Dallas, Meadville, Pa.

20. Willard A. Cutter to Brother, Washington, D.C., August 11, 1863, transcript courtesy of Mike Dallas, Meadville, Pa.

21. Abraham Lincoln to Ulysses S. Grant, August 9, 1863, *Collected Works* 6: 374.

22. Reply to Emancipation Memorial, September 13, 1862, *Collected Works* 5: 423.

23. John W. Blassingame et al., eds., *The Frederick Douglass Papers*, 5 vols. (New Haven, Conn.: Yale University Press, 1985), 3: 606.

24. Frederick Douglass, "Lincoln and the Colored Troops," in Rice, *Reminiscences of Abraham Lincoln*, 319.

25. The explanation for the strange check remains elusive. See Roland T. Carr, "The Mysteries of Lincoln's Bank Accounts," *The Bankers Magazine* [undated], Riggs National Bank Archives, Washington, D.C.

26. Frederick Douglass, "Lincoln and the Colored Troops," in Rice, *Reminiscences of Abraham Lincoln*, 323.

27. Quoted in Roy Morris, Jr., *The Better Angel: Walt Whitman in the Civil War* (New York: Oxford University Press, 2000), 147.

28. Quoted in Roy P. Basler, ed., *Walt Whitman's Memoranda during the War (&) Death of Abraham Lincoln; reproduced in facsimile* (Bloomington: Indiana University Press, 1962), 6–7. In this case, Whitman observed Lincoln on Fourteenth Street.

29. *Specimen Days*, "Abraham Lincoln," No. 45 [August 12, 1863], Walt Whitman, *Prose Works* (Philadelphia: David McKay, 1892); Bartleby.com, 2000. www.bartleby.com/229/ [October 29, 2002]. Whitman first published the entry on Lincoln in the *New York Times* on August 16, 1863. He included it in *Memorandum during the War* (1875) and later revised the passage again as part of his prose series, *Specimen Days*, which was collected in *Prose Works* (1892). In *Specimen Days*, Whitman made minor changes to the language of his wartime journal entry but also added a key phrase; "They say this guard was against his personal wish, but he let his counselors have their way."

30. Miers, *Lincoln Day by Day*, 202.

31. Interview with *Washington Post*, August 3, 1924. The eighty-four-year-old Mangan believed that the episode took place in the summer of 1864, but it appears that he simply mixed up the years in question.

32. Diary entry, Sunday, August 23, 1863, in Burlingame and Ettlinger, *Inside Lincoln's White House*, 75–76.

33. Abraham Lincoln to James C. Conkling, Executive Mansion, August 26, 1863, *Collected Works*, 6: 406–410.

34. Dennett, *Lincoln and the Civil War*, 76.

35. Edwin Stanton to Ellen Stanton, August 25, 1863, quoted in Benjamin P. Thomas and Harold Hyman, *Stanton: The Life and Times of Lincoln's Secretary of War* (New York: Knopf, 1962), 383–384.

36. Thomas and Hyman, *Stanton*, 384.

37. Diary entry [July–August 1863] in Burlingame and Ettlinger, *Inside Lincoln's White House*, 78.

38. Dispatch of May 2, 1863, appearing in *Sacramento Daily Union*, May 27 1863, in Burlingame, *Lincoln Observed*, 48.

39. Diary entry, Thursday, July 16, 1863, in Burlingame and Ettlinger, *Inside Lincoln's White House*, 63.

40. Abraham Lincoln to Robert H. Milroy, Executive Mansion, June 29, 1863, *Collected Works*, 6: 308. Diary entry, Thursday, July 16, 1863, in Burlingame and Ettlinger, *Inside Lincoln's White House*, 63.

41. Donn Piatt, "Lincoln the Man," in Rice, *Reminiscences of Abraham Lincoln*, 355–358. Bates, *Lincoln in the Telegraph Office*, 113.

42. Diary entry, Monday, September 21, 1863, Beale, *Diary of Gideon Welles*, 1: 438; Abraham Lincoln to William S. Rosecrans, Washington, D.C., September 21, 1863, 12:35 A.M., *Collected Works*, 6: 472; Diary entry, Sunday, September 27, 1863, in Burlingame and Ettlinger, *Inside Lincoln's White House*, 85.

43. Abraham Lincoln to Mary Lincoln, September 21, 22, 1863, *Collected Works* 6: 471–472, 474.

44. The two primary accounts of this evening come from David Bates and John Hay. Bates claimed in a recollection that a War Department employee named John C. Hatter was the man who delivered the message to Lincoln at the Soldiers' Home. Bates, *Lincoln in the Telegraph Office*, 172–175. For Hay's more contemporaneous account, see Diary entry, Sunday, September 27, 1863, in Burlingame and Ettlinger, *Inside Lincoln's White House*, 85–86.

45. Katherine Helm, *The True Story of Mary, Wife of Lincoln* (New York: Harper & Brothers, 1928), 225.

46. McPherson, *Ordeal by Fire*, 337.

47. Willard A. Cutter to Elizabeth Cutter, Soldiers' Home, October 8, 1863, Willard A. Cutter Papers, Allegheny College, Meadville, Pa.

48. Willard A. Cutter to Elizabeth Cutter, Camp at the White House, November 4, 1863, Willard A. Cutter Papers, Allegheny College, Meadville, Pa. Entry for November 4, 1863, Miers, *Lincoln Day By Day*, 217.

49. Diary entry, Monday, November 9, 1863, in Burlingame and Ettlinger, *Inside Lincoln's White House*, 110, 325n–326n.

50. Noah Brooks, "Glimpses of Lincoln in War Time," *Century* 49 (January 1895), 467.

51. Carpenter, *The Inner Life of Abraham Lincoln*, 58–59; John Hay, "Life in the White House in the Time of Lincoln," *Century* 41 (November 1890), 36.

Chapter 7. "Present at Fort Stevens"

1. The Lincolns wrote a joint letter of recommendation for Stackpole from the Soldiers' Home in 1862. He also earned several references in the letters and recollections of the infantrymen who guarded the cottage. See Mary Lincoln and Abraham Lincoln to John E. Wool, Soldiers' Home, July 3 [1862], *Collected Works Supplement*, 140. Photocopy of original provided courtesy of Carol Ayres, De Paul Library, St. Mary College, Leavenworth, Kan.

2. Invoices from John Alexander, upholsterer, Washington, May 21, 1864, Record Group 217, Records of the U.S. General Accounting Office (GAO), Records of the First Auditor, Audit 151.223, October 24, 1864, National Archives.

3. Roland T. Carr, *32 President's Square: Part I of a Two-Part Narrative of the Riggs Bank and Its Founders* (Washington, D.C.: Acropolis Books, 1980), 66–67.

4. David Schuyler, *Apostle of Taste: Andrew Jackson Downing 1815–1852* (Baltimore, Md.: Johns Hopkins University Press, 1996), 1, 56–61, 67–68.

5. Carr, *32 President's Square*, 104.

6. Paul R. Goode, *The United States Soldiers' Home: A History of Its First Hundred Years* (Richmond, Va.: William Byrd Press, 1957), 62–63.

7. Benjamin B. French to John H. Rice, June 16, 1864, Volume 14: September 7, 1861–June 9, 1865, pp. 373–376, National Archives Microfilm Publication M371, reel 7, Records of the Office of Public Buildings and Public Parks of the National Capital, Record Group 42, National Archives and Records Administration. I owe special thanks to Michelle Krowl for helping to identify this document.

8. See Edward Steers, Jr., "President Lincoln's Summer White House: The 'President's Villa' or 'Anderson Cottage'?" *The Lincolnian* 2 (January–February 1984), 1–7.

9. *San Francisco Bulletin*, May 20, 1865, quoted in Milton H. Shutes, *Lincoln and California* (Stanford, Calif.: Stanford University Press, 1943), 254–256.

10. *Washington Chronicle*, July 3, 1864. Willard A. Cutter to Elizabeth Cutter, Washington, D.C., July 11, 1864, Willard A. Cutter Papers, Allegheny College, Meadville, Pa.

11. Donald, *Lincoln*, 513, 515.

12. Benjamin Franklin Cooling, *Symbol, Sword, and Shield: Defending Washington during the Civil War* (Shippensberg, Pa.: White Mane Publishing, 1991), 106–107.

13. *Official Records*, Series 1, Vol. 21, pp. 390–392, quoted in Cooling, *Symbol, Sword, and Shield*, 134.

14. John Henry Cramer, *Lincoln under Enemy Fire: The Complete Account of His Experiences during Early's Attack on Washington* (Baton Rouge: Louisiana State University Press, 1948), 1–10.

15. W. W. Goldsborough, *The Maryland Line in the Confederate Army: 1861–1865* (orig. pub. 1900; Gaithersburg, Md.: Olde Soldier Books, 1987), 203. After the Civil War, Johnson emerged as a leading exponent of the southern "Lost Cause" and a popular lecturer, which suggests that his recollection needs to be handled with care. He had obvious political and financial motives for exaggerating the significance of his wartime role.

16. Edwin M. Stanton to Abraham Lincoln, July 9, 1864, Abraham Lincoln Papers, Library of Congress. Transcribed and annotated by the Lincoln Studies Center, Knox College, Galesburg, Ill.

17. Lieutenant Frank Wilkeson, *Recollections of a Private Soldier in the Army of the Potomac*, quoted in Byron Stinson, "The Invalid Corps," *Civil War Times Illustrated* 10 (May 1971), 25–26.

18. *Official Records*, Series 1, Vol. 37, Part 1, p. 196, quoted in Cramer, *Lincoln under Enemy Fire*, 11.

19. William E. Doster, *Lincoln and Episodes of the Civil War* (New York: G. P. Putnam's Sons, 1915), 248.

20. Edwin M. Stanton to Abraham Lincoln, July 10, 1864, Abraham Lincoln Papers, Library of Congress. Transcribed and annotated by the Lincoln Studies Center, Knox College, Galesburg, Ill.

21. See, *Autobiography of Albert Nelson See*, [25–26].

22. Willard A. Cutter to Elizabeth Cutter, Washington D.C., July 11, 1864, Willard A. Cutter Papers, Allegheny College, Meadville, Pa. Diary entry, Sunday, July 10, 1864, in Burlingame and Ettlinger, *Inside Lincoln's White House*, 221.

23. Dispatch of July 12, 1864, appearing in *Sacramento Daily Union* August 10, 1864, in Burlingame, *Lincoln Observed*, 126.

24. Noah Brooks, "Two War-Time Conventions," *Century* 49 (March 1895), 730.

25. William B. Roe to Captain Joseph H. Spencer, Washington, August 1, 1864, in *Official Records* Series 1, Vol. 37 (part 2), pp. 563–564.

26. *Official Records*, Series 1, Vol. 37, Part 2, pp. 202, 209.

27. Quoted in Bates, *Lincoln in the Telegraph Office*, 250.

28. H. H. Atwater quoted in Bates, *Lincoln in the Telegraph Office*, 253–254.

29. Diary entry, Monday, July 11, 1864, in Burlingame and Ettlinger, *Inside Lincoln's White House*, 221–222.

30. Jubal Early quoted in Cramer, *Lincoln under Enemy Fire*, 12.

31. Jubal Anderson Early, *Autobiographical Sketch and Narrative of the War between the States* (Philadelphia: J. B. Lippincott, 1912), 391.

32. Doster, *Lincoln and Episodes of the Civil War*, 250.

33. Bates, *Lincoln in the Telegraph Office*, 252–253.

34. Diary entry, Monday, July 11, 1864, in Burlingame and Ettlinger, *Inside Lincoln's White House*, 221–222.

35. Charles A. Dana to Ulysses S. Grant, July 11, 1864, in *Official Records* Series 1, Vol. 37 (part 2), pp. 192–194.

36. Doster, *Lincoln and Episodes of the Civil War*, 251; Early, *Autobiographical Sketch*, 391.

37. Quoted in Bates, *Lincoln in the Telegraph Office*, 253–254.

38. Diary entry, July 12, 1864, in Doster, *Lincoln and Episodes of the Civil War*, 252.

39. Diary entry, Tuesday, July 12, 1864, in Pease and Randall, *The Diary of Orville Hickman Browning*, 1: 675–676.

40. Diary entry, July 12, 1864, 1:30 P.M., quoted in Doster, *Lincoln and Episodes of the Civil War*, 253.

41. Diary entry, Tuesday, July 12, 1864, in Burlingame and Ettlinger, *Inside Lincoln's White House*, 222.

42. George Thomas Stevens quoted in Cramer, *Lincoln under Enemy Fire*, 28–29; Robert W. McBride, "Lincoln's Body Guard: The Union Light Guard of Ohio," *Indiana Historical Society Publications* 5 (1911), 32–33.

43. David T. Bull to wife [Fort Stevens], July 14, 1864, in private possession (Professor Sleeter Bull, University of Illinois) quoted in Cramer, *Lincoln Under Enemy Fire*, 26–27.

44. Alexander Woollcott, "Get Down, You Fool!" *Atlantic Monthly* 164 (February 1938), 169–173. Diary entry, Wednesday, July 13, 1864, in Burlingame and Ettlinger, *Inside Lincoln's White House*, 222–223.

45. Horatio Wright, quoted in Cramer, *Lincoln under Enemy Fire*, 30–31.

46. P. H. Kaiser, "Lincoln at Fort Stevens," *National Magazine* 10 (February 1910), 525–526.

47. Diary entry, July 12, 1864, John T. Morse, Jr., ed., *Diary of Gideon Welles: Secretary of the Navy under Lincoln and Johnson* (4 vols., Boston: Houghton Mifflin, 1911), 2: 75.

48. Quoted in Cramer, *Lincoln Under Enemy Fire*, 26–27.

49. Aldace F. Walker to Father, Fort Stevens, July 13, 1864, transcripts available from Fort Ward Museum Library, Alexandria, Va.

50. Testimony Concerning Shelling of Houses Near Fort Stevens, Executive Mansion, October 10, 1864, *Collected Works* 8: 42.

51. Elizabeth Thomas quoted in Washington, *They Knew Lincoln*, 163–165.

52. T. E. Morrow to Father, camp near Darkesville, August 2, 1864, quoted in Cooling, *Symbol, Sword, and Shield*, 212.

53. Aldace F. Walker to Father, Fort Stevens, July 13, 1864, transcripts available from Fort Ward Museum Library, Alexandria, Va.

54. Diary entry, Wednesday, July 13, 1864, in Burlingame and Ettlinger, *Inside Lincoln's White House*, 222–223.

55. Diary Entry, July 11, 1864, Morse, *Diary of Gideon Welles*, 2: 73.

56. Henry W. Halleck to Edwin Stanton, July 13, 1864, Abraham Lincoln Papers, Library of Congress. Transcribed and annotated by the Lincoln Studies Center, Knox College, Galesburg, Ill.

57. Abraham Lincoln to Edwin Stanton, July 14, 1864, and Memorandum for Cabinet, July 14, 1864, Abraham Lincoln Papers, Library of Congress. Transcribed and annotated by Lincoln Studies Center, Knox College, Galesburg, Ill. It is not clear whether Lincoln actually read this memorandum to his cabinet. Diary entry, Thursday, July 14, 1864, in Burlingame and Ettlinger, *Inside Lincoln's White House*, 223.

58. Willard A. Cutter to Elizabeth Cutter, Washington, D.C., July 11, 1864, Willard A. Cutter Papers, Allegheny College, Meadville, Pa. *Official Records*, Series 1, Vol. 37 (Part 1), pp. 279, 307, 310.

59. Diary entry, Sunday, July 17, 1864, in Cole and McDonough, *Witness to the Young Republic*, 453.

60. Quoted in Carpenter, *The Inner Life of Abraham Lincoln*, 301–302.

61. Quoted in Allen Clark, "Abraham Lincoln in the National Capital," *Records of the Columbia Historical Society* 27 (1925), 60.

62. Lizzie W. S. to Abraham Lincoln, July 1864, Abraham Lincoln Papers, Library of Congress. Transcribed and annotated by the Lincoln Studies Center, Knox College, Galesburg, Ill.

63. Proposal Calling for 500,000 Volunteers, July 18, 1864, *Collected Works*, 7: 448–449. To Whom It May Concern, Executive Mansion, July 18, 1864, *Collected Works*, 7: 451.

Chapter 8. "Damned in Time & in Eternity"

1. Diary entry, July 26, 1864, Morse, *Diary of Gideon Welles*, 2: 87–88.

2. Mary Lincoln to Robert T. Lincoln, Executive Mansion, July 29 [1864], in Turner and Turner, *Mary Todd Lincoln*, 178.

3. Mary Lincoln to Mercy Levering Conkling, Soldiers' Home, July 29 [1864], in Turner and Turner, *Mary Todd Lincoln*, 178.

4. Turner and Turner, *Mary Todd Lincoln*, 177, 178n.

5. Ulysses S. Grant to Abraham Lincoln, July 25, 1864, Abraham Lincoln Papers, Library of Congress. Transcribed and annotated by the Lincoln Studies Center, Knox College, Galesburg, Ill.

6. John Y. Simon, "Grant, Lincoln, and Unconditional Surrender," in Gabor S. Boritt, ed., *Lincoln's Generals* (New York: Oxford University Press, 1994), 180.

7. John Y. Simon's penetrating essay on the Lincoln-Grant relationship is especially strong on this point. See Boritt, *Lincoln's Generals*, 179.

8. *Collected Works* 7: 476n.

9. Abraham Lincoln to Ulysses S. Grant, August 3, 1864, *Collected Works* 7: 476.

10. John S. Goff, *Robert Todd Lincoln: A Man in His Own Right* (Norman: University of Oklahoma Press, 1969), 56–57.

11. Quoted in Randall, *Lincoln's Sons*, 177.

12. Quoted in diary entry, Emilie Todd Hardin [December 1863] reprinted in Katherine Helm, *The True Story of Mary, Wife of Lincoln* (New York: Harper & Brothers, 1928), 227.

13. Burlingame, *Lincoln Observed*, 46–47; Bates, *Lincoln in the Telegraph Office*, 397–398.

14. Diary entry, July 15, 1864, Morse, *Diary of Gideon Welles*, 2: 78; John P. Usher, *President Lincoln's Cabinet* (Omaha, Nebr.: Nelson H. Loomis, 1925), 22.

15. Charles M. Derickson recollection, December 15, 1897, courtesy of Jane Westenfeld and Michael Burlingame, Ida M. Tarbell Papers, Allegheny College, Meadville, Pa.

16. Thomas and Hyman, *Stanton*, 384–385.

17. Joshua F. Speed, *Reminiscences of Abraham Lincoln* (Louisville, Ky.: John P. Morton, 1884), 32–33.

18. Joseph Gillespie to Ida M. Tarbell, February 7, 1876, Ida M. Tarbell Papers, Allegheny College, Meadville, Pa. I owe special thanks to Michael Burlingame for identifying and transcribing this letter.

19. Willard A. Cutter to Elizabeth Cutter, Washington, D.C., January 24, 1864, Willard A. Cutter Papers, Allegheny College, Meadville, Pa.; George C. Ashmun, "Recollections of a Peculiar Service," in *Sketches of War History, 1861–1865; Papers Read Before the Ohio Commandery of the Military Order of the Loyal Legion of the United States* (Cincinnati: Robert Clark, 1888), 279.

20. Smith Stimmel, *Personal Reminiscences of Abraham Lincoln* (Minneapolis, Minn.: William H. M. Adams, 1928), 18–20.

21. Robert W. McBride, "Lincoln's Body Guard: The Union Light Guard of Ohio," *Indiana Historical Society Publications* 5 (1911), 28–29.

22. Stimmel, *Personal Reminiscences of Abraham Lincoln*, 29–30.

23. McBride, "Lincoln's Body Guard," 34.

24. Stimmel, *Personal Reminiscences of Abraham Lincoln*, 25–27.

25. McBride, "Lincoln's Body Guard," 9–12.

26. Ibid., 35.

27. Judge Advocate General's Office Records, Record Group 153, File No. NN3022, July 1, 1864, George A. Bennett, National Archives, Washington, D.C. I owe special thanks to Tom and Beverly Lowry and the Index Project Inc. for helping to identify this case.

28. Judge Advocate General's Office Records, Record Group 153, File No. LL2712, October 1, 1864, Arthur W. White, National Archives, Washington, D.C. I owe special thanks to Tom and Beverly Lowry and the Index Project Inc. for helping to identify this case.

29. *New York Tribune*, August 5, 1864.

30. *Collected Works* 8: 550.

31. John G. Nicolay to Abraham Lincoln, March 30, 1864, Abraham Lincoln Papers, Library of Congress. Transcribed and annotated by the Lincoln Studies Center, Knox College, Galesburg, Ill.

32. Frederic Bancroft and William A. Dunning, eds., *The Reminiscences of Carl Schurz* (3 vols., New York: McClure Co., 1907–1908), 3: 103–104. Schurz claimed that his reconstruction of Lincoln's conversation came mainly from a confidential letter that he had written to a friend shortly after their meeting.

33. "To Whom It May Concern," July 18, 1864, *Collected Works*, 7: 451. Greeley was not regarded as a conservative, but he was unpredictable and considered the Niagara Falls overture to be a real one.

34. Charles D. Robinson, *Collected Works* 7: 501n.

35. William P. Dole to Abraham Lincoln, August 18, 1864, Abraham Lincoln Papers, Library of Congress. Transcribed and annotated by the Lincoln Studies Center, Knox College, Galesburg, Ill.

36. Abraham Lincoln to Charles D. Robinson [pencil draft], August 17, 1863, Abraham Lincoln Papers, Library of Congress. Transcribed and annotated by the Lincoln Studies Center, Knox College, Galesburg, Ill. Please note that the editors of Lincoln's *Collected Works* include only the second draft of this letter in his official writings; *Collected Works* 7: 499–501.

37. Frederick Douglass to Theodore Tilton, October 15, 1864, Philip S. Foner, *The Life and Writings of Frederick Douglass* (5 vols; New York: International Publishers, 1952), 3: 423–424.

38. Frederick Douglass to Abraham Lincoln, August 29, 1864, Abraham Lincoln Papers, Library of Congress. Transcribed and annotated by the Lincoln Studies Center, Knox College, Galesburg, Ill.

39. David W. Blight, *Frederick Douglass' Civil War* (Baton Rouge: Louisiana State University Press, 1989), 183–184.

40. Douglass to Tilton, October 15, 1864, Foner, *Life and Writings*, 3: 424. "When there was any shadow of a hope that a man of a more decided anti-slavery conviction and policy could be elected," Douglass wrote, "I was not for Mr. Lincoln." The abolitionist measured his support for Lincoln in purely practical terms, not only on the slavery question, but also for personal reasons. On the same day that he replied to the president's suggestion about a new Underground Railroad, for example, Douglass asked for a favor on behalf of his son Charles, a Union soldier who was gravely ill. Understanding the implications of this "great favor," Lincoln immediately ordered a discharge for Charles Douglass. See William S. McFeely, *Frederick Douglass* (New York: W. W. Norton, 1991), 230.

41. Diary of Joseph T. Mills, State Historical Society of Wisconsin, Madison.

42. *Collected Works* 7: 506.

43. *Collected Works* 7: 507.

44. *Collected Works* 7: 507–508.

45. *Collected Works* 7: 508; Diary of Joseph T. Mills, State Historical Society of Wisconsin, Madison.

46. Abraham Lincoln to Charles D. Robinson, August 17, 1864 [second draft], Abraham Lincoln Papers, Library of Congress. Transcribed and annotated by the Lincoln Studies Center, Knox College, Galesburg, Ill.

47. "Interview with Alexander W. Randall and Joseph T. Mills," August 19, 1864, *Collected Works* 7: 506.

48. Abraham Lincoln to Isaac M. Schermerhorn, September 12, 1864,

Chapter 9. "Whatever is, is right"

1. Carpenter, *The Inner Life of Abraham Lincoln*, 62–63; Willard A. Cutter to Elizabeth Cutter, Washington, D.C., March 31, 1864, Willard A. Cutter Papers, Allegheny College, Meadville, Pa.

2. Diary entry, Friday, May 13, 1864, in Burlingame and Ettlinger, *Inside Lincoln's White House*, 195.

3. Originally from Wheeling, W. Va., *Register*, reprinted in *New York Times*, April 6, 1887, 8: 2. The headline in the *New York Times* mistakenly places the story in 1862, but the text clearly indicates that the event occurred in 1864. A different version of this story appeared in Ward Lamon's recollections, published in 1895. According to Lamon, the near miss happened in 1862 and Lincoln told him about it afterward. It appears that Lamon's memory was influenced by the published Nichols account. See Ward Hill Lamon, *Recollections of Abraham Lincoln* (Chicago: A. C. McClurg, 1895), 261–263.

4. U.S. Patent No. 6469. For a good discussion of Lincoln's interest in technology, see Robert V. Bruce, *Lincoln and the Tools of War* (Indianapolis, Ind.: Bobbs-Merrill, 1956).

5. Bates, *Lincoln in the Telegraph Office*, 264–265.

6. Diary entry, March 29, 1857, "Diary and Memorandum of William L. Marcy," *American Historical Review* 24 (July 1919), 644.

7. Charles J. M. Gwinn to Montgomery Blair, August 28, 1864, Abraham Lincoln Papers, Library of Congress. Transcribed and annotated by the Lincoln Studies Center, Knox College, Galesburg, Ill.

8. Reverdy Johnson to Abraham Lincoln, August 27, 1864, and Charles J. M. Gwinn to Abraham Lincoln, August 29, 1864, Abraham Lincoln Papers, Library of Congress. Transcribed and annotated by the Lincoln Studies Center, Knox College, Galesburg, Ill.

9. Order to Henry S. Huidekoper, September 1, 1864, *Collected Works* 7: 530–531. Huidekoper's brief recollection of the episode appears in H[enry] S. Huidekoper, "On Guard at White House," *National Magazine* 9 (February 1909), 512.

10. Quoted in Thomas and Hyman, *Stanton*, 387.

11. Abraham Lincoln to Ulysses S. Grant, September 22, 1864, *Collected Works* 8: 17.

12. David V. Derickson to Abraham Lincoln, [September] 1864, Abraham Lincoln Papers, Library of Congress. Transcribed and annotated by the Lincoln Studies Center, Knox College, Galesburg, Ill. See additional letters by Solomon N. Pettis to Lincoln, [September and] September 26, 1864.

13. Quoted in Long, *The Civil War Day by Day: An Almanac 1861–1865*.

14. Donald Bruce Johnson, ed., *National Party Platforms, vol. 1, 1840–1956* (Urbana: University of Illinois Press, 1978 rev. ed.), 34–35.

15. David E. Long, *The Jewel of Liberty: Abraham Lincoln's Re-election and the End of Slavery* (orig. pub. 1994; New York: Da Capo, 1997), 230.

16. Abraham Lincoln to Mary Lincoln, Washington, August 31 and September 8, 1864, *Collected Works* 7: 526, 544.

17. Goode, *The United States Soldiers' Home*, 67.

18. Board Meeting, Washington, June 9, 1862, Soldiers' Home Commissioners Board Meeting minutes, typescripts courtesy of Beryl X. Smith, U.S. Soldiers' and Airmen's Home, Washington, D.C.

19. Goode, *The United States Soldiers' Home*, 67; Lincoln to Henry W. Halleck, Executive Mansion, March 3, 1864 in *Collected Works: First Supplement*, 228.

20. George W. Hazzard to Abraham Lincoln, Cincinnati, Ohio, October 21, 1860, and Leslie Combs to Abraham Lincoln, Frankfort, Kentucky, September 6, 1861, Abraham Lincoln Papers, Library of Congress. Transcribed and annotated by the Lincoln Studies Center, Knox College, Galesburg, Ill.

21. Benjamin King to Board of Commissioners, March 2, 1859, quoted in Goode, *The United States Soldiers' Home*, 70–71.

22. Board Meeting, Washington, June 9, 1862, Soldiers' Home Commissioners Board Meeting minutes, typescripts courtesy of Beryl X. Smith, U.S. Soldiers' and Airmen's Home, Washington, D.C.

23. Information compiled from the Quarterly Reports of Inmates, Entry 18, Record Group 231, National Archives, Washington, D.C.

24. *Washington Sunday Chronicle*, April 14, 1861, 3: 6. I owe special thanks to Michael Burlingame for sharing this newspaper clipping.

25. *San Francisco Bulletin*, May 20, 1865, quoted in Milton H. Shutes, *Lincoln and California* (Stanford, Calif.: Stanford University Press, 1943), 254–256.

26. Patrick J. Kelly, *Creating A National Home: Building the Veteran's Welfare State 1860–1900* (Cambridge, Mass.: Harvard University Press, 1997), 13.

27. Congressional Globe, 35th Congress, 1st Session, April 12, 1858, 1552.

28. Goode, *The United States Soldiers' Home*, 83–84.

29. Unidentified resident quoted in Editor's Desk, *Harper's New Monthly Magazine* 71 (July 1885), 312.

30. Comments on residents from Aldace F. Walker to Father, Fort Massachusetts, October 5, 1862, transcripts available from Fort Ward Museum Library, Alexandria, Va. Demographic conclusions drawn from the Quarterly Reports of Inmates, Entry 18, Record Group 231, National Archives, Washington, D.C.

31. Annual Message to Congress, December 6, 1864, *Collected Works*, 8: 141.

32. Memorandum Concerning Ward H. Lamon and the Antietam Episode [c. September 12, 1864], *Collected Works*, 7: 548–549.

33. Quoted in Niall Ferguson, *The House of Rothschild: The World's Banker 1849–1999* (New York: Viking, 1999), 115.

34. F[ernando Wood] to Abraham Lincoln, New York, September 10, 1864, Abraham Lincoln Papers, Library of Congress. This meeting is not mentioned in any of the three book-length studies on the 1864 contest: William Frank Zornow, *Lincoln and the Party Divided* (Norman: University of Oklahoma Press, 1954); Long, *The Jewel of Liberty*; and John C. Waugh, *Reelecting Lincoln: The Battle for the 1864 Presidency* (New York: Crown, 1997).

35. Quoted in Burlingame, *Lincoln Observed*, 263n. Brooks placed the meeting in August 1864, but some of the text suggests it must have happened after the fall of Atlanta. Yet the memory is jumbled and at least part of the story also appears borrowed from earlier encounters. Both John Hay and John Nicolay reported in contemporary documents on an earlier conversation between Lincoln and Wood that concerned the fate of Vallandigham—whom Woods secretly despised; see diary entry [June 17, 1864] in Burlingame and Ettlinger, *Inside Lincoln's White House*, 208, 350. Even if Brooks was conflating several meetings, however, the underlying point, unless he invented the entire tale, is that Lincoln and Wood had an ongoing private dialogue over how much leeway to grant Copperheads during the war.

36. The day after his meeting with Lincoln at the Soldiers' Home, Wood also wrote a critical letter, breaking ranks with other Copperheads and endorsing McClellan as the Democratic nominee—despite the general's refusal to support the antiwar plank of the party platform. See Zornow, *Lincoln & the Party Divided*, 137.

37. Melvin G. Holli, *The American Mayor: The Best & The Worst Big-City Leaders* (University Park: Penn State University Press, 1999). Wood was ranked the eighth worst.

38. Ernest A. McKay, "New York City: Both Booster, Bane of Union," *Washington Times* November 25, 1995.

39. Diary entry, Sunday, September 25, 1864, and Monday September 26, 1864, in Burlingame and Ettlinger, *Inside Lincoln's White House*, 232–232. For the letter written by Governor Smith after the election, John G. Smith to Abraham Lincoln, December 30, 1864, at the University of Vermont Library, see Ibid., 360n–361n.

40. Abraham Lincoln to Mary Lincoln, September 11, 1864, *Collected Works* 7: 547.

41. Willard A. Cutter to George Cutter, Washington, D.C., September 17, 1864, Willard A. Cutter Papers, Allegheny College, Meadville, Pa.

42. Mary Lincoln to Abram Wakeman, Soldiers' Home, September 23 [1864], Turner and Turner, *Mary Todd Lincoln*, 180.

43. Mary Lincoln to Abram Wakeman, October 23 [1864], Turner and Turner, *Mary Todd Lincoln*, 181.

44. Stimmel, *Personal Reminiscences of Abraham Lincoln*, 37.

45. Howard K. Beale, *The Diary of Edward Bates* (Washington, D.C.: Government Printing Office, 1933), 422.

46. George Borrett, "An Englishman in Washington in 1864," *The Magazine of History with Notes and Queries* 38 (Extra no. 149; 1929), 11–15.

47. Brooks recounted two slightly different versions of this evening. See Noah Brooks, "Washington in Lincoln's Time," *Century* 49 (November 1894), 147–148, and Noah Brooks, "Personal Reminiscences of Lincoln," *Scribners Monthly* 15 (February 1878), 563–564.

48. Noah Brooks, "Washington in Lincoln's Time," *Century* 49 (November 1894), 148.

49. Hugh McCulloch, "The Lincoln-Douglas Debates and the Gettysburg Oration," in Rice, *Reminiscences of Abraham Lincoln*, 156–157.

50. Hugh McCulloch to Abraham Lincoln, October 13, 1864, Abraham Lincoln Papers, Library of Congress. Transcribed and annotated by the Lincoln Studies Center, Knox College, Galesburg, Ill.

51. Orders, C. H. Raymond, Washington, July 2, 1864, in *Official Records* Series 1, Vol. 37 (Part 2), p. 8. Endorsement Concerning Escort [Washington], July 4, 1864, *Collected Works* 7: 423.

52. Rebecca Pomroy to unidentified person, Washington, October 1864, quoted in Boyden, *War Reminiscences*, 228–229.

53. Thomas N. Conrad, *A Confederate Spy: A Story of the Civil War* (New York: J. S. Ogilvie Publishing, 1892), 69–71.

54. Ibid., 72–73.

55. Ibid., 74.

56. William A. Tidwell with James O. Hall and David Winfred Gaddy, *Come Retribution: The Confederate Secret Service and the Assassination of Lincoln* (Jackson: University of Mississippi Press, 1988), 273.

57. Robert W. McBride, "Lincoln's Body Guard: The Union Light Guard of Ohio," *Indiana Historical Society Publications* 5 (1911), 37–38.

58. McPherson, *Ordeal by Fire*, 457.

59. Willard A. Cutter to George Cutter, Camp at the White House, November 9, 1864, Willard A. Cutter Papers, Allegheny College, Meadville, Pa.

60. Response to a Serenade, November 10, 1864, *Collected Works*, 8: 101.

61. Diary entry, Tuesday, November 8, 1864, in Burlingame and Ettlinger, *Inside Lincoln's White House*, 245.

Conclusion

1. Diary entry, April 15, 1865, in Beale, *Diary of Gideon Welles*, 2: 290.

2. Baker, *Mary Todd Lincoln*, 263–267.

3. Ibid., 341–342.

4. *Washington Post*, July 27, 1963.

Bibliography

Archival Collections

Allegheny College, Meadville, Pennsylvania
    Ida M. Tarbell Papers
    Willard A. Cutter Papers
Crawford County Historical Society, Meadville, Pennsylvania
    Genealogical Files
Fort Ward Museum Library, Alexandria, Virginia
    Aldace F. Walker Papers (transcripts only)
Historical Society of Washington, D.C.
    City Directories
    Historical Maps
Huntington Library, San Marino, California
    Herndon-Lamon Papers
    Gideon Welles Papers
    Ward H. Lamon Papers
Illinois State Historical Society, Springfield, Illinois
    Albert N. See Autobiography
    Company K, 150th Pennsylvania Volunteers Photo Album
    David Davis Family Papers
    Orville Hickman Browning Papers
    Lyman Trumbull Family Papers
Library of Congress, Washington, D.C.
    Albert Beveridge Papers
    Blair Family Papers
    Salmon Chase Papers
    Corcoran Family Papers
    Benjamin B. French Papers
    John Hay Papers
    Samuel Heintzelman Papers
    Herndon-Weik Collection
    Abraham Lincoln Papers

John G. Nicolay Papers
Riggs Family Papers
Edwin Stanton Papers
Lyman Trumbull Papers
James Wadsworth Family Papers
Gideon Welles Papers
Levi Woodbury Papers
Lincoln National Life Foundation, Ft. Wayne, Indiana
    Soldiers' Home Files
National Archives, Washington, D.C.
    Office of Public Buildings Records (RG 42)
    Judge Advocate General's Office Records (RG 153)
    General Accounting Office Records (RG 217)
    United States Soldiers' Home Records (RG 231)
New York Public Library, New York, New York
    J. G. Holland Papers
New York State Library, Albany, New York
    Preliminary Emancipation Proclamation
Riggs National Bank Archives, Washington, D.C.
    Roland T. Carr Papers
State Historical Society of Wisconsin, Madison, Wisconsin
    Joseph T. Mills Papers
United States Soldiers' and Airmen's Home, Washington, D.C.
    Beryl X. Smith Files
    Ray Colvard Files
    Vertical Files

Newspapers and Periodicals

Baltimore Sun
Charleston Mercury
Chicago Tribune
Frank Leslie's Illustrated Newspaper
Harper's New Monthly Magazine
Harper's Weekly
The Independent (New York)
National Intelligencer (Washington, D.C.)
New York Evening Post
New York Herald
New York Times
New York Tribune
North American Review
San Francisco Bulletin
Union County (Penna.) Star and Lewisburg Chronicle
Washington Chronicle
Washington Post
Washington Star

Published Collections and Reference Works

Basler, Roy P., et al., eds. *The Collected Works of Abraham Lincoln*. 11 vols. New Brunswick, N.J.: Rutgers University Press, 1953–1990.

———. *Walt Whitman's Memoranda During the War (&) Death of Abraham Lincoln; reproduced in facsimile*. Bloomington: Indiana University Press, 1962.

Beale, Howard K., ed. *The Diary of Edward Bates*. Washington, D.C.: U.S. Government Printing Office, 1933.

———. *Diary of Gideon Welles: Secretary of Navy Under Lincoln and Johnson*. 3 vols. New York: W. W. Norton, 1960.

Blassingame, John W., et al., eds. *The Frederick Douglass Papers: Series One*. 5 vols. New Haven: Yale University Press, 1979–1992.

Booker, Richard. *Abraham Lincoln in Periodical Literature, 1860–1940*. Chicago: Fawley-Brost, 1941.

Burlingame, Michael, ed. *Lincoln Observed: The Civil War Dispatches of Noah Brooks*. Baltimore: Johns Hopkins University Press, 1998.

———. *Lincoln's Journalist: John Hay's Anonymous Writings for the Press, 1860–1864*. Carbondale: Southern Illinois University Press, 1998.

———. *At Lincoln's Side: John Hay's Civil War Correspondence and Selected Writings*. Carbondale: Southern Illinois University Press, 2000.

Burlingame, Michael, and John R. Turner Ettlinger, eds. *Inside Lincoln's White House: The Complete Civil War Diary of John Hay*. Carbondale: Southern Illinois University Press, 1997.

Cole, Donald B., and John J. McDonough, eds. *Benjamin Brown French, Witness to the Young Republic: A Yankee's Journal, 1828–1870*. Hanover, N.H.: University Press of New England, 1989.

Dennett, Tyler, ed. *Lincoln and the Civil War in the Diaries and Letters of John Hay*. Orig. pub. 1939. New York: Da Capo, 1988.

Donald, David H., ed. *Inside Lincoln's Cabinet: The Civil War Diaries of Salmon P. Chase*. New York: Longman's, 1954.

Downing, A[ndrew] J. *Cottage Residences, Rural Architecture & Landscape Gardening*. Orig. pub. 1842. With introduction by Michael Hugo-Brunt. Watkins Glen, N.Y.: Library of Victorian Culture, 1967.

Foner, Philip S., ed. *The Life and Writings of Frederick Douglass*. 5 vols. New York: International Publishers, 1952.

Halleck, Fitz Greene. *The poetical works of Fitz-Greene Halleck. Now first collected. Illustrated with steel engravings, from drawings by American artists*. 2d ed. New York: D. Appleton, 1848.

Johnson, Donald Bruce, ed. *National Party Platforms, Vol. 1, 1840–1956*. Urbana: University of Illinois Press, 1978.

Laas, Virginia Jeans, ed. *Wartime Washington: The Civil War Letters of Elizabeth Blair Lee*. Urbana: University of Illinois Press, 1991.

Lawton, Eba Anderson, ed. *History of the "Soldiers' Home" Washington, D.C.* New York: G. P. Putnam's Sons, 1914.

Lomax, Elizabeth Lindsay. *Leaves from an old Washington diary, 1854–1863*. Edited by Lindsay Lomax Wood. [New York]: E. P. Dutton, 1943.

Long, E. B., ed. *The Civil War Day by Day: An Almanac 1861–1865*. New York: Doubleday, 1971.

Meigs, M[ontgomery] C. "General M. C. Meigs on the Conduct of the Civil War." *American Historical Review* 26 (1920–1921): 285–303.

Miers, Earl S., ed. *Lincoln Day by Day: A Chronology 1809–1865*. Dayton, Ohio: Morningside, 1990.

Mitgang, Herbert, ed. *Abraham Lincoln: A Press Portrait*. Orig. pub. 1956. New York: Fordham University Press, 2000.

Monaghan, Jay. *Lincoln Bibliography, 1839–1939*. 2 vols. Springfield: Illinois State Historical Library, 1943.

Morse, John T., Jr., ed. *Diary of Gideon Welles: Secretary of the Navy Under Lincoln and Johnson*. 4 vols. Boston: Houghton Mifflin, 1911.

Neely, Mark E., Jr. *The Abraham Lincoln Encyclopedia*. New York: McGraw-Hill, 1982.

Official Records of the Union and Confederate Armies, the War of the Rebellion Washington, D.C.: U.S. Government Printing Office, 1890–1901.

Pease, Theodore C., and James G. Randall, eds. *The Diary of Orville Hickman Browning*. 2 vols. Springfield: Illinois State Historical Society, 1925–33.

Pittman, Benn, ed. *The Assassination of President Lincoln and the Trial of the Conspirators*. Orig. pub. 1867. New York: Funk & Wagnalls, 1954.

Schwartz, Thomas F., and Kim M. Bauer, eds. "Unpublished Mary Todd Lincoln." *Journal of the Abraham Lincoln Association* 17 (Summer 1996): 1–21.

Sears, Stephen W., ed. *The Civil War Papers of George B. McClellan: Selected Correspondence, 1860–1865*. New York: Ticknor & Fields, 1989.

Turner, Justin G., and Linda Levitt Turner, eds. *Mary Todd Lincoln: Her Life and Letters*. New York: Alfred A. Knopf, 1972.

U.S. Department of State. *The Assassination of Abraham Lincoln*. Washington, D.C.: Government Printing Office, 1867.

Whitman, Walt. *Prose Works*. Philadelphia: David McKay, 1892; Bartleby.com, 2000. www.bartleby.com/229/.

Recollections

Ashmun, George C. "Recollections of a Peculiar Service," in *Sketches of War History, 1861–1865; Papers Read Before the Ohio Commandery of the Military Order of the Loyal Legion of the United States*. Cincinnati: Robert Clark, 1888.

Bancroft, Frederic, and William A. Dunning, eds. *The Reminiscences of Carl Schurz*. 3 vols. New York: McClure, 1907–1908.

Bates, David Homer. *Lincoln in the Telegraph Office: Recollections of the United States Military Telegraph Corps during the Civil War*. Orig. pub. 1907. Lincoln: University of Nebraska Press, 1995.

Bayne, Julia Taft. *Tad Lincoln's Father*. Boston: Little, Brown, 1931.

Benjamin, Marcus, ed. *Washington During War Time*. Washington, D.C.: National Tribune, 1902.

Borrett, George. "An Englishman in Washington in 1864." *The Magazine of History, with Notes and Queries* 38 (Extra No. 149, 1929): 5–15.

Boutwell, George S. *The Lawyer, the Statesman, and the Soldier*. New York: D. Appleton, 1887.

———. *Reminiscences of Sixty Years in Public Affairs*. 2 vols. New York: McClure, Phillips, 1902.

Boyden, Anna L., ed. *War Reminiscences: A Record of Mrs. Rebecca R. Pomroy's Experience in War-times*. Boston: D. Lothrop, 1884.

Brooks, Noah. "Personal Reminiscences of Lincoln." *Scribner's Monthly* 15 (February 1878): 561–69.

———. "Washington in Lincoln's Time." *Century* 49 (November 1894): 140–49.

———. "Glimpses of Lincoln in War Time." *Century* 49 (January 1895): 457–67.

———. "Two War-Time Conventions." *Century* 49 (March 1895): 723–37.

———. *Washington in Lincoln's Time*. New York: Century, 1895.

Brown, R[obert] C. *History of Crawford County: Part II*. Chicago: Warner, Beers, 1885.

Browne, Francis F., ed. *The Every-Day Life of Abraham Lincoln*. New York: N. D. Thompson, 1886.

Burlingame, Michael, ed. *An Oral History of Abraham Lincoln: John G. Nicolay's Interviews and Essays*. Carbondale: Southern Illinois University Press, 1996.

Burt, Silas W. "Lincoln on His Own Story-Telling." *The Century Magazine* 73 (February 1907): 499–502.

Chamberlin, Thomas. *History of the One Hundred and Fiftieth Regiment Pennsylvania Volunteers, Second Regiment, Bucktail Brigade*. Philadelphia: McManus, 1905.

Carpenter, F[rancis] B. *The Inner Life of Abraham Lincoln: Six Months at the White House*. Orig. pub. 1866. Lincoln: University of Nebraska Press, 1995.

Chittenden, L.E. *Recollections of President Lincoln and His Administration*. New York: Harper & Brothers, 1891.

Clay-Clopton, Virginia. *A Belle of the Fifties: Memoirs of Mrs. Clay of Alabama, Covering Social and Political Life in Washington and the South, 1853–66*. Edited by Ad Sterling. New York: Doubleday, 1904.

Clemmer, Mary. *Ten Years in Washington: Life and Scenes in the National Capital As a Woman Sees Them*. Hartford, Conn.: A. D. Worthington, 1873.

Conrad, Thomas N. *A Confederate Spy: A Story of the Civil War*. New York: J.S. Ogilvie, 1892.

Cooke, Jay. "Interview with Lincoln." *American History Illustrated* 7 (November 1972): 10–11.

Cox, Samuel S. *Eight Years in Congress, from 1857–1865*. New York: D. Appleton, 1865.

Cozzens, Peter, and Robert I. Girardi, eds. *The Military Memoirs of General John Pope*. Chapel Hill: University of North Carolina Press, 1998.

Croffut, William A. "Lincoln's Washington: Recollections of a Journalist Who Knew Everybody." *Atlantic Monthly* 145 (January 1930): 55–65.

———. *An American Procession 1855-1914: A Personal Chronicle of Famous Men*. Orig. pub. 1931. Freeport, N.Y.: Books for Libraries Press, 1968.

Curtis, George Ticknor. "McClellan's Last Service to the Republic, Part III." *North American Review* 130 (June 1880): 565–85.

Dahlgren, Madeleine Vinton, ed. *Memoir of John A. Dahlgren, Rear-Admiral United States Navy*. Boston: James R. Osgood, 1882.

Dana, Charles Anderson. *Lincoln and His Cabinet*. Cleveland, Ohio: De Vinne Press, 1896.

Dicey, Edward. "Washington During the War." *Macmillan's Magazine* 6 (May 1862): 16–29.

———. *Spectator of America*. Edited by Hebert Mitgang. Orig. pub. 1863. Chicago: Quadrangle Books, 1971.

Doster, William E. *Lincoln and Episodes of the Civil War*. New York: G. P. Putnam's Sons, 1915.

Dudley, Edgar S. *A Reminiscence of Washington and Early's Attack in 1864*. Cincinnati, Ohio: P. G. Thompson, 1884.

Early, Jubal A. *A Memoir of the Last Year of the War for Independence*. Lynchburg, Va.: C.W. Button, 1867.

Editor's Desk. *Harper's New Monthly Magazine* 71 (July 1885): 308–13.

Ellet, E. F. *The Court Circles of the Republic*. Hartford, Conn.: Hartford Publishing, 1869.

Fehrenbacher, Don E., and Virginia Fehrenbacher, eds. *Recollected Words of Abraham Lincoln*. Stanford, Calif.: Stanford University Press, 1996.

Field, Maunsell B. *Memories of Many Men and of Some Women*. New York: Harper & Brothers, 1874.

Forney, John W. *Anecdotes of Public Men*. 2 vols. New York: Harper & Brothers, 1874–1881.

French, John R. "Reminiscences of Famous Americans." *North American Review* 141 (September 1885): 226–41.

Gemmill, Jane W. *Notes on Washington, or Six Years at the National Capital*. Philadelphia: E. Claxton, 1884.

Gerry, Margarita Spalding, ed. *Through Five Administrations: Reminiscences of Colonel William H. Crook, Body-Guard to President Lincoln.* New York: Harper & Brothers, 1910.

Glyndon, Howard [Laura Redden Searing]. "The Truth About Mrs. Lincoln." *The Independent,* August 10, 1882.

Goldsborough, W. W. *The Maryland Line in the Confederate Army: 1861–1865.* Orig. pub. 1900. Gaithersburg, Md.: Olde Soldier Books, 1987.

Good, Timothy S., ed. *We Saw Lincoln Shot: One Hundred Eyewitness Accounts.* Jackson: University Press of Mississippi, 1995.

Grimsley, Elizabeth Todd. "Six Months at the White House." *Journal of the Illinois State Historical Society* (October-January 1926–27): 43–73.

Hamlin, Charles E. *The Life and Times of Hannibal Hamlin.* 2 vols. Orig. pub. 1899. Port Washington, N.Y.: Kennikat Press, 1971.

Hanaford, P[hoebe] A. *Abraham Lincoln: His Life and Public Services.* Boston: B. B. Russell, 1866.

Hay, John. "Life in the White House in the Time of Lincoln." *Century* 41 (November 1890): 33–37.

Helm, Katherine. *The True Story of Mary, Wife of Lincoln: Containing the Recollections of Mary Lincoln's Sister Emilie (Mrs. Ben Hardin Helm).* New York: Harper & Brothers, 1928.

Holzer, Harold, ed. *Lincoln as I Knew Him: Gossip, Tributes, and Revelations from His Best Friends and his Worst Enemies.* Chapel Hill, N.C.: Algonquin Books, 1999.

Huidekoper, H. S. "On Guard At White House." *National Magazine* 9 (February 1909): 510–12.

Johnson, Albert E. H. "Reminiscences of Honorable Edwin M. Stanton, Secretary of War." *Records of the Columbia Historical Society Records* 13 (1910): 69–97.

Kaiser, P. H. "Lincoln at Fort Stevens." *National Magazine* 10 (February 1910): 525–26.

Keckley, Elizabeth. *Behind the Scenes, or Thirty Years a Slave, and Four Years in the White House.* Orig. pub. 1868. New York: Oxford University Press, 1988.

Kelly, Joseph T. "Memories of a Lifetime in Washington." *Columbia Historical Society Records* 31–32 (1930): 117–49.

Kieffer, Harry M. *The Recollections of a Drummer-Boy.* 6th ed. rev. Boston: Ticknor, 1889.

Lamon, Ward Hill. *Recollections of Abraham Lincoln, 1847–1865.* Chicago: A. C. McClurg, 1895.

McBride, Robert W. "Lincoln's Body Guard: The Union Light Guard of Ohio." *Indiana Historical Society Publications* 5 (1911): 5–39.

McCulloch, Hugh. "Memories of Some Contemporaries." *Scribner's* 4 (September 1888): 279–95.

Neill, Edward D. *Abraham Lincoln and His Mailbag.* Edited by Theodore C. Blegen. St. Paul: Minnesota Historical Society, 1964.

Nicolay, J[ohn] G., and John Hay. "A History of Abraham Lincoln." *Century* 39 (January 1890): 428–43.

———. *Abraham Lincoln: A History.* 10 vols. New York: Century, 1890.

Pendel, Thomas F. *Thirty-Six Years in the White House.* Washington, D.C.: Neal Publishing, 1902.

Poore, Ben[jamin] Perley. *Perley's Reminiscences of Sixty Years in the National Metropolis.* 2 vols. Philadelphia: Hubbard Brothers, 1886.

Rice, Allen Thorndike, ed. *Reminiscences of Abraham Lincoln by Distinguished Men of His Time.* Orig. pub. 1885. Rev. ed. New York: Harper & Brothers, 1909.

Smith, Thomas West. *The Story of a Cavalry Regiment: Scott's 900 Eleventh New York Cavalry.* N.p.: Veteran's Association, 1897.

Speed, Joshua F. *Reminiscences of Abraham Lincoln and Notes of a Visit to California, Two Lectures.* Louisville, Ky.: John P. Morton & Co., 1884.

Stimmel, Smith. *Personal Reminiscences of Abraham Lincoln.* Minneapolis: William H. M. Adams, 1928.

Stoddard, William O. "White House Sketches." *New York Citizen*, August 25, 1866.

———. *Inside the White House in War Times*. New York: Charles L. Webster, 1890.

Swett, Leonard. "The Conspiracies of the Rebellion." *North American Review* 144 (February 1887): 179–90.

Tarbell, Ida M. *All in the Day's Work: An Autobiography*. Orig. pub. 1939. Boston: G. K. Hall, 1985.

Usher, John P. *President Lincoln's Cabinet*. Omaha, Nebr.: Nelson H. Loomis, 1925.

Washington, John E. *They Knew Lincoln*. New York: E. P. Dutton, 1942.

Welles, Gideon. "History of Emancipation." *Galaxy* 14 (December 1872): 838–52.

Wilson, Douglas L., and Rodney O. Davis, eds. *Herndon's Informants: Letters, Interviews, and Statements about Abraham Lincoln*. Urbana: University of Illinois Press, 1998.

Wilson, Rufus Rockwell, ed. *Lincoln among His Friends*. Caldwell, Idaho: Caxton Printers, 1942.

Woollcott, Alexander. "Get Down, You Fool!" *Atlantic Monthly* 164 (February 1938): 169–73.

Secondary Sources

Anbinder, Tyler G. "Fernando Wood and New York City's Secession from the Union: A Political Reappraisal." *New York History* 68 (January 1987): 67–92.

Baker, Jean H. *Mary Todd Lincoln: A Biography*. New York: W. W. Norton, 1987.

Baxter, Maurice G. *Orville H. Browning: Lincoln's Friend and Critic*. Bloomington: Indiana University Press, 1957.

Belz, Herman. *Abraham Lincoln, Constitutionalism, and Equal Rights*. New York: Fordham University Press, 1998.

Bennett, Lerone, Jr. *Forced into Glory: Abraham Lincoln's White Dream*. Chicago: Johnson Publishing, 2000.

Billings, Elden E. "Social and Economic Conditions in Washington During the Civil War." *Records of the Columbia Historical Society* 63–65 (1966): 191–209.

Bishop, Jim. *The Day Lincoln Was Shot*. New York: Harper, 1955.

Boritt, G[abor] S. *Lincoln and the Economics of the American Dream*. Memphis, Tenn.: Memphis State University Press, 1978.

———, ed. *Lincoln's Generals*. New York: Oxford University Press, 1994.

———. *The Lincoln Enigma: The Changing Faces of an American Icon*. New York: Oxford University Press, 2001.

Brennan, John C. "The Confederate Plan to Abduct President Lincoln." *Surratt Society News* (March 1981): 4-6.

Bruce, Robert V. *Lincoln and the Tools of War*. Indianapolis: Bobbs-Merrill Co., 1956.

Burlingame, Michael. *The Inner World of Abraham Lincoln*. Urbana: University of Illinois Press, 1994.

Carr, Roland T. *32 President's Square: Part I of a Two-Part Narrative of the Riggs Bank and Its Founders*. Washington, D.C.: Acropolis Books, 1980.

Clark, Allen C. "Abraham Lincoln in the National Capital." *Records of the Columbia Historical Society* 27 (1925): 1–174.

Conlin, Michael F. "The Smithsonian Abolition Lecture Controversy: The Clash of Antislavery Politics with American Science in Wartime Washington." *Civil War History* 46 (December 2000): 301–23.

Cooling, Benjamin Franklin. *Symbol, Sword, and Shield: Defending Washington during the Civil War*. 2d rev. ed. Shippensberg, Pa.: White Mane Publishing, 1991.

Coulson, Thomas. *Joseph Henry: His Life and Work*. Princeton, N.J.: Princeton University Press, 1950.

Cramer, John Henry. *Lincoln under Enemy Fire: The Complete Account of His Experiences during Early's Attack on Washington.* Baton Rouge: Louisiana State University Press, 1948.

Davis, William C. *Lincoln's Men: How President Lincoln Became Father to an Army and a Nation.* New York: Free Press, 1999

Donald, David Herbert. *Lincoln.* New York: Simon & Schuster, 1995.

———. *Lincoln at Home: Two Glimpses of Abraham Lincoln's Domestic Life.* Washington, D.C.: White House Historical Association, 1999.

Eberstadt, Charles. *Lincoln's Emancipation Proclamation.* New York: Duschness Crawford, 1950.

Ferguson, Niall. *The House of Rothschild: The World's Banker 1849–1999.* New York: Viking, 1999.

Fisher, Perry G. *Anderson Cottage Museum Feasibility Study.* Prepared for Geier Brown Renfrow Architects as part of Contract DACA 31-83-D-0033 with the Department of the Army, June 1, 1985.

Franklin, John Hope. *The Emancipation Proclamation.* New York: Anchor, 1965.

Friedel, Frank, and William Pencak, eds. *The White House: The First Two Hundred Years.* Boston: Northeastern University Press, 1994.

George, Joseph Jr. "Black Flag Warfare: Lincoln and the Raids against Richmond and Jefferson Davis." *Pennsylvania Magazine of History and Biography* 115 (July 1991): 291–318.

Goff, John S. *Robert Todd Lincoln.* Norman: University of Oklahoma Press, 1969.

Goode, Paul R. *The United States Soldiers' Home: A History of Its First Hundred Years.* Richmond, Va.: William Byrd Press, 1957.

Green, Constance McLaughlin. *Washington: A History of the Capital, 1800–1950.* Princeton, N.J.: Princeton University Press, 1962.

Greier Brown Renfrow Architects. *Preservation Plan: United States Soldiers' and Airmen's Home, Washington, D.C.* Project No. 223. July 19, 1985.

Groat, William. *United States Soldiers' Home.* Washington, D.C.: National Capital Press, 1931.

Guelzo, Allen C. *Abraham Lincoln: Redeemer President.* Grand Rapids, Mich.: William B. Eerdmans Publishing, 1999.

Hanchett, William. *Lincoln Murder Conspiracies.* Urbana: University of Illinois Press, 1983.

———. *Out of the Wilderness: The Life of Abraham Lincoln.* Urbana: University of Illinois Press, 1994.

Hendrick, Burton J. *Lincoln's War Cabinet.* Boston: Little, Brown, 1946.

Holli, Melvin G. *The American Mayor: The Best and the Worst Big-City Leaders.* University Park: Pennsylvania State University Press, 1999.

Holzer, Harold. *Lincoln Seen and Heard.* Lawrence: University Press of Kansas, 2000.

Jacob, Kathryn Allamong. *Capital Elites: High Society in Washington, D.C., after the Civil War.* Washington, D.C.: Smithsonian Institution Press, 1995.

Johnston, Allan John. "Surviving Freedom: The Black Community of Washington, D.C., 1860–1880." Ph.D. dissertation, Duke University, 1980.

Jones, Howard. *Abraham Lincoln and a New Birth of Freedom: The Union and Slavery in the Diplomacy of the Civil War.* Lincoln: University of Nebraska Press, 1999.

Kelly, Patrick J. *Creating a National Home: Building the Veterans' Welfare State, 1860–1900.* Cambridge: Harvard University Press, 1997.

Kimmel, Stanley P. *Mr. Lincoln's Washington.* New York: Coward-McCann, 1957.

Kincaid, Robert L. *Joshua Fry Speed: Lincoln's Most Intimate Friend.* Harrogate, Tenn.: Lincoln Memorial University Press, 1943.

Kunkel, Mabel. *Abraham Lincoln: Unforgettable American.* Charlotte, N.C.: Delmar, 1976.

Kurtz, Michael. "Emancipation in the Federal City." *Civil War History* 26 (September 1978): 250–67.

Lee, Richard M. *Mr. Lincoln's City: An Illustrated Guide to the Civil War Sites of Washington.* McLean, Va.: EPM Publications, 1981.

Leech, Margaret. *Reveille in Washington, 1860–1865*. New York: Harper & Brothers, 1941.

Lewis, Thomas A. "There, in the heat of July, was the shimmering Capitol; Jubal Anderson Early's Maryland Invasion, 1864." *Smithsonian* 19 (July 1988): 66-74.

Lichten, Frances. *Decorative Art of Victoria's Era*. New York: Charles Scribner's Sons, 1950.

Long, David. *The Jewel of Liberty: Abraham Lincoln's Re-Election and the End of Slavery*. Orig. pub. 1994. New York: Da Capo, 1997.

Mason, Victor Louis. "Four Lincoln Conspiracies." *Century* 51 (April 1896): 889–912.

McFeely, William S. *Frederick Douglass*. New York: W. W. Norton, 1991.

McKay, Ernest A. "New York City: Both booster, bane of Union." *Washington Times*, November 25, 1995.

McMurtry, R. Gerald. "The Soldiers' Home: The Lincolns' Summer Retreat." *Lincoln Lore* 1589 (July 1970): 1–4.

McPherson, James M. *Ordeal by Fire: The Civil War and Reconstruction*. 2d ed. New York: McGraw-Hill, 1982.

———. *Battle Cry of Freedom*. New York: Oxford University Press, 1988.

———. *For Cause and Comrades: Why Men Fought in the Civil War*. New York: Oxford University Press, 1997.

Morris, Roy, Jr. *The Better Angel: Walt Whitman in the Civil War*. New York: Oxford University Press, 2000.

Mushkat, Jerome. *Fernando Wood: A Political Biography*. Kent, Ohio: Kent State University Press, 1990.

Neely, Mark E., Jr. *The Fate of Liberty: Abraham Lincoln and Civil Liberties*. New York: Oxford University Press, 1991.

———. *The Last Best Hope of Earth: Abraham Lincoln and the Promise of America*. Cambridge: Harvard University Press, 1993.

Nickell, Joe. "Paranormal Lincoln; Abraham Lincoln's Premonitions of His Assassination." *Skeptical Inquirer* 23 (May 1, 1999): 16–20.

Nicolay, Helen. *Lincoln's Secretary: A Biography of John G. Nicolay*. New York: Longmans, Green, 1949.

Ogilvie, Philip W. "Elizabeth Thomas (1821–1917)." Unpublished paper, 2000.

Otto, Celia Jackson. *American Furniture of the Nineteenth Century*. New York: Viking, 1965.

Paludan, Phillip S. *The Presidency of Abraham Lincoln*. Lawrence: University Press of Kansas, 1994.

Penney, O.E. *Transportation to the Soldiers' Home*. Washington, D.C.: Capital Transit, 1953.

Perry, Leslie J. "Lincoln's Home Life in Washington." *Harper's* (February 1897), 353–59.

Pratico, John. *Moments in the History of the Soldiers' Home*. N.p.: self-published, 1996.

Pratt, Harry E. *The Personal Finances of Abraham Lincoln*. Springfield, Ill.: Abraham Lincoln Association, 1943.

Randall, Ruth Painter. *Mary Lincoln: Biography of a Marriage*. Boston: Little, Brown, 1953.

———. *Lincoln's Sons*. Boston: Little, Brown, 1955.

Rietveld, Ronald D. "The Lincoln White House Community." *Journal of the Abraham Lincoln Association* 20 (1999): 17-48.

Robbins, Mary Caroline. "Park-Making as a National Art." *The Atlantic Monthly* 79 (January 1897): 86–98.

Ross, Ishbel. *The President's Wife: Mary Todd Lincoln*. New York: Putnam, 1973.

Safire, William. *Freedom: A Novel of Abraham Lincoln and the Civil War*. Orig. pub. 1987. New York: Avon Books, 1988.

Sandburg, Carl. *Abraham Lincoln: The War Years*. 4 vols. New York: Harcourt, Brace, 1939.

Schuyler, David. *Apostle of Taste: Andrew Jackson Downing 1815–1852*. Baltimore: Johns Hopkins University Press, 1996.

Seale, William. *The President's House: A History*. Washington, D.C.: White House Historical Association, 1986.

Sears, Stephen W. *George B. McClellan: The Young Napoleon*. New York: Ticknor & Fields, 1988.

Shutes, Milton H. *Lincoln and California*. Stanford, Calif.: Stanford University Press, 1943.

Smith, William E. *The Francis P. Blair Family in Politics*. 2 vols. New York: Macmillan, 1933.

Steers, Edward, Jr. "President Lincoln's Summer White House: The 'President's Villa' or 'Anderson Cottage'?" *The Lincolnian* 2 (January–February 1984): 1–7.

Stinson, Byron. "The Invalid Corps." *Civil War Times Illustrated* 10 (May 1971): 20–27.

Tarbell, Ida M. *The Life of Abraham Lincoln*. 4 vols. New York: S. S. McClure, 1895.

Temple, Wayne C. "Mary Todd Lincoln's Travels." *Journal of the Illinois State Historical Society* 52 (Spring 1959): 180–94.

————. *Abraham Lincoln: From Skeptic to Prophet*. Mahomet, Ill.: Mayhaver Publishing, 1995.

Thomas, Benjamin P. *Lincoln's New Salem*. Carbondale: Southern Illinois University Press, 1954.

Thomas, Benjamin P., and Harold Hyman. *Stanton: The Life and Times of Lincoln's Secretary of War*. New York: Knopf, 1962.

Tidwell, William A. *April '65: Confederate Covert Action in the American Civil War*. Kent, Ohio: Kent State University Press, 1995.

Tidwell, William A., James O. Hall, and David Winfred Gaddy. *Come Retribution : The Confederate Secret Service and the Assassination of Lincoln*. Jackson: University Press of Mississippi, 1988.

Townsend, George Alfred. "How Wilkes Booth Crossed the Potomac." *Century* 27 (April 1884): 822–32.

Turner, Thomas Reed. *The Assassination of Abraham Lincoln*. Melbourne, Fla.: Krieger Publishing Co., 1999.

Waugh, John C. *Reelecting Lincoln: The Battle for the 1864 Presidency*. New York: Crown, 1997.

Whyte, James H. "Divided Loyalties in Washington during the Civil War." *Columbia Historical Society Records* 60–62 (1963): 103–22.

Wilson, Douglas L. *Honor's Voice: The Transformation of Abraham Lincoln*. New York: Alfred A. Knopf, 1998.

Wilson, Francis. *John Wilkes Booth: Fact and Fiction of Lincoln's Assassination*. Boston: Houghton Mifflin, 1929.

Zornow, William Frank. *Lincoln and the Party Divided*. Norman: University of Oklahoma Press, 1954.

Acknowledgments

I HAVE MORE PEOPLE TO THANK THAN USUAL, BECAUSE THIS BOOK IS AN EXAMPLE OF what might be labeled *intra*-disciplinary history. Preservationists, archivists, college professors, independent historians, local historians, Civil War buffs, reenactors, and even a few helpful descendants have contributed to the making of *Lincoln's Sanctuary*. All of them deserve abundant praise for their generosity and acknowledgment of their particular brand of historical expertise. It is rare when historians of different types cross the invisible boundaries that separate them. I hope that this book might offer some encouragement for more co-mingling in the future.

First, I must confess that it was not I who made the initial overture. A few summers ago, I received a phone call from Sophie Lynn at the National Trust for Historic Preservation asking me to venture down to Washington for a meeting with Richard Moe. The purpose was to discuss plans for renovating and preserving the Lincoln cottage at the Soldiers' Home. Their hope was that I could research and write something like a guide book that would help put the Lincoln era at the Soldiers' Home into better context. A few years and a few hundred pages later, we had the manuscript for a book and the window into a richer, more poignant story than any of us fully anticipated.

There are a number of people at the National Trust who were tireless in their support for this project and in their help to me. I would like to single out three for special mention: William Dupont, James Vaughan, and Max van Balgooy. Bill Dupont is the Graham Gund Architect for the National Trust and my principal resource on physical details about the cottage where the Lincolns stayed. Jim Vaughan, the vice president for stewardship of historic sites, watched over the project carefully and chaired several interpretive planning sessions that benefited me enormously. Max van Balgooy, the director of interpretation and education, pitched in repeatedly, offering everything from research assistance to expert mapmaking. I owe him special thanks.

There are two other figures at the National Trust who probably deserve more credit for this book than anyone else. The first is Dick Moe, the president of the organization and the person whose vision and influence made the entire project possible. A historian himself, Dick understood the value of this story from the beginning and fought for it when fighting was needed. The other is Sophia Lynn, the project manager and my principal point of contact in the organization. By last count, my computer archive contains over three hundred e-mails from Sophie—all of them smart, curious, and enthusiastic. She did literally everything: organizing, researching, cajoling, paying, reminding, photo-hunting, editing, and so much more. I cannot praise her enough, so I must fall back on the one compliment that means the most to me. She is a true scholar. She is also, in more personal terms, a *mensch*, who knows what it means to offer support in a crisis.

The National Trust organized an advisory committee of scholars to help review my draft manuscripts and to provide plenty of advice and guidance. The members formed an all-star cast of Lincoln and Civil War–era scholars and included Jean Baker, James Basker, David Blight, Gabor Boritt, David Donald, Allen Guelzo, Harold Holzer, David Long, Phillip Paludan, Gary Scott, and Douglas Wilson. All of them were helpful, but I want to highlight special contributions from David Donald and Gabor Boritt. Professor Donald was my first mentor in the Lincoln field, a wonderful teacher and a memorable role model. Gabor Boritt has been an equally important mentor and friend to me in the years since college. In fact, it was probably Gabor's endorsement more than anything else that helped place me in this project. It was certainly his support and encouragement that kept me going to the end.

Mary Beth Corrigan, Edward Daniels, and April Weber constituted a veritable rapid deployment force of professional research assistance. Their help was invaluable and their future as historians is unlimited. Jared Peatman served as a super-competent fact-checker. Karen Needles offered timely aid in photo research. Tom and Beverly Lowry of the Index Project provided access to their groundbreaking database of Civil War court-martial cases. Other scholars volunteered assistance at critical junctures. As always, Michael Burlingame proved to be one of the most generous Lincoln scholars, offering insight and newspaper clippings from his vast collection of research materials. Allen Guelzo and Harold Holzer also made specific contributions to the research that dramatically improved the book. Edward Steers, Jr., provided a wonderful photograph. David Schuyler reviewed the chapter on Andrew Jackson Downing and the

Lincolns' cottage with his usual good humor and sharp intelligence. Dr. C. A. Tripp graciously shared with me his insights on Lincoln's relationship with David Derickson. Christopher Bates, Steve Carson, Michael Hill, Michelle Krowl, and Michael Maione each helped locate some of the harder to find sources that might otherwise have eluded me.

Part of the benefit of working with the National Trust was in receiving access to their wide network of experts in architecture, landscape design, material culture, interpretation, and preservation. Some of the professionals who provided key insights at various stages in the process are Matthew Chalifoux, Vincent Ciulla, Thomas Frye, Andrea Lowery, Laurie Matthews, Amber Moulton, Beth Newberger, Patricia O'Donnell, Susan Oyler, Rick Ortega, Clement Price, Judy Robinson, George Skarmeas, Susan Schreiber, Glenn Stach, Judy Vannais, Elizabeth Waters, and Gail Winkler

Great archivists and librarians are heroes to anyone preparing a historical monograph. Along the way in writing this book, I encountered several heroes: Jane Westenfeld, Special Collections, Pelletier Library, Allegheny College, Meadville, Pennsylvania; Laura Wickstead Polo and Anne Stewart, Crawford County Historical Society, Meadville, Pennsylvania; Gail Redman, Historical Society of Washington, D.C.; Kim Bauer, Kathryn Harris, Thomas Schwartz, and Cheryl Schnirring, Illinois State Historical Library at Springfield; John Sellers at the Library of Congress; Michael Musick at the National Archives; Kathi Stanley and James Lane, New York State Library at Albany; and Carol Ayres, DePaul Library, St. Mary College, Leavenworth, Kansas.

In some ways, the project's principal archive was not at an official repository at all, but rather the Soldiers' Home in Washington, D.C., which is still a functioning retirement community for U.S. military veterans. I want to thank Hal Grant, director of residence services, for his assistance in securing my access to materials and the facilities. I also want to offer special praise to three residents who helped preserve the institutional memory of this important place: Ray Colvard, John Pratico, and Beryl X. Smith. And finally, though I never met her, Kerri Childress, the former public relations officer of the Soldiers' Home, merits recognition for her early efforts at focusing public attention on the historic significance of the Lincoln cottage.

For me, the most wonderful development of this project was the discovery of the Willard Cutter letters. A group of dedicated historians, the reenactors of Companies C, F, and K of the 150th Pennsylvania Volunteers, deserve all the credit for this achievement. Three men from this group helped lead me to this cache of unexamined materials: Joe Conroy, John Kevin, and Mike Dallas. In particular, I owe special gratitude to Mike Dallas of Meadville, who is a tireless historical detective of the first order.

The descendants of Willard Cutter have also been especially helpful. Robert Lang, Sr., played a pivotal role in the final stages of my research. I also want to thank the Lang family of Meadville for their assistance, and I want to honor the memory of Irene Sprout, Willard Cutter's granddaughter, who preserved his letters and helped make them available for future generations of students. Thanks are also due Dorothea Derickson Midgett, a descendant of Captain David V. Derickson, for her generous assistance.

The people at Oxford University Press have also been generous and wonderful to work with, beginning with Peter Ginna, my editor and fellow BNC alum. Peter has the one quality that I imagine is a prerequisite for all great editors—patience. He waited out my writer's angst and then helped make a much better book possible. I owe him a great deal. I also owe special debts of gratitude to Joellyn Ausanka, Furaha Norton, Kate Pruss, and Matthew Sollars.

Finally, I must acknowledge my wonderful family. To my new in-laws, Ellen and Bruce Haynes, to Robyn and Ben, and to Fran and Sidney Borowsky, I want to express my thanks for their love and enthusiastic support. To my grandmother, Edith Getson, who has clipped every single Lincoln article that has appeared in the *Fort Lauderdale Sun-Sentinel* over the last several years, I offer my deepest respect, appreciation, and love. To my sister, Beth Pinsker, a truly wonderful writer, I can only say thank-you for everything. To my little brother, Curt Allison, who asked to be in the acknowledgments but who deserves a book of his own, I offer my continued best wishes for his bright future. For my parents, Ann and Sandy Pinsker, both wonderful teachers and great role models, I have nothing but love and respect. They created an atmosphere in our household that inspired ambition but still made having fun a priority. And finally, for my wife, Rachel, who took me on as something of a renovation project herself, I am eternally grateful. She is my best editor and best friend and truly does offer me all the sanctuary that I need in this world.

Index

Note: Page references in italics refer to photographs or illustrations.